QUESTIONS & ANSWERS:
SECURED TRANSACTIONS

QUESTIONS & ANSWERS:
SECURED TRANSACTIONS

Second Edition

Multiple-Choice and Short-Answer Questions and Answers

HON. BRUCE A. MARKELL
United States Bankruptcy Judge, District of Nevada and
Senior Fellow in Bankruptcy and Commercial Law
William S. Boyd School of Law
University of Nevada, Las Vegas

TIMOTHY R. ZINNECKER
Harry and Helen Hutchens Research Professor
South Texas College of Law

NOTE TO USERS

To ensure that you are using the latest materials available in this area, please be sure to periodically check the LexisNexis Law School web site for downloadable updates and supplements at www.lexisnexis.com/lawschool.

Editorial Offices
121 Chanlon Rd., New Providence, NJ 07974 (908) 464-6800
201 Mission St., San Francisco, CA 94105-1831 (415) 908-3200
www.lexisnexis.com

MATTHEW BENDER

ABOUT THE AUTHORS

Bruce A. Markell has been a bankruptcy judge since 2004, and a member of the Ninth Circuit's Bankruptcy Appellate Panel since 2007. He came to the bench from the academy; since 1999, he had been the Doris S. and Theodore B. Lee Professor of Law at the William S. Boyd School of Law at the University of Nevada, Las Vegas, where he taught Contracts, Commercial Law, Securitization, and Bankruptcy. He maintains a position at the Boyd School of Law as its Senior Fellow in Bankruptcy and Commercial Law. Judge Markell is the author of numerous articles on bankruptcy and commercial law. He is a member of the editorial board of *Collier on Bankruptcy*, and contributes several chapters to that publication. In 2001, he published a casebook on Contracts, *Making and Doing Deals: Contracts in Context*, with Professor David Epstein and Dean Lawrence Ponoroff; a second edition of that book was published in 2006, and a third edition is scheduled for 2011. In 2004, he published *Core Concepts of Commercial Law: Past, Present & Future*, a commercial law casebook with Professor John Dolan and Dean Larry Ponoroff, and *Securitization, Structured Finance and Capital Markets*, a set of teaching materials on securitization, with Professors Steven L. Schwarcz and Lissa Broome. *Securitization* is scheduled to be translated into Japanese in 2010. In early 2005, he published another casebook, *Bankruptcy: 21st Century Debtor-Creditor Law*, with David Epstein, Steve Nickles, and Elizabeth Perris; due to the enactment of BAPCPA, a second edition was published in late 2005, and a third edition is scheduled for 2010. In 2009, Oxford University Press published *International Cooperation in Bankruptcy and Insolvency Matters*, which he co-authored with Bob Wessels and Jason J. Kilborn. He is also the co-author, with Professor and Dean Mary Jo Wiggins, of the forthcoming *Questions & Answers: Bankruptcy* (LexisNexis 2011).

Professor Markell has served as an advisor on bankruptcy and secured transaction reform to the Republic of Indonesia, and was the International Bar Association's representative to the sessions of United Nations Commission on International Trade Law (UNCITRAL) that led to the creation of UNCITRAL's model law on the assignment of international receivables. He was also asked by the United Nations to be an expert consultant to its project to create a legislative guide for secured transactions.

Timothy R. Zinnecker is the Harry and Helen Hutchens Research Professor at South Texas College of Law, where he teaches Secured Transactions, Payment Systems, and other courses. Professor Zinnecker graduated with honors from the J. Reuben Clark Law School, Brigham Young University, in 1986, where he served as lead note and comment editor of the law review and was a member of the Order of the Coif. He then served as a judicial clerk for the Hon. Frank X. Gordon, chief justice of the Arizona Supreme Court, and the Hon. Edith H. Jones, United States Court of Appeals for the Fifth Circuit.

Professor Zinnecker practiced commercial law in Dallas and Houston for five years before joining the faculty at South Texas College of Law in 1994. He also has taught at the law schools of Samford University, Florida State University, the University of Richmond, and the University of Houston. His scholarship has appeared in *The Business Lawyer* and the primary law journals at Arizona State, Chapman, Gonzaga, Kansas, Missouri, Richmond, and Tennessee. He also is the author of *The Default Provisions of Revised Article 9 of the Uniform Commercial Code* (ABA 1999), the co-author of *Payment Systems, Banking and Documentary Transactions* (Carolina Academic Press 2d ed. 2007), and the co-author of *Questions and Answers: Payment Systems* (LexisNexis 2003; second edition forthcoming). Professor Zinnecker also is a frequent blogger at *The Faculty Lounge* website (http://thefacultylounge.org).

DEDICATIONS

To Douglass G. Boshkoff, a better mentor and friend there never was.

B.A.M.

To my beloved wife, Lisa, truly a "Proverbs 31" woman.

T.R.Z.

PREFACE

The primary source of law for Secured Transactions is Article 9 of the Uniform Commercial Code. This study guide uses multiple-choice and short-answer questions to test your knowledge of Article 9 and its occasional intersection with other sources of law (*e.g.*, the Federal Tax Lien Act [part of the Internal Revenue Code], and the Bankruptcy Code). These materials are based on the uniform version of Article 9 (sometimes referred to as "Revised Article 9"), which became effective in every (or almost every) state on July 1, 2001. Our occasional citations to other UCC articles (such as Articles 1, 2, and 8) are to the versions most recently approved by the American Law Institute and the National Conference of Commissioners on Uniform State Laws (*warning*: these versions may not yet be enacted into law in your jurisdiction). Our materials do not reflect non-uniform amendments enacted by any particular state. You will find a copy of the UCC in any of the several softback statutes books adopted for use by most commercial law professors.

The short-answer questions should be answered in no more than ten sentences and under twenty minutes. We believe that you will better understand the materials if you prepare your own answer before peeking at the model answer.

We love teaching Secured Transactions and are delighted that you are using our study guide to supplement your understanding of this challenging subject. We invite you to contact us with your questions and comments.

HON. BRUCE A. MARKELL
bruce.markell@unlv.edu
Las Vegas, Nevada
November 2010

PROFESSOR TIMOTHY R. ZINNECKER
tzinnecker@stcl.edu
Houston, Texas
November 2010

TABLE OF CONTENTS

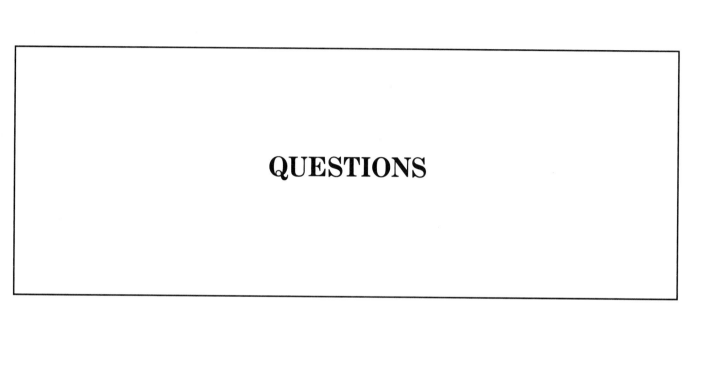

QUESTIONS

1.   Article 9 does *not* apply to sales of

   (A)   credit card receivables.

   (B)   automobile lease contracts.

   (C)   negotiable promissory notes secured by real estate.

   (D)   computer software diskettes.

2.   Grace wants to borrow $15,000 from her parents to upgrade the bathroom in her residence. Her parents insist on collateral. Grace offers her AKC-registered and prize-winning Dalmatian, her automobile (which is already securing repayment of its purchase price), and her right to a federal income tax refund.

   Article 9 will cover the parents' property interest in

   (A)   all three items of collateral.

   (B)   only the Dalmatian and the federal income tax refund.

   (C)   only the Dalmatian and the automobile.

   (D)   only the automobile.

3.   BizCorp wants to borrow $10 million from MidBank for general corporate purposes. The parties agree that the loan will be secured by all of BizCorp's assets. BizCorp's assets include (i) a claim against a competitor for patent infringement that will go to trial next month, (ii) rights as a beneficiary on a life insurance policy covering BizCorp's founder and chief executive officer, and (iii) a corporate airplane registered with the Federal Aviation Administration.

   Article 9 will cover MidBank's property interest in

   (A)   only the patent infringement claim.

   (B)   only the patent infringement claim and the airplane.

   (C)   only the rights under the life insurance policy and the airplane.

   (D)   all three assets.

4.   Three months ago, Ingrid Garcia borrowed $600 from Matt Johnson. Ingrid used the money to pay

several personal expenses (including two overdue payments on her car note). Ingrid and Matt agreed, in writing, that repayment of the debt was secured by Ingrid's claim against her employer for wages earned.

Ingrid has failed to pay the $600 to Matt, who is asserting rights as a "secured party" under Article 9. Ingrid claims that Article 9 is inapplicable to an assignment of a claim for wages. Matt argues, however, that his interest in Ingrid's claim for wages has transformed into an Article 9 security interest in Ingrid's personal bank account for amounts equal to the payroll checks which Ingrid has recently deposited.

Assuming that Matt can overcome any tracing challenges, does Article 9 cover Matt's alleged security interest in payroll amounts deposited by Ingrid into her personal bank account?

ANSWER:

5.   Last year, Norman lost his high-paying management position when his corporate employer merged with a competitor. Unable to find a similar position, Norman has suffered significant financial hardships and his creditors have turned aggressive. The county assessor has placed a statutory lien on his boat for unpaid property taxes. A neighbor who won a dog bite lawsuit against Norman in recent months has received a judgment lien on some of Norman's non-exempt investment property. Two nights ago his car was seized from the street in front of his home by an agent of the dealer exercising its rights as a creditor under the only contract signed by Norman (a "Promissory Note" under which the dealer retained title to the car until the purchase price was paid in full). And just this morning, the bank posted a foreclosure notice on his residence under a mortgage document executed by Norman at the time of purchase.

Article 9 governs the property interest claimed by

(A)   the county assessor, because boats can serve as collateral under Article 9.

(B)   the neighbor, because investment property can serve as collateral under Article 9.

(C)   the car dealer, even though Norman did not execute a formal "security agreement" contract.

(D)   the bank, because its interest in the residence arises contractually.

6. Yesterday, BizCorp sold a unit of inventory to Grace, who used her credit card to pay for the purchase. After swiping her card through the machine, Grace signed a piece of paper, acknowledging her payment obligations under the credit card agreement.

This payment receivable now held by BizCorp is

(A) chattel paper, if the piece of paper evidences both the monetary obligation and a security interest retained by BizCorp in the unit of inventory.

(B) an instrument, if the writing meets the requirements of a "negotiable instrument" under Article 3.

(C) a payment intangible.

(D) an account.

7. John is a professional photographer who lives in Chicago. He wants to borrow $2,000 from his mother, who insists on collateral.

Which of the following assets offered by John is a "consumer good"?

(A) His wedding album.

(B) A certificate of deposit.

(C) A photocopier that he uses half the time for personal reasons and half the time for professional purposes.

(D) A claim against the State of Illinois for an income tax refund.

8. Which of the following assets offered by John is "investment property"?

(A) A $10,000 certificate of deposit issued to John by MegaBank, bearing an annual interest rate of 4% and a five-year maturity date.

(B) A rare comic book that he purchased solely for investment purposes (i.e., appreciation in market value over time).

(C) Five hundred shares of BizCorp capital stock (not evidenced by a tangible certificate, and having a market value less than 20% of what John paid for it).

(D) His condominium in Vail, Colorado (which generates annual rental income to him in an amount greater than what he earns annually as a photographer).

9.   Which of the following assets offered by John is *not* a "general intangible"?

(A) A claim against his brother, who orally agreed to repay a $2,500 loan from John.

(B) John's domain name: thepictureperfectphotographer.com.

(C) A registered copyright held by John on a photography book that he wrote.

(D) John's right to receive $150 each month for the next ten years, arising from a winning lottery ticket that he purchased.

10. All of the following are examples of a "registered organization" *except*

(A) a limited partnership.

(B) a sole proprietorship that has filed a "d/b/a" ("doing business as") certificate with the appropriate state official.

(C) a limited liability company (created under the laws of Florida) that is delinquent in paying its property taxes.

(D) a corporation (chartered under the laws of Texas) that recently filed a bankruptcy petition.

11. Lender has an enforceable security interest in BizCorp's current and future inventory. This morning, BizCorp sold a unit of inventory to Jessalyn. The sale did *not* create a "cash proceed" if Jessalyn

(A) paid with her personal check.

(B) swiped her debit card.

(C) paid with a cashier's check payable to her, which she indorsed to BizCorp.

(D) used a non-merchant credit card (e.g., Visa, American Express, etc.).

12. Yesterday, Allison bought a new computer. She will *not* be an "account debtor" if she bought the computer on credit and

(A) executed a negotiable, but unsecured, promissory note to evidence the debt.

(B) executed the seller's standard sales agreement which evidenced the debt and reserved in the seller's favor a security interest in the computer.

(C) orally agreed to repay the debt in ninety days.

(D) executed a non-negotiable writing, and the debt is unsecured.

13. Article 9 applies to consignments, but only if the transaction falls within the Article 9 definition of that term. Which of the following transactions could fall within the definition of "consignment"?

(A) Annie, a professional musician, delivers one of her two pianos (with a fair market value of at least $7,800) to a piano dealer for resale.

(B) Now that Maggie's quadruplets are ten years old, Maggie delivers four toddler bicycles (each with a fair market value of at least $300) to a bike dealer for resale.

(C) BizCorp delivers twenty framed and matted vintage movie posters (with an aggregate estimated value of $22,000) to an auction house for resale to the public at an upcoming weekly auction.

(D) ZinnCo delivers several used desktop photocopiers (with an aggregate estimated value of $1,300) to Joe's Consignment Shoppe for resale.

14. In which of the following transactions is corporate entity BAMCO *not* a "debtor"?

(A) BAMCO sells 40% of its outstanding accounts to Finance Company.

(B) BAMCO is the primary obligor on a $1 million loan that is secured by the assets of BAMCO's two subsidiaries.

(C) BAMCO purchased from Seller a piece of equipment that (unknown to BAMCO) is subject to a perfected security interest held by Seller's primary lender.

(D) BAMCO holds for resale several units of inventory delivered to it by Supplier under a transaction that is a "consignment" as defined by Article 9.

15. What action must Lender take in order to achieve "control" of a deposit account maintained by Debtor with Bank?

ANSWER:

16. Each of the following is a "good" as defined by Article 9 except

(A) a chandelier that has become a fixture in a residence.

(B) a twenty-dollar bill ($20) kept in a purse.

(C) a collection of rare postage stamps held for investment purposes.

(D) the gas in a plastic container used by the owner as fuel for his lawn mower and snow blower.

17. Meredith is the president and chief executive officer of ZinnCo. Last year, Meredith borrowed $15,000 from the company, memorializing the loan and its repayment terms in writing. Several months ago, ZinnCo delivered the writing to Lender as collateral for a secured loan. Lender never filed a financing statement, so its possession of the writing perfects its security interest only if the writing is a "negotiable instrument" under the UCC.

Which of the following writings (properly executed by Meredith) will *not* create a "negotiable instrument" under the UCC?

(A) "Maker hereby promises to pay $15,000 to the order of ZinnCo on _____."

(B) "The undersigned promises to pay $15,000 to ZinnCo on demand."

(C) "Maker agrees to pay $15,000 to _____ on July 20, 2017."

(D) "The undersigned agrees to pay $15,000 to the order of ZinnCo on May 15, 2015; provided that all amounts shall be immediately due and payable if the undersigned is no longer employed by ZinnCo."

18. Lender has an enforceable security interest in the debtor's current and after-acquired "inventory." Lender's security interest will *not* include

(A) a fleet of vehicles that the debtor leases at an airport site to customers for short periods of time.

(B) thousands of grape clusters on the vines of a debtor that operates a prize-winning winery.

(C) 100 gallons of cooking oil used every week by a debtor that operates a restaurant.

(D) several shelves of board games held for sale by a toy company to customers, the overwhelming majority of whom are humans who will acquire the games for personal, family, or household use.

19. Section 9-317(a) is a statute that resolves priority disputes between an Article 9 creditor and a "lien creditor." Which of the following is an example of a lien creditor?

(A) A purchase-money creditor that fails to take the steps necessary to achieve superpriority.

(B) A lender claiming an interest in the debtor's fixtures under a real estate mortgage.

(C) A tort victim that has obtained a property interest in the debtor's investment portfolio pursuant to a court-issued writ.

(D) A mechanic that holds a statutory lien on a vehicle in its possession until the owner pays for services rendered.

20. Lender has a perfected security interest in the debtor's current and after-acquired "payment intangibles." The collateral will include a right to payment claimed by the debtor

(A) as a credit card receivable arising from the debtor's sale of a unit of inventory.

(B) under a photocopier lease executed by the debtor as lessor.

(C) under a patent-licensing agreement executed by the debtor as licensor.

(D) as a refund of a cash deposit previously paid as part of an unsuccessful request for tickets to an extremely popular college basketball tournament.

21. In which of the following transactions is corporate entity ZinnCo *not* a "secured party"?

    (A) ZinnCo purchased 173 lease contracts from Dealer (who executed the contracts as a lessor of office equipment).

    (B) ZinnCo sold a vehicle on credit to a buyer, who executed an unsecured promissory note in favor of ZinnCo and delivered the original certificate of title to ZinnCo to hold until the loan is repaid.

    (C) ZinnCo sold computer equipment on credit to a customer, who executed ZinnCo's standard sales contract which includes a provision under which ZinnCo reserves title to the equipment until the purchase price is paid in full.

    (D) ZinnCo and a customer have an oral understanding that a rare, autographed baseball card owned by the customer and delivered to ZinnCo will serve as collateral for the customer's past-due bills until the outstanding balance falls below $300.

22. What action must Lender take in order to achieve "control" of a certificated stock certificate that has been issued to, and registered in the name of, Debtor?

ANSWER:

23. Part Six of Article 9 gives specific statutory rights to a secured party upon "default." Which statement concerning that term is true?

    (A) The UCC does not define the term, leaving the definition to the contractual agreement of the secured party and the debtor.

    (B) The UCC defines the term to include the debtor's nonpayment of principal when due and nonpayment of interest for a period beyond any agreed-upon grace period.

    (C) The UCC defines the term to include the death of a human debtor.

    (D) The UCC defines the term to include the voluntary filing of a bankruptcy petition by the debtor, but not an involuntary bankruptcy petition filed against the debtor.

24. The following are examples of "accessions," *except*

    (A) the addition of two rear tires to a farm tractor that is subject to a pre-existing perfected security interest.

    (B) the mixing of flour, water, eggs, and other ingredients to create a chocolate cake.

    (C) the matting and framing of a law license that will be displayed on the wall of a lawyer's office.

    (D) the sewing of decorative buttons onto a woman's jacket.

25. Erin is borrowing $10,000 from her parents. The loan will be secured by Erin's various investments, including:

> 100 shares of MegaCorp common stock purchased by Erin directly from MegaCorp and evidenced by a stock certificate;

> 100 mutual fund shares of the LRGZ Global Investments Fund, purchased directly by Erin from the issuer (ownership is evidenced by a confirmation statement and quarterly performance reports); and

> 100 shares of ZeeMart common stock, the sole investment in an account maintained for Erin by the brokerage firm, Marbury Madison Group.

Which statement is true?

(A) The MegaCorp stock certificate is an example of a "certificated security," but only if the certificate is in registered form (rather than in blank form).

(B) The mutual fund shares in the LRGZ Global Investments Fund are an example of a "security entitlement."

(C) Marbury Madison Group is an example of a "securities intermediary."

(D) The ZeeMart shares are an example of an "uncertificated security."

26. A secured party may obtain a "purchase-money security interest" in each of the following assets *except*

(A) a rare book, kept by the owner in a safety deposit box at a bank.

(B) a bottle of champagne, stored in a collection outside the United States.

(C) a motorcycle that is subject to a certificate-of-title law.

(D) 300 shares of BAMCO common stock, purchased on "margin."

27. BigBank is lending $10 million to ZinnCorp for general corporate purposes. The loan will be secured by all of ZinnCorp's current and after-acquired personal property.

   To create an enforceable security interest in ZinnCorp's assets, the written security agreement

   (A) must state the maximum principal debt to be secured.

   (B) must state the expected final payment date.

   (C) must state both the maximum principal debt to be secured and the expected final payment date, unless the promissory note evidencing the loan is a "negotiable instrument" as defined by UCC Article 3.

   (D) need not describe the amount, any interest rate, any repayment dates, or any other specific details of the debt to be secured.

28. To create an enforceable security interest in ZinnCorp's property, the written security agreement must be executed

   (A) by both BigBank and ZinnCorp.

   (B) by only ZinnCorp.

   (C) by ZinnCorp and, if BigBank is chartered under federal (rather than state) law, BigBank.

   (D) by ZinnCorp and, if BigBank anticipates exercising statutory (rather than merely contractual) rights and remedies following any default by ZinnCorp, BigBank.

29. To create an enforceable security interest in ZinnCorp's assets, the written security agreement must describe the collateral in a manner that

   (A) is "commercially reasonable."

   (B) is "not manifestly unreasonable."

   (C) "reasonably identifies" the collateral.

   (D) utilizes Article 9's defined terms, such as "inventory" and "equipment."

30. To create an enforceable security interest in ZinnCorp's assets that fall within the following defined terms, the parties cannot rely solely on the term

(A) "commercial tort claims."

(B) "investment property."

(C) "deposit accounts."

(D) "payment intangibles."

31. The purpose of including an after-acquired property clause in the written security agreement is to include within the "collateral" any assets in which ZinnCorp acquires rights after the date on which

   (A) ZinnCorp authenticates the security agreement.

   (B) BigBank first gives value.

   (C) ZinnCorp first borrows any funds.

   (D) ZinnCorp executes the promissory note that evidences the $10 million loan.

32. Notwithstanding BigBank's inclusion of an after-acquired property clause in the written security agreement, the clause is not effective to encumber any of ZinnCorp's future

   (A) federally registered copyrights.

   (B) patent infringement claims against business competitors.

   (C) lease agreements that qualify as "electronic chattel paper."

   (D) motor vehicles that are subject to certificate-of-title laws.

33. For some unknown reason, BigBank and ZinnCorp never produce a written security agreement. Both parties are willing to testify that they had an oral understanding that the $10 million loan would be secured by all of ZinnCorp's assets. Nevertheless, this oral understanding will fail to create an enforceable security interest in ZinnCorp's

   (A) patents.

   (B) promissory notes executed by customers.

   (C) computer equipment.

   (D) corporate bank account.

34. Oliver Jenkins recently graduated from law school and has moved to Seattle to begin a judicial clerkship. To furnish his apartment, Oliver borrowed $5,000 on June 1 from his parents. The loan is secured by all of the furnishings that Oliver will acquire with his parents' funds. The written security agreement, authenticated by Oliver on (and dated) June 6, included an after-acquired property clause and otherwise reasonably described the collateral. Oliver used his parents' funds to purchase the following:

kitchen table and four chairs	June 2
bedroom furniture	June 9
washer/dryer	June 18

In which of the items will Oliver's parents have an enforceable security interest?

ANSWER:

35. Graham Excavation Corporation ("GEC") builds roads and clears land for governmental, commercial, and private parties. In February, Hoover Finance loaned $1 million to GEC. To secure repayment of the loan, GEC granted to Hoover Finance a security interest in its excavation equipment. During the year, Hoover Finance funded additional advances to GEC. Also during the year, GEC bought additional excavation equipment. A summary of the activity follows:

February 1	Parties execute security agreement and other loan papers
	Hoover Finance advances $1 million
	Value of existing excavation equipment is $1.2 million
April 10	Hoover Finance advances $200,000
May 20	GEC buys road grader for $350,000
June 25	GEC buys bulldozer for $400,000
August 15	Hoover Finance advances $350,000

In November, GEC defaulted on its obligations to Hoover Finance, having repaid none of the loans.

Ignoring any market changes in the value of the equipment, and assuming that the security agreement included an after-acquired property clause but not a future advance clause, calculate the amount of Hoover Finance's secured claim.

ANSWER:

36. Ignoring any market changes in the value of the equipment, and assuming that the security agreement included a future advance clause but not an after-acquired property clause, calculate the amount of Hoover Finance's unsecured claim.

ANSWER:

37. Tim borrowed $2,500 from his friend, Bruce, last week. Tim and Bruce orally agreed that Tim's baseball card collection would serve as collateral for the loan.

Which statement is true?

(A) Bruce does not have an enforceable security interest in the baseball card collection because Article 9 does not permit oral security agreements.

(B)   Bruce does not have an enforceable security interest in the baseball card collection because Article 9 does not permit oral security agreements if the debtor is a consumer and the secured debt exceeds $1,000.

(C)   The oral understanding is sufficient to create an enforceable security interest in the baseball card collection, but only if Bruce takes possession of the collection.

(D)   The oral understanding is sufficient to create an enforceable security interest in the baseball card collection, but only if Bruce — or a third party that is neither under Tim's control nor too closely associated with Tim — takes possession of the collection.

38.   Assume, instead, that Tim borrowed the $2,500 from LawProf Credit Union. To secure repayment of the loan, the Credit Union insisted on taking a security interest in Tim's personal checking account maintained with the Credit Union. Tim orally agreed to this arrangement, which was never memorialized in writing or otherwise authenticated.

Which statement is true?

(A)   The Credit Union does not have an enforceable security interest in Tim's checking account because Article 9 requires a written security agreement for this type of collateral.

(B)   Article 9 does not apply to this transaction because Article 9 excludes from its scope of coverage a transaction in which a checking account serves as collateral.

(C)   The Credit Union does not have an enforceable security interest in Tim's checking account because Article 9 does not permit oral security agreements if the debtor is a consumer and the secured debt exceeds $1,000.

(D)   The Credit Union has an enforceable security interest in Tim's checking account if Tim uses the loan proceeds for a business purpose — even if Tim uses the checking account primarily for personal, family, or household expenses.

39.   BizCorp sells various musical instruments. BizCorp's customers include symphonies, houses of worship, schools and colleges, professional musicians, and many consumer households. Friendly Finance has agreed to make a $5 million loan to BizCorp that will be secured by the musical instruments.

If the parties desire to use Article 9 terminology when describing the musical instruments, the security agreement should describe the collateral as

(A)   instruments.

(B)   inventory.

(C)   inventory, equipment, and consumer goods.

(D)   goods.

40. MegaBank will loan $5 million to Friendly Furniture Corp. (a corporation chartered under California law that operates furniture stores in Los Angeles and San Francisco, California; Las Vegas, Nevada; and Phoenix, Arizona). Repayment of the loan will be secured by all of Friendly's personal property, including accounts, inventory, equipment, chattel paper, instruments, documents, general intangibles, investment property, letter-of-credit rights, commercial tort claims, and deposit accounts.

   The MegaBank loan officer asks its lawyer to determine whether any other parties have non-fixture security interests in the collateral. In response, the lawyer should order a UCC search report against Friendly from the appropriate filing officer in

   (A) California only.

   (B) California, Nevada, and Arizona.

   (C) California and, if different, the state in which Friendly maintains its chief executive office.

   (D) California and, if different, the state in which its stores generate the greatest percentage of Friendly's gross sales revenues.

41. MegaBank's lawyer submits a written request for a search report on Monday, July 20, and each filing officer receives the request on Wednesday, July 22.

   Each filing officer must communicate the results of its search to MegaBank's lawyer no later than

   (A) Friday, July 31.

   (B) Wednesday, July 29.

   (C) Monday, July 27.

   (D) Friday, July 24.

42. The information on the search report(s) must be current through at least

   (A) Monday, July 20.

   (B) Friday, July 17.

   (C) Friday, July 10.

   (D) Wednesday, July 1.

43.   MegaBank's lawyer receives the requested information and sends a copy to its client. MegaBank's loan officer forwards a copy to Friendly's general counsel. The general counsel reviews the information and concludes that two filings pertain to the assets of "Friendly's Furniture, Inc.," a different legal entity.

Article 9 permits Friendly's general counsel to

(A) file a termination statement against the two filings.

(B) take no unilateral filing action.

(C) file a correction statement that explains the problem, provided that the correction statement is authenticated by an authorized officer of "Friendly's Furniture, Inc."

(D) unilaterally file a correction statement.

44.   MegaBank's lawyer is preparing the financing statement. The financing statement

(A) will not perfect a security interest in any of Friendly's "fixtures" unless the filing is recorded in the real estate records of the county where the fixture is (or will be) located.

(B) cannot be filed before Friendly authenticates the security agreement.

(C) must be authenticated by Friendly.

(D) need not include an after-acquired property clause in order to perfect a security interest in Friendly's future personalty.

45.   To be effective, the financing statement must

(A) provide the name of the secured party (MegaBank).

(B) describe the secured debt.

(C) avoid using a supergeneric collateral description (such as "all assets" or "all personal property").

(D) be filed in each state where Friendly maintains its inventory, equipment, and other tangible property.

46.   MegaBank's lawyer prepares the financing statement and submits it, along with the necessary fees, to the appropriate filing officer(s) on Monday, August 10. Each filing officer receives the filing on Wednesday, August 12. Give three of the reasons why a filing officer may *rightfully* reject the filing.

ANSWER:

47.   A filing officer rightfully rejects the financing statement on Thursday, August 13. That filing officer must communicate its decision to MegaBank's lawyer no later than

(A) Friday, August 14.

(B) Tuesday, August 18.

(C) Thursday, August 20.

(D) Monday, August 31.

48. Ignoring any proceeds-related arguments, the filed financing statement will *not* perfect MegaBank's security interest in Friendly's

(A) stocks, bonds, and other investment property managed by a person or entity subject to regulatory oversight by the Securities and Exchange Commission.

(B) bank accounts, unless the bank accounts are insured by the Federal Deposit Insurance Corporation.

(C) fleet of delivery trucks.

(D) domain name (http://www.FriendlyFurniture.com).

49. A filed financing statement is the only method by which MegaBank will perfect its security interest in Friendly's

(A) rights under a life insurance policy that will pay Friendly over $1 million upon the death of its founder and chief executive officer, Felix Friendly.

(B) cash that is received from customers and prior to its deposit into a bank account.

(C) payment claims arising when customers use a credit card as the method of payment.

(D) lease contracts executed by local entities that lease furniture from Friendly to furnish apartment units.

50. A filing officer records MegaBank's financing statement on August 12, 2010. The parties contemplate that Friendly will be making periodic loan payments through December 2018. MegaBank's lawyer anticipates filing a continuation statement sometime prior to Friendly's last loan payment. Which of the following will be the best date on which to file the continuation statement?

(A) Any date after Friendly has paid more than 50% of the original principal amount of the loan.

(B) March 6, 2015.

(C) February 23, 2016.

(D) July 20, 2016.

51. MegaBank's lawyer files the continuation statement ten days after the original filing has expired. The original filing remains in the public records, and the filing clerk records the continuation statement.

Which statement is true?

(A) MegaBank enjoys continuous and uninterrupted perfection because both the original filing and the continuation statement are in the public records and provide a searcher with the intended notice.

(B) MegaBank enjoys continuous and uninterrupted perfection because the ten-day mistake falls within Article 9's statutory grace period applicable to untimely filed continuation statements.

(C) MegaBank will enjoy continuous and uninterrupted perfection if it files a new financing statement no later than thirty days following the date on which the effectiveness of its original filing lapsed.

(D) MegaBank does not have, and is unable to take any filing action that will result in, continuous and uninterrupted perfection.

52. Friendly makes its last monthly loan payment to MegaBank in December 2018. What filing action (if any) must MegaBank take, and what penalties (if any) might MegaBank incur for failing to do so?

ANSWER:

53. Alex Garza borrowed $15,000 from Essex Financing for the purpose of opening a restaurant. The loan is secured by an enforceable interest in Alex's personal and business assets. In addition to a central filing, Essex Financing should consider a county filing if

(A) Alex is a debtor.

(B) the collateral includes the restaurant equipment.

(C) Alex is married, and he and his wife maintain their primary residence in a community property state.

(D) the collateral includes his personal automobile, on which Alex pays county property taxes each calendar year.

54. BigBank, MidBank, and SmallBank are the sole members of a syndicate that is making a $25 million loan to ZinnCorp. The loan is secured by an enforceable security interest in ZinnCorp's accounts, inventory, and equipment. The security agreement includes an after-acquired property clause. The three banks have appointed MegaBank as the collateral agent for the syndicate.

All of the loan papers were executed earlier today, and the financing statement has been mailed to the appropriate filing office. BigBank's loan officer (your client) just called to express concern that the secured party is identified on the filing as "MEGABANK, AS AGENT" — but the names of the three syndicate banks do not appear anywhere on the filing.

Should you and your client be concerned that the filing fails to perfect BigBank's security interest?

ANSWER:

55. Robert W. Zimmer lives in Kansas City, Missouri (Jackson County). Zimmer operates a consulting service ("RWZ Consulting") that he has incorporated under the laws of Delaware. The sole business office is located in Kansas City, Kansas (Johnson County). Yesterday, Zimmer, acting on behalf of his consulting service, bought a new computer system on credit from Bradford Computer Co. ("BCC"). To secure repayment of the loan, BCC retained an enforceable security interest in the computer system (which BCC installed at the business location of the consulting service).

   To perfect its security interest BCC should file its financing statement

   (A) against "Robert W. Zimmer" in Jackson County, Missouri.

   (B) against "Robert W. Zimmer" in Missouri's central filing office.

   (C) against "RWZ Consulting" in Kansas's central filing office.

   (D) against "RWZ Consulting" in Delaware's central filing office.

56. Why is BCC's security interest in the computer system not automatically perfected?

ANSWER:

57. BizCorp sells office equipment to businesses and consumers, often on credit. These credit purchases are evidenced by a single-page contract (captioned "PROMISSORY NOTE AND SECURITY AGREEMENT") that memorializes the buyer's monetary obligation and BizCorp's retention of title in the item(s) until the buyer has fulfilled all monetary obligations.

   BizCorp wants to use these contracts to obtain necessary financing from Lender. The parties are contemplating two possible transactions. First, Lender will extend credit that will be secured by the contracts. Second, Lender will purchase the contracts for a discounted price.

   Discuss whether Article 9 applies to both proposed transactions and what action Lender must take to perfect any Article 9 interest in the contracts.

ANSWER:

58. Would any of your analysis change if the single-page contracts were negotiable, but unsecured, promissory notes?

ANSWER:

59. On August 1, The Book Nook ("TBN"), a retail bookseller, executed a written security agreement granting to Bank a security interest in TBN's existing and future equipment to secure repayment of a loan in an amount not yet agreed upon by the parties. On August 4, Bank filed a proper financing statement against "equipment" with the proper official. Loan negotiations concluded on August 7, when Bank executed a binding commitment to lend up to $500,000 to TBN in one or more advances. On August 10, TBN requested the

initial advance of $100,000. Bank funded the $100,000 advance on August 12.

Bank's interest in a new computer system, purchased by TBN on August 3 and delivered and installed on August 11, became perfected on

(A) August 4.

(B) August 7.

(C) August 11.

(D) August 12.

60. When did Bank obtain a perfected security interest in a shipment of children's books that TBN ordered on August 2 and received on August 8?

ANSWER:

61. Maria Garza, a resident of Dallas, Texas, intends to borrow $25,000 from SmallBank. The loan will be secured by the following collateral:

100 shares of 3X stock, represented by a certificate in Maria's possession;

200 shares of the Franklin Large Cap Fund (the Fund is organized under Delaware law; the account agreement is governed by New York law); and

all of the investments in her brokerage account managed by the Houston office of Providence Securities, an entity organized under Delaware law (the account agreement is governed by New York law).

SmallBank wants to perfect its security interest in all of these investments by filing. To do so, it must file its financing statement

(A) in the county records in Dallas County, Texas.

(B) in the central filing office of Texas.

(C) in the central filing offices of Texas, Delaware, and New York.

(D) in the county records of Dallas County, Texas, and in the central filing offices of Texas, Delaware, and New York.

62. Three years after funding the loan, SmallBank discovers that Maria had recently sold all shares of her 3X stock to her father, Arturo, who lives in Rochester, New York.

What filing action, if any, should SmallBank take to continue to perfect its interest in the shares of 3X stock, following Maria's unauthorized transaction?

ANSWER:

63. A few weeks after Maria sold all of her shares of 3X stock to her father, Maria moved from Dallas,

Texas, to Santa Fe, New Mexico.

What filing action, if any, should SmallBank take to continue to perfect its security interest in Maria's investment property, following Maria's relocation to a different state?

ANSWER:

64. VegasBank wants to perfect an enforceable security interest in BAMCO's inventory, accounts, equipment, investment property, and deposit accounts. BAMCO does business in Nevada, Colorado, and Utah. Its chief executive office is located in Las Vegas.

Explain why this statement is true or false: *If BAMCO is a corporation organized under Delaware law, then VegasBank should file in Delaware to perfect its security interest in inventory and equipment and in Nevada to perfect its security interest in accounts and investment property.*

ANSWER:

65. Explain why this statement is true or false: *If BAMCO is a general partnership, then VegasBank should file in each state where inventory and equipment are located to perfect its security interest in that collateral and in Nevada to perfect its security interest in accounts and investment property.*

ANSWER:

66. Explain why this statement is true or false: *BAMCO's relocation of its chief executive office to Denver has no impact on the continued effectiveness of VegasBank's financing statement if BAMCO is a corporation.*

ANSWER:

67. In which transaction does Bank have a perfected security interest?

(A) Bank has an enforceable PMSI in Tom's boat (which is not subject to any certificate-of-title laws). Bank never files a financing statement. Tom uses the boat equally for personal and business purposes.

(B) Bank has an enforceable security interest in 100 shares of BAMCO stock owned by Meredith. The shares are evidenced by a certificate issued in Meredith's name. Meredith delivers the certificate to Bank without indorsing it. Bank never files a financing statement.

(C) Bank has an enforceable security interest in all of the motor vehicles owned by Zippy Rental Agency that it leases to travelers, on a short-term basis, from its facility at Reagan National Airport in Washington, D.C. Bank files a financing statement against Zippy's vehicle inventory, rather than complying with certificate-of-title laws.

(D)   Bank has an enforceable security interest in BizCorp's deposit accounts maintained with other financial institutions. Bank files a financing statement.

68.   Copyrights, trademarks, and patents are often registered by their owners with national registries in Washington, D.C. Under current case law, a lender can perfect its security interest in these forms of intellectual property by filing a financing statement (rather than registering its property interest in the relevant national registry) when the collateral is

(A)   patents and trademarks, but not copyrights.

(B)   trademarks and copyrights, but not patents.

(C)   trademarks, but not patents or copyrights.

(D)   patents, copyrights, or trademarks.

69.   Bank makes a $25,000 loan to BAM Corp. (a Delaware corporation) in January. The loan is secured by a security interest in BAM's accounts, inventory, and equipment, and the security agreement includes an after-acquired property clause. Bank promptly files a proper financing statement with the appropriate Delaware clerk.

BAM Corp. changes its name to "ZinnCo" on March 15. Bank knows of the name change, but takes no action in response. Thereafter, ZinnCo acquires three pieces of equipment (Item #1 in May, Item #2 in July, and Item #3 in September).

As of November 1, Bank has

(A)   no security interest in Items #1, #2, and #3.

(B)   unperfected security interests in each of the three items.

(C)   a perfected security interest in Item #1.

(D)   unperfected security interests in Items #2 and #3.

70.   Assume that BAM Corp. does not change its name. Instead, in March, and without Bank's knowledge or permission, BAM sells a piece of equipment (the "Item") to Purchaser.

As of November 1, Bank's security interest in the Item

(A)   no longer exists.

(B)   remains perfected, but only if the Item remains located in Delaware.

(C)   remains perfected, regardless of where Purchaser is located.

(D)   remains perfected, but only if Purchaser is located in Delaware.

71.   Give an example of collateral in which a security interest can be perfected three different ways.

ANSWER:

72. GetSmart! is a Nevada corporation that operates several tutorial clinics in Las Vegas. Most of its customers are individuals who want to maximize their score on any of a number of standardized tests (such as the ACT, the SAT, the GMAT, the LSAT, etc.). GetSmart! owns or leases office furniture, photocopiers, and computers, and its customers pay — with cash, checks, or credit cards — prior to each tutorial. GetSmart! also maintains an up-to-date, and rather lengthy, customer list.

GetSmart! wants to open several tutorial clinics in Reno, Nevada. It approaches Omega Bank for a $1 million loan. Omega Bank agrees to fund the loan, and GetSmart! executes a promissory note and a security agreement that describes the collateral as "all accounts, equipment, and general intangibles." The security agreement includes an after-acquired property clause. Omega Bank files its financing statement (describing the collateral as "all of Debtor's personal property") with the appropriate office.

Upon filing the financing statement, Omega Bank has (or, upon attachment, will have) a perfected security interest in

(A) none of GetSmart!'s assets because its financing statement fails to provide a proper collateral description.

(B) everything, other than the customer list and the cash.

(C) everything, other than the cash and the checks and the customer list.

(D) everything, other than the cash and the checks.

73. Katherine Grace Johnson has lived in Iowa all of her life. Her birth certificate and Social Security Card list her name as "Katherine Grace Johnson." Her Iowa driver's license lists her name as "K. Grace Johnson." Since birth, family and friends have called her "Grace."

Grace has operated a bakery, as a sole proprietorship, for several years in Des Moines. She needs some new ovens and other equipment, so she approaches Hawkeye Bank for a $300,000 loan. Hawkeye Bank agrees to make the loan, on a secured basis over a four-year term, on one condition: Grace must incorporate her business and transfer all of her business assets to the corporate entity.

Which of the following is the best reason for Hawkeye Bank's request?

(A) Secured loans to human debtors violate Federal Trade Commission regulations.

(B) A corporate debtor's name can be determined with more accuracy than can the name of a human debtor.

(C) Transferring ownership of the business assets from a sole proprietorship to a corporate entity will terminate any pre-existing security interests originally granted by Grace.

(D) A financing statement is effective for five years against a corporate debtor, but only three years against a human debtor.

74. BizCorp is in the business of selling and leasing photocopiers to individuals and businesses. In February, Omega Bank extended credit to BizCorp, in return for an enforceable security interest in BizCorp's inventory. Omega Bank perfected its security interest in BizCorp's inventory by filing a financing statement with the appropriate state official. The security agreement and the financing statement described the collateral as "inventory"; neither description mentioned an after-acquired property clause.

In June, BizCorp sold one of its photocopiers in the ordinary course of its business to a law firm, which paid for the purchase by tendering a cashier's check for the full price.

Evidence reveals that BizCorp owned the photocopier for six months before selling it to the law firm.

Omega Bank

(A) cannot claim an enforceable security interest in the cashier's check because the loan papers failed to mention an after-acquired property clause, and BizCorp did not acquire rights in the cashier's check until after it had authenticated the security agreement.

(B) cannot claim an enforceable security interest in the cashier's check because the loan papers describe the collateral merely as "inventory" and fail to use language (such as "checks" or "proceeds") that would cover the check.

(C) can claim an enforceable security interest in the cashier's check, but the security interest will not be perfected if the sale of the photocopier to the law firm effectively terminated Omega Bank's security interest in the photocopier.

(D) can claim an enforceable and perfected security interest in the cashier's check, assuming it is identifiable as a proceed of the photocopier.

75. Trinity Finance holds a perfected security interest in the inventory of The Avid Reader bookstore. Both the security agreement and the financing statement describe the collateral as "debtor's current and after-acquired inventory."

Last month a hurricane caused significant damage to the bookstore, including $1 million in lost, damaged, or destroyed inventory. The bookstore is insured against this loss.

Trinity Finance has

(A) a perfected security interest in the bookstore's insurance claim.

(B) a perfected security interest in the bookstore's insurance claim, but only for twenty days from the date of the hurricane damage, after which the security interest will become unperfected.

(C) an unperfected security interest in the bookstore's insurance claim.

(D) no security interest in the bookstore's insurance claim because Article 9 excludes from its coverage a debtor's interest arising under an insurance policy.

76. A month goes by, and the bookstore receives a $1 million check from its insurance company. Trinity Finance has

(A) a perfected security interest in the check.

(B) a perfected security interest in the check, but only for twenty days after the bookstore's receipt of the check, after which the security interest is unperfected unless Trinity Finance takes possession of the check.

(C) an unperfected security interest in the check, unless and until the bookstore indorses and delivers the check to Trinity Finance.

(D) no security interest in the check because the check is "money" under the UCC and Article 9 excludes from its coverage a debtor's rights in money.

77. Assume, instead, that the insurance company does not pay the claim by delivering a check to the bookstore. Instead, the insurance company sends a $1 million wire transfer (a "funds transfer" under UCC Article 4) directly to the bookstore's general operating bank account that the bookstore maintains with ZinnBank.

Assuming that Trinity Finance can satisfy its tracing burden, Trinity Finance has

(A) a perfected security interest in the bookstore's bank account for $1 million.

(B) a perfected security interest in the bookstore's bank account for $1 million, but only for twenty days, after which the security interest is unperfected unless Trinity Finance obtains control over the bank account.

(C) an unperfected security interest in the bookstore's bank account, unless and until Trinity Finance obtains control over the bank account.

(D) no security interest in the bookstore's bank account because Article 9 excludes from its coverage the debtor's interest in a bank account arising from a funds transfer covered by UCC Article 4.

78. MediCorp is a Delaware corporation that owns and operates hospitals and clinics in San Francisco, Los Angeles, and San Diego. A few months ago, BAM Technologies sold three pieces of medical equipment to MediCorp on credit, retaining an enforceable security interest in the equipment to secure the aggregate purchase price. BAM Technologies filed its financing statement with California's central filing office.

Yesterday, without the knowledge or consent of BAM Technologies, MediCorp sold one of the three pieces of equipment to HealthNet for $1.5 million. HealthNet paid $500,000 in cash and executed and delivered a short-term $1 million negotiable promissory note for the balance.

Assuming that BAM Technologies can satisfy its tracing burden, BAM Technologies has

(A) no security interest in either the cash or the note.

(B) an unperfected security interest in both the cash and the note.

(C) a perfected security interest in both the cash and the note, but only if BAM Technologies filed its financing statement within twenty days after MediCorp took possession of the equipment.

(D) a perfected security interest in both the cash and the note.

79. On July 20, Omega Bank obtained an enforceable security interest in the current and after-acquired inventory of Gershwin Pianos, a business that sells and leases pianos. Omega Bank filed its financing statement in the appropriate place against Gershwin's inventory on August 1.

On November 1, Lauren bought an upright piano from Gershwin. Lauren operates a sole proprietorship that sells office equipment, and she paid for the piano by delivering to Gershwin (for in-store use) a photocopier of comparable value.

As of December 1, does Omega Bank have a perfected security interest in the photocopier?

ANSWER:

80. Discuss whether your answer to the preceding question would change if Lauren paid cash for her piano, and, later that day, Gershwin used that cash to purchase the photocopier from Dealer.

ANSWER:

81. Lender has a perfected security interest in Debtor's inventory and accounts. Contrary to the terms of the security agreement, Debtor deposited cash proceeds in a bank account in April that contained non-proceeds. Evidence reveals the following activity during April:

- the opening balance on April 1 was $8,000 ($2,000 of which is proceeds)

- Debtor deposited cash proceeds into the account as follows:

    $6,000 on April 5

    $3,000 on April 24

- Debtor deposited non-proceeds into the account as follows:

    $4,000 on April 15

    $2,000 on April 28

- Debtor made the following withdrawals from the account:

    $7,000 on April 7

    $5,000 on April 20

As of April 30, under the lowest intermediate balance rule, Lender can claim a security interest in

(A) $8,000.

(B) $9,000.

(C) $10,000.

(D) $11,000.

82. Assume that Debtor also deposited cash proceeds of $4,000 on April 12 and non-proceeds of $2,000 on April 22, and withdrew $8,000 on April 17. Calculate the amount of Lender's security interest as of April 30 under the lowest intermediate balance rule.

ANSWER:

83. Tim, an avid chess player, borrowed $15,000 from his parents in August 2009 to purchase a Civil War chess set later that month on an internet auction site. At his parents' insistence, Tim authenticated a security agreement that granted to his parents a security interest in the chess set (which was adequately described). Tim also executed a promissory note payable to his parents, with a maturity date of December 31, 2011. His parents filed a financing statement against Tim and the chess set in Ohio, where Tim lived and worked. Tim never told his parents that someone else won the auction, or that he then used his parents' money to take a vacation to New Zealand and pay off some credit card debt.

In October 2009, Tim purchased an identical Civil War chess set at the same internet auction site.

In July 2010, Tim was promoted by his employer; that month he moved to Rochester, New York, to assume his new responsibilities.

In February 2011, Tim sold the Civil War chess set to another collector in exchange for three baseballs, each in mint condition and autographed by a different member of baseball's Hall of Fame.

Tim failed to repay the $15,000 to his parents when the promissory note came due on December 31, 2011.

On that date, his parents have

(A) no security interest in the baseballs.

(B) an unperfected security interest in the baseballs.

(C) a perfected security interest in the baseballs, but only if the chess set was a consumer good as used by Tim.

(D) a perfected security interest in the baseballs, whether or not the chess set was a consumer good as used by Tim.

84. Which of the following examples of collateral is most likely to merit a fixture filing?

    (A) Coal in the ground.

    (B) A large video screen that drops down from the ceiling of a church.

    (C) A grand piano that cannot be removed from its location without removing one or more doors and related door frames or, alternatively, disassembling the piano.

    (D) Daily revenues earned by a hotel for making its rooms available to travelers.

85. Unlike a standard financing statement, a fixture filing must

    (A) include a description of real estate.

    (B) be authorized by the record owner of the real estate if the debtor does not have an interest of record in the real estate.

    (C) be authenticated by the debtor, if the debtor is a consumer.

    (D) be notarized by the county clerk.

86. Molly, a resident of Minneapolis, has hired Quality Contractors to install granite countertops and new cabinets and lighting in the kitchen of her vacation home in Phoenix. Quality Contractors is financing the remodeling on a secured basis. The countertops, cabinets, and lights will serve as collateral. Once installed, all of these items will be "fixtures" under local law.

    Quality Contractors

    (A) has no reason to file a fixture filing because its PMSI is automatically perfected in the consumer goods.

    (B) has no reason to file a fixture filing because Article 9 excludes from its scope a security interest in residential fixtures.

    (C) should file a fixture filing in the appropriate Minnesota county.

    (D) should file a fixture filing in the appropriate Arizona county.

87. Grappino Corporation ("GC"), chartered under Delaware law, owns and operates three wineries and related vineyards in the Sonoma Valley, north of San Francisco. Bay Area

Bank holds a mortgage on the real estate and "all fixtures now or hereafter affixed thereto." The mortgage (which is not a construction mortgage) was filed in the local property records in January.

On July 8, GC purchased four storage tanks on credit from BAMCO (with BAMCO retaining an enforceable security interest in the tanks). BAMCO delivered and installed the tanks (each a "fixture" under applicable law, and not readily removable) on August 5.

In November, GC defaulted on his obligations to Bay Area Bank and BAMCO. The two creditors are disputing whose property interest in the storage tanks enjoys priority.

Which statement is true?

(A) BAMCO has perfected its security interest in the tanks if it filed a standard financing statement with the central filing office in California.

(B) BAMCO will win the priority dispute with Bay Area Bank if BAMCO filed a standard financing statement on July 20.

(C) BAMCO will win the priority dispute with Bay Area Bank if BAMCO filed a fixture filing on August 23.

(D) BAMCO's security interest in the tanks is automatically perfected because BAMCO is a purchase-money creditor.

88. Now that GC is in default, BAMCO wants to enforce its rights and remedies. Which statement is true?

(A) Because the tanks are fixtures, BAMCO's rights and remedies are provided by real estate law, rather than Article 9.

(B) Because the tanks are fixtures, BAMCO cannot remove the tanks (absent GC's consent).

(C) BAMCO can remove the tanks, but only if its security interest in the tanks enjoys priority over the claim asserted by Bay Area Bank.

(D) BAMCO cannot remove the tanks if GC has paid off more than 60% of the purchase-money debt associated with the tanks.

89. Assume that BAMCO exercises due care in removing the tanks under applicable law, but still causes damage of $6,000. In addition, the absence of the three tanks has caused GC's property to decrease in value by $36,000.

Bay Area Bank and GC each contend that BAMCO owes $42,000 to it.

Which statement is true?

(A) BAMCO owes $42,000 to Bay Area Bank, and nothing to GC.

(B) BAMCO owes $6,000 to Bay Area Bank, and nothing to GC.

(C) BAMCO owes $36,000 to Bay Area Bank, and $6,000 to GC.

(D) BAMCO owes nothing to Bay Area Bank, and $6,000 to GC.

90. Markell & Zinnecker, L.P. ("M&Z"), obtained a $3 million loan in February from Gilmore Finance to buy an urban lot and build a restaurant. The loan is secured by a construction mortgage on the property (and all buildings, improvements, and fixtures then or thereafter added to the property) filed in the real property records at the time of the loan. Gilmore Finance made no other filings.

In July, as construction progressed, FrigiTech agreed to sell two large walk-in refrigerator/freezer units to M&Z for $400,000. M&Z paid $100,000 in cash and agreed to pay the balance, with interest, over the next twelve months. To secure the deferred part of the purchase price, M&Z granted to FrigiTech an enforceable security interest in the units. FrigiTech promptly filed a financing statement with the central filing office, but it did not file any fixture filings.

Under applicable local law, the two walk-in refrigerator/freezer units — when installed — will be "fixtures" (and will not be readily removable).

As agreed, FrigiTech delivered the units to the building site on July 15, with the one-week installation expected to begin in early August. On July 24, however, M&Z defaulted on all of its material contracts and filed a bankruptcy petition. Further construction immediately ceased.

In a priority contest between Gilmore Finance and FrigiTech concerning the two walk-in refrigerator/freezer units,

(A) FrigiTech will win because Gilmore Finance has no interest in the units.

(B) Gilmore Finance will win because FrigiTech never filed a fixture filing.

(C) Gilmore Finance will win because FrigiTech's PMSI never secured the full purchase price of $400,000.

(D) Gilmore Finance will win because its mortgage is a construction mortgage.

91. Assume the same facts, except M&Z filed its bankruptcy petition in mid-August, after FrigiTech had completed its installation of the two walk-in refrigerator/freezer units (but before construction of the restaurant had concluded). Who will win the dispute between Gilmore Finance and FrigiTech under these revised facts?

ANSWER:

92. Continue to assume the revised facts. The bankruptcy trustee seeks to convert FrigiTech's secured claim into an unsecured claim by exercising its avoidance powers under the strong-arm clause of the Bankruptcy Code. Will the trustee be successful?

ANSWER:

93. Meredith, a veterinarian, bought her first home in April 2010. To finance part of the down payment, she borrowed $15,000 from her parents (Tim and Lisa). Rather than encumber the real estate with a second mortgage, Meredith granted to her parents an enforceable security interest in her grand piano that she had purchased several years ago.

A few months later, Meredith borrowed $10,000 from her sister (Grace) to pay off some of her student loans, at which time Meredith granted to Grace an enforceable security interest in the same grand piano.

Within a year, Meredith had defaulted on both loans (still owing $15,000 to her parents and $10,000 to Grace). A priority dispute arose over the piano between Grace and her parents. With everyone's consent, Meredith sold the piano for $20,000, and the funds are held in trust by Meredith's brother, Ethan.

If Grace and her parents hold unperfected security interests in the piano, then Ethan should award

(A) $15,000 to his parents and $5,000 to Grace.

(B) $10,000 to his parents and $10,000 to Grace.

(C) $12,000 to his parents and $8,000 to Grace.

(D) $10,000 to Grace and $10,000 to Meredith; his parents are not entitled to any proceeds because their secured debt arose from a real estate transaction that is excluded from the scope of Article 9.

94. Assume that Tim and Lisa perfected their security interest in the piano by filing a financing statement in April 2010, and Grace perfected her security interest in the piano by taking possession of it (with Meredith's consent) in September 2010. As before, Meredith defaults on both loans. For the first time, Grace and her parents discover that the piano serves as collateral on two loans. With everyone's consent the piano is sold, and Ethan is holding the proceeds of $20,000.

Under these revised facts, Ethan should award

(A) $15,000 to his parents (whose security interest enjoys priority), and the remaining $5,000 to Grace.

(B) $10,000 to Grace (whose security interest enjoys priority because possession trumps filing), and the remaining $10,000 to his parents.

(C) $10,000 to Grace (whose security interest enjoys priority because she took possession of the piano with no knowledge of her parents' security interest), and the remaining $10,000 to his parents.

(D) $15,000 to his parents and the remaining $5,000 to Meredith; Grace is not entitled to any proceeds because possession of collateral cannot protect a security interest that has been perfected by a previous filing.

95. Assume, under the original facts, that Tim and Lisa perfected their security interest by filing a financing statement in April 2010, and Grace perfected her security interest in the piano by filing a financing statement in December 2010. Tim, Lisa, and Grace know that the piano serves as collateral for both loans.

Meredith files a bankruptcy petition on October 1, 2015, when the two family loans remain unpaid. The trustee has received a UCC search report that reveals a continuation statement filed by Tim and Lisa in June 2015 and no continuation statement filed by Grace.

As of the petition date, which security interest in the piano enjoys priority?

ANSWER:

96. MegaHealth is a Delaware corporation with a chief executive office in the Seattle area, from which it operates three local hospitals.

In April, First Bank obtained an enforceable security interest in MegaHealth's "equipment." First Bank promptly filed its financing statement (with the same collateral description) in Delaware.

In September, Second Bank obtained an enforceable security interest in MegaHealth's "equipment, whether now owned or hereafter acquired." Second Bank promptly filed its financing statement (with the same collateral description) in Washington.

In December, MegaHealth defaulted on its material contracts. A priority dispute soon erupted between First Bank and Second Bank over an item of equipment (the "Item") that MegaHealth had acquired in February with its own funds.

First Bank will

(A) win the priority dispute because its security interest in the Item is perfected, and Second Bank's security interest is unperfected.

(B) win the priority dispute because Second Bank has no security interest in the Item.

(C) lose the priority dispute because its security interest in the Item is unperfected, and Second Bank's security interest is perfected.

(D) neither win nor lose the priority dispute, but instead "tie" with Second Bank because both security interests in the Item are unperfected.

97. First Bank and Second Bank are also involved in a priority dispute over a second piece of equipment (the "Item") that MegaHealth had acquired in July with its own funds.

First Bank will

(A) win the priority dispute in the Item because it filed its financing statement before Second Bank filed its financing statement.

(B) win the priority dispute because its security interest in the Item attached before Second Bank's security interest attached.

(C) lose the priority dispute because it has no security interest in the Item, and Second Bank has an enforceable security interest in the Item.

(D) lose the priority dispute because its security interest in the Item is unperfected, and Second Bank's security interest is perfected.

98. Would your analysis to the preceding question change if MegaHealth executed a second security agreement (identical to the first, other than its date) in favor of First Bank in November of the same calendar year?

ANSWER:

99. Beginning in early May, Alpha Bank and Debtor began negotiating the terms of a possible $2 million loan. With Debtor's permission, Alpha Bank filed a financing statement on May 23 against Debtor's "current and after-acquired equipment."

Meanwhile, on May 20, Debtor borrowed $1 million from Omega Bank. To secure repayment of the loan, Debtor granted to Omega Bank a security interest in its current and after-acquired equipment. Debtor authenticated the security agreement that day. Omega Bank (with knowledge of Alpha Bank's earlier filing) filed its financing statement against Debtor's "equipment" on May 27.

Loan negotiations between Alpha Bank and Debtor wrapped up on May 31. On that date, Debtor borrowed $2 million from Alpha Bank and authenticated a security agreement in favor of Alpha Bank that covered Debtor's current and after-acquired equipment. Before funding the loan, Alpha Bank was aware of Omega Bank's earlier loan and prior filing.

A few months passed, and Debtor defaulted on both loans. The default triggered a priority dispute in a piece of equipment that Debtor had acquired with its own funds on May 29.

Whose security interest enjoys priority?

(A) Omega Bank enjoys priority because its security interest attached first.

(B) Omega Bank enjoys priority because its security interest became perfected first.

(C) Omega Bank enjoys priority because Alpha Bank funded its loan with knowledge of Omega Bank's earlier loan and prior filing.

(D) Alpha Bank enjoys priority.

100. On March 24, First Finance obtained an enforceable security interest in the existing and future accounts of Odyssey Furniture, a business that sells home furnishings. First

Finance filed its financing statement against the accounts on March 29.

On June 7, Midway Bank obtained an enforceable security interest in the current and after-acquired inventory of Odyssey Furniture. Midway Bank filed its financing statement against the inventory on June 13.

On September 9, AmeriBank obtained an enforceable security interest in a "proceeds only" deposit account maintained by AmeriBank for Odyssey Furniture. AmeriBank never filed a financing statement.

On November 1, Bonnie bought several pieces of bedroom furniture that had been part of Odyssey's inventory for eight months. Bonnie paid for the furniture with her personal check for $3,500.

Prior to any deposit of the check,

(A) First Finance wins the two-party dispute over the check.

(B) AmeriBank wins the two-party dispute over the check.

(C) Midway Bank wins the one-party dispute over the check.

(D) AmeriBank wins the three-party dispute over the check.

101. Assume that Odyssey Furniture has deposited Bonnie's check into the "proceeds only" deposit account. With respect to the $3,500 credit entry,

(A) AmeriBank wins the two-party dispute.

(B) AmeriBank wins the three-party dispute.

(C) Midway Bank wins the two-party dispute, but only if the dispute is resolved within twenty days of the deposit.

(D) First Finance wins the three-party dispute.

102. Assume that Bonnie does not pay for the furniture with her personal check. Instead, she pays for the furniture by swiping her credit card.

With respect to this payment claim immediately following the transaction,

(A) Midway Bank wins the two-party dispute.

(B) AmeriBank wins the three-party dispute.

(C) First Finance wins the two-party dispute.

(D) First Finance wins the three-party dispute.

103. Assume that Bonnie pays for the furniture by signing Odyssey's standard form "Retail Installment Contract." The contract describes the furniture, summarizes Bonnie's monthly payment obligations, and reserves title in the furniture to Odyssey until Bonnie discharges her financial

obligations.

Which of Odyssey's three creditors has the senior claim to the contract?

ANSWER:

104. First National Bank ("FNB") loaned $100,000 to ZinnCo, an entity that sells office equipment. The loan was secured by an enforceable security interest in ZinnCo's inventory. The security agreement included an after-acquired property clause. FNB filed its financing statement on February 15, three days after the loan was funded and the security agreement was authenticated.

In need of additional funding, ZinnCo sold numerous accounts and chattel paper contracts to Markell Finance in June for $14,000 (the accounts and chattel paper contracts resulted from inventory sales). Markell Finance, in the business of buying accounts and commercial paper, took possession of the chattel paper contracts. As part of its due diligence, Markell Finance ordered and received a UCC search report that revealed FNB's financing statement.

When FNB discovered what ZinnCo had done, it sued Markell Finance for conversion of the accounts and chattel paper contracts.

The judge should rule that

(A) FNB has priority in the accounts and the chattel paper.

(B) FNB has priority in the accounts, and Markell Finance has priority in the chattel paper.

(C) Markell Finance has priority in the accounts, and FNB has priority in the chattel paper.

(D) Markell Finance has priority in the accounts and the chattel paper.

105. MegaChurch maintains a deposit account at Salem Bank. On May 1, Salem Bank obtained an enforceable security interest in that deposit account pursuant to a security agreement authenticated by MegaChurch.

On September 1, MegaChurch borrowed $150,000 from Trinity Finance to finance new playground construction and parking lot resurfacing. The loan was secured by an enforceable security interest in the playground equipment, as well as all other current and after-acquired equipment. Trinity Finance filed a proper financing statement against "equipment" with the appropriate authority on September 10.

On October 1, MegaChurch purchased a new grand piano for its worship center, paying for the purchase with a $35,000 check drawn on its deposit account at Salem Bank.

In a priority dispute over the grand piano that is resolved as of October 10,

(A) Trinity Finance has priority over Salem Bank, which has no security interest in the grand piano.

(B) Trinity Finance has priority over Salem Bank, which has an unperfected security interest in the grand piano.

(C)   Trinity Finance has priority over Salem Bank, which has a perfected security interest in the grand piano.

(D)   Salem Bank has priority over Trinity Finance.

106.   Assume that Salem Bank discovers on October 15 that MegaChurch purchased the piano and, with MegaChurch's permission, files a financing statement against the piano on October 18.

In a priority dispute over the grand piano that is resolved as of November 1,

(A)   Salem Bank's security interest enjoys priority because Trinity Finance's security interest in after-acquired equipment is unperfected.

(B)   Trinity Finance enjoys priority because Salem Bank never had control over the deposit account on which MegaChurch wrote the $35,000 check that MegaChurch issued as payment for the grand piano.

(C)   Salem Bank's perfected security interest enjoys priority over Trinity Finance's perfected security interest.

(D)   Trinity Finance's perfected security interest enjoys priority over Salem Bank's perfected security interest.

107.   On February 1, 2009, Polk Finance obtained an enforceable security interest in the current and after-acquired equipment of AlphaCorp, a Delaware corporation. Polk Finance filed its financing statement in Delaware on February 4, 2009.

On June 4, 2010, Albany Bank obtained an enforceable security interest in the current and after-acquired equipment of OmegaTech, Inc., a Delaware corporation. Albany Bank filed its financing statement in Delaware on June 10, 2010. The security agreement prohibited any dispositions of the equipment.

On August 10, 2011, OmegaTech sold an item of equipment (the "Item") to AlphaCorp, for use as equipment.

On September 1, 2012, Albany Bank seeks a declaratory judgment that its security interest in the Item enjoys priority over the competing security interest in the Item held by Polk Finance.

The judge should rule that

(A)   Albany Bank enjoys priority.

(B)   Polk Finance enjoys priority because its filing date is earlier than the filing date of Albany Bank.

(C)   Polk Finance enjoys priority because Albany Bank's security interest became unperfected on the date of sale.

(D)   Polk Finance enjoys priority because the sale terminated Albany Bank's security interest.

108.   Assume that Polk Finance filed its financing statement in Texas, rather than Delaware, because

AlphaCorp is a Texas corporation. All other facts remain unchanged.

How should the judge rule under the revised facts?

ANSWER:

109. BAMCO is a Delaware corporation. It has one subsidiary: Zee-Con, incorporated under Texas law.

On August 1, BAMCO executed a valid security agreement in favor of First Bank, granting a security interest in "all shares of Zee-Con capital stock, whether now owned or hereafter acquired" by BAMCO. First Bank gave value for the first time on August 10.

On August 6, Second Bank advanced $23,000 to BAMCO and obtained an enforceable security interest in BAMCO's "investment property, whether now owned or hereafter acquired." Second Bank filed its financing statement with the appropriate authority on August 8.

BAMCO defaulted on both secured loans in early December, triggering a priority dispute in the Zee-Con shares, all evidenced by a single certificate issued in registered form to BAMCO.

First Bank will win the priority dispute if

(A) it filed a financing statement in Texas on August 1.

(B) it filed a financing statement in Delaware on August 9.

(C) it took delivery of the Zee-Con stock certificate on November 15.

(D) Second Bank's security interest violates the terms of First Bank's security agreement.

110. Bank made a $1 million loan to HealthNet Corp. (a Delaware corporation) in January. The loan was secured by a security interest in HealthNet's accounts and equipment, and the security agreement included an after-acquired property clause. Bank promptly filed its financing statement.

HealthNet changed its name to "Houston Healthcare Corp." on March 15. Bank knew of the name change, but took no action in response.

Lender made a $1 million loan to Houston Healthcare Corp. in August. The loan was secured by a security interest in Houston Healthcare's accounts and equipment, and the security agreement included an after-acquired property clause. Lender promptly filed its financing statement. Lender was aware of Bank's security interest in the collateral, but the UCC search report that Lender ordered against "Houston Healthcare Corp." did not disclose Bank's filing.

Houston Healthcare defaulted on both loans in December. A priority dispute in three pieces of equipment has erupted. Evidence reveals that the debtor used its own funds to acquire Item #1 on May 10, Item #2 on July 20, and Item #3 on September 18.

As of December 15, Bank has priority in

(A) none of the Items.

(B) Item #1 only.

(C) Items #1 and #2 only.

(D) all three Items.

111. In 2010, Esther borrowed $10,000 from Matthew, her brother. To secure repayment of the loan, Esther authenticated a security agreement that created an enforceable security interest in her collection of chess sets. Matthew perfected his security interest by filing a financing statement in Texas, as Esther lived in San Antonio.

In February 2011, Esther moved to Phoenix. Matthew knew that his sister had left Texas, but he took no filing action.

In April 2011, Esther borrowed $8,000 from Shelby, her sister. To secure repayment of the loan, Esther authenticated a security agreement that created an enforceable security interest in the same collection of chess sets. Shelby perfected her security interest by filing a financing statement in Arizona. Shelby knew of Matthew's earlier loan so she ordered a UCC search report in Texas, which disclosed Matthew's filing.

Thereafter, following several financial setbacks, Esther filed a bankruptcy petition. Matthew and Shelby are fighting over Esther's collection of chess sets. They have asked the bankruptcy court to resolve their priority dispute as of the petition date.

How should the court resolve the dispute, if Esther filed her petition on May 20, 2011?

ANSWER:

112. How should the court resolve the dispute, if Esther filed her petition on September 1, 2011?

ANSWER:

113. Ellie Swanson operates a piano studio in her home, where she gives lessons to several children and a few adults. Her three children also take lessons, and her husband plays for relaxation and personal enjoyment. Ellie's business is a sole proprietorship that has applied for, and received from the appropriate official, a "dba" (doing business as) certificate for the name of "ES Music Studio."

Last July, Ellie borrowed $4,000 from her parents. At the time of the loan, Ellie executed a security agreement that granted to her parents a security interest in "any and all pianos, whether now owned or hereafter acquired" by Ellie. Ellie's parents promptly filed a financing statement with the appropriate clerk.

Earlier this year, Ellie added a second piano to her studio. She purchased the piano on credit from Dealer. Dealer retained an enforceable security interest in the piano that attached on March 3. Dealer delivered the piano to Ellie's home on March 10.

Ellie has defaulted on her financial obligations to her parents and Dealer, and both creditors are claiming a superior interest in the second piano. Evidence reveals that the second piano is used by Ellie's family for personal use 55% of the time, and in Ellie's business 45% of the time. Dealer has never filed a financing statement.

The priority dispute should be resolved in favor of

(A) Ellie's parents, because they are the only creditors with a perfected security interest in the piano.

(B) Ellie's parents, because they are the only creditors who filed a financing statement.

(C) Dealer, because it is the only creditor with an enforceable security interest in the second piano.

(D) Dealer, because its perfected security interest has priority over the perfected security interest claimed by Ellie's parents.

114. Would your analysis change if both percentages were 50%, and all other facts remained the same?

ANSWER:

115. Assume that the second piano is used in Ellie's business 80% of the time, and Dealer filed a financing statement against "ES Music Studio."

Under these revised facts, the priority dispute should be resolved in favor of

(A) Ellie's parents, who hold the only perfected security interest in the second piano.

(B) Ellie's parents, but only if Dealer filed its financing statement more than twenty days after March 3.

(C) Ellie's parents, but only if Dealer filed its financing statement more than twenty days after March 10.

(D) Dealer.

116. ZinnCo borrowed $1 million from Alpha Bank last year. The loan is secured by a perfected security interest in ZinnCo's current and after-acquired equipment.

In March of this year, ZinnCo began leasing from BizCorp three photocopiers for general use at its corporate headquarters. The leases are true leases (and not disguised secured financings).

ZinnCo's employees loved the new photocopiers, so ZinnCo and BizCorp agreed on July 1 that ZinnCo would cease leasing the photocopiers and instead purchase them. BizCorp agreed to finance the purchase price, which ZinnCo agreed to pay in monthly installments for three years. ZinnCo executed a security agreement that created an enforceable security interest in the three photocopiers. BizCorp perfected its security interest by filing a financing statement on July 17.

By November, ZinnCo had defaulted on its obligations to Alpha Bank and BizCorp. The two creditors are fighting over the three photocopiers that BizCorp leased, and then sold, to ZinnCo.

The priority dispute should be resolved in favor of

(A) Alpha Bank, because its filing is earlier than BizCorp's filing.

(B) Alpha Bank, because BizCorp's security interest is not a PMSI.

(C) Alpha Bank, because BizCorp failed to timely perfect its PMSI.

(D) BizCorp, because its perfected PMSI qualifies for superpriority.

117. In February 2009, Clinic borrowed $2 million from Bank. The loan was secured by Clinic's current and after-acquired equipment. Bank filed its financing statement on February 4.

In July 2010, Clinic bought a $250,000 machine on credit from Dealer. Dealer retained a security interest in the machine, which attached on July 2 when Clinic authenticated the security agreement. Dealer did not deliver and install the machine until July 15. Dealer failed to file its financing statement until August 2.

In April 2011, without Dealer's consent, Clinic sold the machine to a competitor for $150,000.

Assuming that both Bank and Dealer can satisfy any tracing burden, which creditor has the superior claim to the $150,000?

(A) Dealer, because its PMSI in the machine qualified for superpriority that extends to the proceeds.

(B) Bank, because its filing date is earlier than Dealer's filing date and perfection date.

(C) Bank, because Dealer failed to file its financing statement on a date that would have made its PMSI in the machine eligible for superpriority that would have extended to proceeds.

(D) Bank, because Dealer's superpriority in the machine does not extend to the proceeds.

118. Last year, Debtor borrowed $1 million from Lender. The loan is secured by an enforceable security interest in Debtor's equipment. The security agreement included an after-acquired property clause. Lender perfected its security interest by filing a financing statement shortly after extending credit.

On June 1 of this year, Debtor bought a new piece of equipment on credit from Dealer. Dealer retained an enforceable security interest in the equipment to secure repayment of its purchase price. Dealer delivered and installed the equipment at Debtor's plant on June 5 and filed its financing statement on June 29.

As of July 1,

(A) Dealer has a perfected PMSI that enjoys priority.

(B) Dealer has a perfected PMSI that does not enjoy priority.

(C) Dealer has a perfected non-PMSI that does not enjoy priority.

(D) Dealer has an unperfected non-PMSI that does not enjoy priority.

119. Three years ago, Lender made a $2 million loan to the Metropolis Zoo. The loan is secured by an enforceable security interest in the Zoo's current and future inventory, equipment, and accounts. Lender filed its financing statement against the Zoo and the collateral within days of funding the loan.

Six months ago, ToyCo delivered a shipment of toy animals to the Zoo for sale in its gift shop. The transaction between ToyCo and the Zoo was a true "consignment" under Article 9.

Last month, a priority dispute arose between Lender and ToyCo over ToyCo's shipment of toy animals that remain in the Zoo's gift shop.

Which statement best states the filing duty imposed on ToyCo if ToyCo expects to win the priority dispute?

(A) ToyCo need not file a financing statement because in a true consignment the Zoo (the consignee) never acquired sufficient rights in the goods to make them part of Lender's collateral.

(B) ToyCo must file a financing statement against the toy animals before delivering them to the Zoo.

(C)   ToyCo must file a financing statement against the toy animals no later than twenty days following their delivery date to the Zoo.

(D)   ToyCo need not file a financing statement because it has a PMSI in the toy animals.

120.   Which statement best states the notice duty imposed on ToyCo if ToyCo expects to win the priority dispute?

(A)   ToyCo must send notice of its property interest in the toy animals to Lender before ToyCo delivers the toy animals to the Zoo.

(B)   Lender must receive ToyCo's notice of its property interest in the toy animals before ToyCo delivers the toy animals to the Zoo.

(C)   Lender must receive Toyco's notice of its property interest in the toy animals no later than twenty days following their delivery to the Zoo.

(D)   ToyCo need not send notice of its property interest in the toy animals to Lender.

121.   Which statement best states the result of a priority dispute between Lender and ToyCo in identifiable proceeds from the Zoo's sale of the toy animals to its patrons?

(A)   ToyCo will always win a priority dispute in proceeds arising from debit card transactions.

(B)   ToyCo will always win a priority dispute in proceeds arising from cash transactions.

(C)   Lender will always win a priority dispute in proceeds arising from credit card transactions.

(D)   Lender will always win a priority dispute in proceeds arising from check transactions.

122.   BAM, Inc., is a Nevada corporation that operates a restaurant in Las Vegas. On June 12, it purchased three new food freezers from Dealer. The aggregate purchase price was $120,000. Dealer financed 25% ($30,000) and retained an enforceable security interest in the freezers to secure repayment of the credit. Dealer delivered the freezers on June 20 and filed its financing statement on July 2. BAM financed the remaining 75% ($90,000) with funds borrowed from its principal shareholder, Barbara Martin. Martin, too, retained an enforceable security interest in the freezers to secure repayment of her $90,000 loan. Martin filed her financing statement on June 30.

Several months later, the restaurant failed and BAM defaulted on its payment obligations to Dealer ($20,000) and Martin ($80,000).

If the equipment liquidator sells the freezers for $60,000, then it should distribute

(A) $60,000 to Martin.

(B) $20,000 to Dealer and $40,000 to Martin.

(C) $15,000 to Dealer and $45,000 to Martin.

(D) $12,000 to Dealer and $48,000 to Martin.

123. Assume the same facts as in the preceding question, except Dealer refused to extend any credit. BAM then borrowed the $30,000 from Fidelity Bank, who retained an enforceable security interest in the freezers to secure repayment of the $30,000 loan. Fidelity Bank filed its financing statement on June 27.

Again, the restaurant failed and BAM defaulted on its payment obligations to Fidelity Bank ($20,000) and Martin ($80,000).

How should the liquidator distribute the $60,000 under these revised facts? Would your analysis change if Fidelity Bank filed its financing statement on July 1?

ANSWER:

124. ZinnMark is a corporate entity that operates an upscale resort hotel in Aspen, Colorado. On March 1, ZinnMark and FurniCo entered into a contractual agreement whereby FurniCo agreed to sell to ZinnMark numerous furnishings on credit. FurniCo retained an enforceable security interest in all furnishings that it sold to ZinnMark, and the security agreement included an after-acquired property clause and a future advance clause. The agreement also called for ZinnMark's payments to be applied to the oldest purchase price first. FurniCo filed a proper financing statement with the appropriate official on March 16.

ZinnMark made the following purchases from FurniCo during the year:

April	framed pictures	($40,000)
May	sofa-sleeper beds	($100,000)
June	lamps	($60,000)

Near the end of the year, ZinnMark defaulted on its financial obligations not only to FurniCo ($120,000), but also to BigBank ($1 million), which had extended credit to ZinnMark two years ago, secured by an enforceable security interest in all of ZinnMark's current and future equipment, and perfected by a financing statement filed at the time of the loan.

The two creditors are fighting over the furnishings sold by FurniCo to ZinnMark during the year.

If a liquidator sells the framed pictures for $25,000, then FurniCo should receive

(A) $0.

(B) approximately $2,675.

(C) $12,500.

(D) $25,000.

125. If a liquidator sells the sofa-sleeper beds for $70,000, then FurniCo should receive

(A) $0.

(B) $22,500.

    (C) $60,000.

    (D) $70,000.

126. If a liquidator sells the lamps for $40,000, then FurniCo should receive

    (A) $4,300.

    (B) $20,000.

    (C) $33,333.

    (D) $40,000.

127. Kline Music sold a grand piano to the local youth symphony on credit two years ago for $20,000. Kline Music retained an enforceable security interest in the piano, and perfected its interest by filing a financing statement soon after the sale.

    Due to the symphony's negligence, the keyboard and soundboard become damaged last summer. The symphony bought a new keyboard and soundboard on credit from MusiCorp at a cost of $8,000. MusiCorp installed the replacement parts and then returned the piano to the symphony on August 4. MusiCorp retained a security interest in the keyboard and soundboard and perfected that interest by filing its financing statement on August 17.

    Earlier this year, the symphony defaulted on its obligations to Kline Music ($14,000) and MusiCorp ($7,000). A liquidator has sold the piano for $13,500 (of which $6,000 is attributable to the keyboard and soundboard).

    The liquidator should distribute

    (A) $13,500 to Kline Music.

    (B) $11,500 to Kline Music and $2,000 to MusiCorp.

    (C) $9,000 to Kline Music and $4,500 to MusiCorp.

    (D) $7,500 to Kline Music and $6,000 to MusiCorp.

128. Earlier this year, Farmer Smith sold garlic, rosemary, and other spices on credit to Pasta Company. The spices had a value of $1,000. Farmer Smith took and perfected a security interest in the spices by filing his financing statement before delivering the spices to Pasta Company.

    During the same month, Farmer Jones sold tomatoes on credit to Pasta Company. The tomatoes had a value of $2,000. Farmer Jones took a security interest in the tomatoes and perfected it by filing a financing statement after delivering the tomatoes to Pasta Company, but before the tomatoes became subject to any processing.

    Pasta Company used the spices and tomatoes to create several bottles of a popular pasta sauce used at several restaurants.

    Later, Pasta Company defaulted on its obligations to Farmer Smith and Farmer Jones when Smith's unpaid debt was $800 and Jones's unpaid debt was $1,200.

A liquidator sold the bottles of pasta sauce for $1,500. The liquidator should distribute

(A) $800 to Farmer Smith if he filed first, and the remaining $700 to Farmer Jones.

(B) $1,200 to Farmer Jones if he filed first, and the remaining $300 to Farmer Smith.

(C) $500 to Farmer Smith and $1,000 to Farmer Jones.

(D) $600 to Farmer Smith and $900 to Farmer Jones.

129. How would your analysis change if the liquidator sold the bottles of pasta sauce for $2,100?
ANSWER:

130. Under the original facts, how would your analysis change if Farmer Smith filed his financing statement after his spices had been commingled with other ingredients?
ANSWER:

131. In addition to the original facts, assume that a third creditor (Bank) asserts a claim to the $1,500. Bank produces a security agreement authenticated by Pasta Company last year that describes the collateral as "current and future inventory of pasta sauces" and a financing statement covering the same collateral that is time-stamped by the clerk within days of the security agreement.

How should the liquidator distribute the $1,500 among the three creditors under these revised facts?
ANSWER:

132. On February 1, Texas National Bank ("TNB") made a $1 million loan to Friendly Furniture Company, a corporation that operates a furniture store in Houston. To secure repayment of the loan, TNB obtained an enforceable security interest in Friendly Furniture's inventory, accounts, and equipment. TNB filed its financing statement against the collateral on February 10. An after-acquired property clause appeared in the collateral description found in the security agreement, but not in the financing statement.

On July 1, ZinnMark Corporation sold thirty sofas and twenty-five bookcases to Friendly Furniture. ZinnMark shipped the sofas from its Atlanta warehouse and delivered them to Friendly Furniture on July 15. It shipped the bookcases from its Phoenix warehouse and delivered them to Friendly Furniture on July 22. ZinnMark retained an enforceable security interest in the sofas and bookcases and filed its financing statement against the collateral on July 18. On July 7, ZinnMark sent a written notice of its security interest in the sofas and bookcases to TNB; the contents of the notice satisfied the statutory requirements of UCC Article 9. TNB received the notice on July 14.

After Friendly Furniture defaults on its obligations to both creditors in November, a priority dispute between TNB and ZinnMark arises in the sofas and bookcases sold by

ZinnMark that Friendly Furniture has not yet sold.

Which statement is true?

(A) The absence of the after-acquired property clause from its financing statement leaves TNB with an enforceable, but unperfected security interest in the sofas and bookcases, so it will lose the priority dispute with ZinnMark under the "perfected trumps unperfected" rule.

(B) TNB has a perfected security interest in the sofas and bookcases that enjoys priority over ZinnMark under the "first to file or perfect" rule.

(C) Notwithstanding TNB's earlier filing, ZinnMark's security interest in the sofas and bookcases enjoys purchase-money superpriority.

(D) ZinnMark has priority in the bookcases, and TNB has priority in the sofas.

133. Yesterday, Grace bought one of the sofas and paid with a check. Meredith used her credit card to purchase one of the sofas. Ethan bought one of the bookcases and paid with cash. And Bruce bought three bookcases after executing Friendly Furniture's retail installment contract, in which Friendly Furniture retained title to the bookcase until Bruce completed his obligation to pay the purchase price in installments over a two-year period. All of these proceeds remain identifiable and are in the possession of Friendly Furniture.

Which statement is true?

(A) ZinnMark has priority in Grace's check and Ethan's cash.

(B) ZinnMark has priority in Bruce's retail installment contract and Ethan's cash.

(C) TNB has priority in Meredith's credit card receivable, Bruce's retail installment contract, and Grace's check.

(D) TNB has priority in Ethan's cash, Grace's check, and Meredith's credit card receivable.

134. ZinnMark is a Delaware corporation that operates three retail stores in Seattle, from which it sells and leases computers, photocopiers, and other office equipment to commercial and consumer customers. ZinnMark's current and after-acquired inventory is subject to a perfected security interest held by MegaBank. The security agreement prohibits asset dispositions, other than those in the ordinary course of ZinnMark's business.

Two months ago, ZinnMark engaged in a routine cash sale of three photocopiers to a Seattle law firm (structured as a limited liability company organized under Washington law) for an aggregate sales price of $30,000.

In a priority dispute between MegaBank and the law firm over the three photocopiers,

(A) MegaBank will lose because it never filed a financing statement in Washington, the state in which the law firm is located.

(B) MegaBank will win if the law firm had knowledge, before it purchased the photocopiers, of MegaBank's security interest.

(C) MegaBank will win if the law firm had knowledge, before it took possession of the photocopiers, of MegaBank's filing in Delaware.

(D) MegaBank will lose under the terms of its security agreement.

135. Assume that the law firm did not pay cash, but instead executed ZinnMark's standard form of a ninety-day, negotiable promissory note (a form that comports with industry-wide standards). While MegaBank's security agreement permits ZinnMark to dispose of its assets in the ordinary course of its business, the agreement expressly prohibits non-cash dispositions (loosely defined as a disposition to a customer who does not pay with cash, a check, a credit card, or a debit card).

How would your analysis change, under these revised facts?

ANSWER:

136. Assume that the law firm paid for the three photocopiers at the time of purchase with a cashier's check for $30,000. ZinnMark promptly deposited the cashier's check into its general operating account that it maintains with SmallBank.

If MegaBank can satisfy its tracing burden,

(A) it cannot claim a security interest in the $30,000 unless the collateral description in its security agreement mentions "proceeds" or "cash proceeds" or "deposit accounts" (or similar language).

(B) it cannot claim a security interest in the $30,000 unless its security interest in the photocopiers survived the sale to the law firm.

(C) it can claim a perfected security interest in the $30,000, but only for twenty days following ZinnMark's receipt of the check.

(D) it can claim a perfected security interest in the $30,000 for twenty days following ZinnMark's receipt of the check, and thereafter.

137. Eight months ago, Sandra bought a dining room suite on credit from Friendly Furniture for everyday use in her home. To secure repayment of the purchase price, Friendly Furniture retained a security interest in the furniture. Friendly Furniture never filed a financing statement, but its security agreement expressly prohibited Sandra from disposing of the furniture or using it as collateral to secure any other debt.

Two months ago, and without the permission of Friendly Furniture, Sandra sold the dining room suite. Friendly Furniture discovered the sale and has sued the buyer for conversion of its collateral.

Friendly Furniture will

(A) lose the lawsuit because its security interest in the furniture was never perfected.

(B) lose the lawsuit if the sale generated cash proceeds that remain identifiable.

(C) lose the lawsuit if the buyer was a good-faith purchaser, with no knowledge of Friendly Furniture's interest, who is using the dining room suite as a consumer good.

(D) win the lawsuit.

138. Assume that Friendly Furniture timely filed a financing statement against Sandra and the dining room suite at the time of her purchase.

How would your analysis change, under these revised facts?

ANSWER:

139. Two years ago, Omega Bank loaned $1 million to Allegro Music Company ("AMC"), a Texas corporation that operates two retail stores in Dallas, from which it sells musical instruments, songbooks, and related items. The loan was secured by an enforceable security interest in AMC's inventory, equipment, and accounts. The security agreement included an after-acquired property clause and prohibited AMC from selling any unit of collateral, except for inventory sales to customers who paid with cash, a check, or a debit card. Omega Bank perfected its security interest by filing a financing statement within days after funding the loan.

Six months ago, AMC sold a $35,000 harp to Ima Virtuoso (a Dallas resident). Ima executed a promissory note (an industry practice for such an expensive purchase), agreeing to make equal monthly payments for five years. Ima is a professional musician and will use the harp in a studio where she earns her livelihood by giving private lessons. Ima has no knowledge of the business relationship between Omega Bank and AMC.

Two months ago, AMC sold some in-house computer equipment to Hewey Dell, an employee (and Dallas resident), for his personal use. Hewey was not aware of the business relationship between Omega Bank and AMC.

In a priority dispute between Omega Bank and Ima over the harp,

(A) Omega Bank wins, because its security interest in the harp survived AMC's disposition of it.

(B) Omega Bank wins, because Ima is not using the harp as a consumer good.

(C) Ima wins, because she can invoke the protections afforded to a buyer in the ordinary course of business.

(D) Ima wins, because Omega Bank never filed a new financing statement against her.

140. In a priority dispute between Omega Bank and Hewey over the computer equipment,

(A) Hewey wins, because he is using the computer equipment as a consumer good.

(B) Hewey wins, because he is a buyer in the ordinary course of business.

(C) Omega Bank wins, because AMC's sale of the computer equipment violated the terms of its security agreement.

(D) Omega Bank wins, because Hewey is AMC's employee.

141. Redbird Bank has a perfected security interest in the current and after-acquired inventory of Dealer, a merchant that sells baseball cards, autographed sporting goods, and other sports memorabilia. The security agreement permits Dealer to sell its goods to customers who pay with cash, a debit card, a credit card, or a check. Credit sales (excluding credit card transactions) are prohibited.

Last week, Mickey bought two autographed baseballs from Dealer (which he intends to add to his collection that he displays at his law office). At Mickey's request, Dealer allowed him to pay by executing a negotiable, unsecured promissory note for the purchase price, payable in ninety days.

After Redbird Bank discovered the transaction and its terms, it sued Mickey for conversion. Mickey responded by invoking the protection afforded by section 9-320(a) to buyers in the ordinary course of business.

Mickey cannot be a buyer in the ordinary course of business

(A) because the sale violated Redbird Bank's security agreement.

(B) because the baseballs are not inventory in Mickey's hands.

(C) if Mickey had actual knowledge of Redbird Bank's filing.

(D)   if negotiable, unsecured promissory notes are not typical forms of payment for Dealer or the sports memorabilia industry.

142. Markells is a Texas corporation that operates a high-end camera equipment store in Houston. Last year, Markells borrowed $500,000 from ZinnBank. The loan was secured by an enforceable security interest in Markells' inventory, equipment, and accounts. The security agreement included an after-acquired property clause and authorized collateral dispositions in the ordinary course of business. ZinnBank perfected its security interest by filing in Texas.

Two months ago, Markells sold camera equipment valued at $4,000 to Gwen (an amateur photographer), who sells photocopiers. The parties agreed that Gwen would pay the purchase price by delivering and installing a photocopier of comparable value at Markells' store. Gwen did so.

Last month, Gwen gave a $2,200 DigiCon camera to her favorite nephew, Ethan, as a birthday present. The DigiCon camera was part of the camera equipment sold by Markells to Gwen.

A priority dispute now exists between ZinnBank and Ethan over the DigiCon camera.

How should the dispute be resolved?

ANSWER:

143. Assume that Markells later sold Gwen's photocopier to BizSmart (an entity that sells office equipment), which then sold it for cash to a customer, Ashley.

If ZinnBank sues Ashley for conversion of the photocopier,

(A)   Ashley should win because she paid cash, and ZinnBank can claim a perfected security interest in the cash if it remains identifiable.

(B)   Ashley should win if she uses the photocopier primarily as a consumer good.

(C)   Ashley should win because she was a buyer in the ordinary course of business.

(D)   Ashley should lose.

144. For two years, MegaBank has had an enforceable security interest in ZinnCorp's inventory, equipment, and accounts. The security agreement included an after-acquired property clause. MegaBank perfected its security interest by filing a financing statement soon after making the initial advance.

Six months ago, BAMCO won a lawsuit against ZinnCorp for property damage negligently caused by one of ZinnCorp's employee-drivers. Notwithstanding the adverse judgment, ZinnCorp has never paid the monetary penalty. As a result, a court official visited ZinnCorp's warehouse three days ago and constructively seized its contents, including inventory and equipment that serve as MegaBank's collateral. At the moment of the constructive seizure, BAMCO became a "lien creditor" as defined by UCC Article 9. Evidence reveals that ZinnCorp acquired rights in some of the assets in the warehouse before BAMCO won its lawsuit (the "pre-lawsuit assets"), while ZinnCorp did not acquire rights in some of the assets in the warehouse until after BAMCO won its lawsuit (the "post-lawsuit assets").

In a priority dispute between MegaBank and BAMCO over the inventory and equipment that were constructively seized by the court official,

(A) MegaBank enjoys priority in both the pre-lawsuit assets and the post-lawsuit assets.

(B) MegaBank enjoys priority in the pre-lawsuit assets, but not the post-lawsuit assets.

(C) MegaBank enjoys priority in the pre-lawsuit assets, and any post-lawsuit assets in which ZinnCorp acquired rights within forty-five days after the court entered judgment in favor of BAMCO.

(D) BAMCO enjoys priority in the pre-lawsuit assets and the post-lawsuit assets because BAMCO is an involuntary creditor (as contrasted with a consensual or contractual creditor).

145. On September 1, Allegro Music Company ("AMC") sold a violin on credit to Timmy Zee. To secure payment of the purchase price, AMC retained an enforceable security interest in the violin pursuant to agreement executed by both parties on that date. AMC delivered the violin to Timmy Zee on September 5.

On September 13, Timmy Zee's neighbor, Ima Victum, acquired the status of "lien creditor" against Timmy Zee (a status that arose from Ima's successful lawsuit against Timmy Zee following an unfortunate canine encounter). Ima's lien encumbers the violin.

On October 1, AMC seeks a declaratory judgment that its security interest in the violin enjoys priority over Ima's lien.

The court should rule in favor of

(A) AMC, if Timmy Zee uses the violin as equipment and AMC filed its financing statement on September 28.

(B) AMC, if Timmy Zee uses the violin as a consumer good, with no relevance attached to when (or if) AMC filed a financing statement.

(C) Ima, if Timmy Zee uses the violin as equipment and AMC filed its financing statement on September 24.

(D) Ima, if Timmy Zee uses the violin as a consumer good and AMC filed its financing statement on September 27.

146. ZeeTech is a corporation chartered under Delaware law. It operates three retail outlets in Detroit.

   In June 2010, Omega Bank loaned money to ZeeTech. To secure repayment of the loan, Omega Bank took an enforceable security interest in all of ZeeTech's current and after-acquired equipment.

   In February 2011, ZeeTech changed its legal name to "Quantum Technologies." ZeeTech timely informed Omega Bank of the change, but Omega Bank never took any action in response.

   In August 2011, a constable constructively seized two pieces of Quantum's equipment pursuit to a writ of execution obtained by Meredith, a tort creditor of Quantum. At the moment of seizure Meredith became a "lien creditor" under UCC Article 9.

   Evidence reveals that Quantum had acquired one of the pieces of equipment ("Item #1") on April 15, 2011, and the other piece of equipment ("Item #2") on July 15, 2011.

   A priority dispute now exists between Omega Bank and Meredith in the two pieces of seized equipment.

   If the dispute is resolved as of September 1, 2011, then

   (A) Omega Bank has priority in both Item #1 and Item #2.

   (B) Meredith has priority in both Item #1 and Item #2.

   (C) Omega Bank has priority in Item #1, and Meredith has priority in Item #2.

   (D) Omega Bank has priority in Item #1, but priority in Item #2 cannot be resolved without additional information.

147. On September 1, Debtor granted to Bank a security interest in equipment worth $150,000 (the "Equipment") to secure a $50,000 loan. The security agreement had a future advance clause, but Bank was not obligated to make any future advances. Bank filed its financing statement on September 5.

   On September 10, Hannah obtained a $75,000 judgment against Debtor. Hannah became a "lien creditor" under UCC Article 9 on September 20 when the sheriff seized the Equipment to satisfy the judgment.

   Bank advanced another $35,000 on October 1, another $25,000 on November 1, and another

$20,000 on November 15.

With the consent of both Bank and Hannah, the sheriff sold the Equipment for $120,000 on December 1.

How should the sheriff distribute the proceeds if evidence reveals that Bank was aware of Hannah's lien and the property seizure as early as October 15?

ANSWER:

148. Assume that the security agreement between Bank and Debtor included the following statement:

"Secured Party agrees to loan $150,000 to Debtor in one or more advances; provided that Secured Party may refuse to fund an advance if an Event of Default exists."

Assume that *"Event of Default"* is defined to include judgments against Debtor in excess of $25,000.

Would these assumptions affect the sheriff's distribution of the $120,000?

ANSWER:

149. In January 2007, Redbird Bank made a $1 million loan to Friendly Furniture Company, a corporate entity that sells furniture through several retail outlets in the St. Louis area. Repayment of the loan was secured by an enforceable security interest in Friendly's inventory, equipment, and accounts. The security agreement included an after-acquired property clause. Redbird Bank perfected its security interest by filing a financing statement on January 18, 2007.

In December 2011, a law enforcement official constructively seized all of the furniture inventory located at one of Friendly's stores, pursuant to court order arising from a successful lawsuit initiated earlier that year by Bradford Industries against Friendly. At the moment of the constructive seizure, Bradford Industries became a "lien creditor" under UCC Article 9.

With the permission of all interested parties, a professional liquidator sold all of the furniture for $700,000 on February 15, 2012, an amount considerably less than what Friendly owes to Redbird Bank.

Redbird Bank has priority in the $700,000

(A) if it filed a continuation statement on July 10, 2011.

(B) if it filed a continuation statement on January 24, 2012.

(C) only if it timely filed a continuation statement before the constructive seizure.

(D) even if it never filed a continuation statement.

150. In early June, Mockingbird Industries and Fidelity Bank began negotiating the terms of a $250,000 secured loan. With Mockingbird's consent, Fidelity Bank filed a financing

statement against Mockingbird, describing the collateral as "all assets."

The parties concluded their negotiations on July 1, when the parties executed several agreements, documents, and instruments, including:

a loan agreement that obligated Fidelity Bank to loan $250,000 to Mockingbird in one or more advances;

a security agreement that described the collateral as "all inventory, equipment, and accounts, in each case whether now owned or existing or hereafter acquired or created"; and

a UCC-3 amendment that changed the collateral description in its original filing to mirror the collateral description found in the security agreement.

Fidelity Bank filed the UCC-3 amendment on July 10, three days after funding Mockingbird's initial borrowing request for $85,000.

Unknown to Fidelity Bank, a court official had validly levied on a significant part of Mockingbird's inventory and equipment on June 25, at which time Heather Finch became a "lien creditor" under UCC Article 9.

In a priority dispute between Fidelity Bank and Heather over the seized assets,

(A)   Fidelity Bank will win because its financing statement covered inventory and equipment when Heather became a lien creditor.

(B)   Heather will win because she became a lien creditor before Fidelity Bank's security interest attached.

(C)   Heather will win because an "all assets" collateral description in a financing statement is ineffective.

(D)   Heather will win if Fidelity Bank cannot claim a PMSI in the seized assets.

151. As a general rule, a creditor's security interest in collateral acquired by the taxpayer-debtor after the IRS files its tax lien notice is subordinate to the tax lien. An exception exists for "commercial financing security" that is timely acquired by the taxpayer-debtor.

Each of the following types of Article 9 collateral is "commercial financing security" except

(A) accounts.

(B) chattel paper.

(C) equipment.

(D) inventory.

152. ZinnMark Fashions operates several retail clothing stores.

On May 1, Bank entered into a binding commitment to make advances to ZinnMark Fashions in an aggregate amount not to exceed $2 million. On that date, ZinnMark Fashions executed a security agreement in which it granted to Bank a security interest in all of its inventory, accounts receivable, and equipment. The security agreement included an after-acquired property clause and a future advance clause. Bank filed a proper financing statement with the appropriate official on May 8. Pursuant to its binding commitment, Bank made the following advances to ZinnMark Fashions (none of which have been repaid):

DATE	AMOUNT
5/8	$300,000
7/12	$200,000
8/3	$400,000
8/22	$100,000
9/9	$300,000

On July 1, the IRS assessed a $700,000 tax lien against ZinnMark Fashions. The IRS filed a tax lien notice with the appropriate officials on August 1. Bank discovered the tax lien notice on August 21.

Assuming that the type and value of collateral are adequate, the IRS lien will be subject to Bank's security interest that secures debt of

(A) $1,300,000.

(B) $1,000,000.

(C) $900,000.

(D) $500,000.

153. In a priority dispute concerning a shipment of dresses and shoes acquired by ZinnMark Fashions on September 7,

     (A)   Bank's security interest enjoys priority.

     (B)   the tax lien enjoys priority because the items are not "commercial financing security."

     (C)   the tax lien enjoys priority because ZinnMark Fashions acquired the items after Bank discovered the tax lien notice.

     (D)   the tax lien enjoys priority because ZinnMark Fashions acquired the items more than forty-five days after the IRS assessed the tax lien.

154. In a priority dispute concerning new computers purchased by ZinnMark Fashions on July 25,

     (A)   the tax lien enjoys priority because the computers are not "commercial financing security."

     (B)   the tax lien enjoys priority because ZinnMark Fashions acquired the computers after the IRS assessed the tax lien.

     (C)   the tax lien enjoys priority because ZinnMark Fashions acquired the computers before Bank acquired knowledge of the tax lien notice.

     (D)   Bank's security interest enjoys priority.

155. Part Six of Article 9 provides the secured party with specific rights and remedies following "default." For a definition of that term, the debtor and secured party should consult

   (A) § 1-201.

   (B) § 9-102.

   (C) § 9-601.

   (D) the security agreement.

156. Following a corporate debtor's default, Article 9 permits the secured party to

   (A) dispose of collateral, whether or not the secured party has possession of it.

   (B) dispose of collateral, but only if the secured party has a perfected security interest in it.

   (C) sue the debtor for breach of contract, but only if the secured party first exhausts its rights and remedies in the collateral.

   (D) propose keeping all or part of the collateral in exchange for forgiving all (but not less than all) of the unpaid secured debt.

157. Lender has an enforceable security interest in Debtor's current and future accounts. Last week, Debtor triggered a default. Lender wants to contact the account debtors and direct their payments to Lender (rather than Debtor) for application against the unpaid secured debt. Lender can do so,

   (A) but must proceed in a commercially reasonable manner.

   (B) but must wait until Debtor has been in default for thirty consecutive calendar days.

   (C) but only if its security interest is perfected.

   (D) but only if its security interest is senior to all other security interests.

158. Dealer sold a car, on credit, to Tim last year. To secure repayment of the purchase price, Dealer timely perfected a security interest in the car.

   Tim recently failed to make his monthly car payment to Dealer, triggering a default. Dealer wants to repossess the car without judicial process. Perhaps rephrased, Dealer wants to engage in a "self-help" repossession.

Which statement is true?

(A) Dealer cannot engage in self-help repossession if the car is a consumer good.

(B) Dealer cannot engage in self-help repossession unless Tim's past-due payments, and any accrued and unpaid interest thereon, exceed $2,000.

(C) Dealer can engage in self-help repossession, but it must avoid breaching the peace while doing so.

(D) Dealer can engage in self-help repossession, but it must timely send an authenticated notice to Tim of Dealer's intent to do so.

159. To minimize the risk of incurring liability arising from the repossession of Tim's car, Dealer should

(A) include a provision in the security agreement that defines behavior that will not trigger a breach of the peace.

(B) immediately cease any repossession in progress if Tim verbally objects.

(C) include a provision in the security agreement that waives any statutory duty imposed on Dealer to avoid breaching the peace.

(D) hire a third-party independent contractor (e.g., Repo Company) to perform the actual repossession.

160. Dealer sends its agent (Repo Company) to Tim's house in the early morning hours to seize the car. Repo Company finds the car locked, and parked on Tim's driveway. Repo Company notices a set of golf clubs in the back seat and correctly assumes that the clubs are not part of Dealer's collateral.

Which statement is true?

(A) Repo Company cannot repossess Tim's car while it is parked on private property.

(B) Repo Company cannot repossess Tim's car because its contents include personal items that are not part of Dealer's collateral.

(C) Repo Company can repossess the car and can refuse to return the golf clubs until Tim pays all past-due amounts on the car note.

(D) Repo Company can repossess the car but must make the golf clubs available to Tim as soon as reasonably possible following the completion of the repossession.

161. Dealer has repossessed Tim's car, which Tim had always driven primarily for personal use. The default that prompted Dealer's repossession was Tim's failure to make a $400 monthly payment. The loan papers included an acceleration clause. Dealer has taken all steps necessary to trigger the acceleration clause. As a result, Tim now owes $11,400. Tim's father, Robert, guaranteed repayment of the debt. Robert has contacted Dealer to discuss the possibility of redeeming the car.

Which statement is true?

(A) Article 9 permits Tim, but not Robert, to redeem the car.

(B) Article 9 permits Robert to redeem the car, but the redemption price will be $11,400 (rather than $400).

(C) Article 9 usually permits Robert to redeem the car, but an exception bars Robert from exercising his redemption rights because the accelerated debt exceeds the statutory cap of $10,000.

(D) Article 9 usually permits Robert to redeem the car, but Robert will be contractually barred from exercising his redemption rights if he waived those rights in the security agreement or other loan paper.

162. The car is never redeemed. Dealer then contemplates the idea of keeping the car and forgiving some or all of the debt (a process that Article 9 refers to as a "strict foreclosure").

Which statement is true?

(A) Dealer cannot propose a partial strict foreclosure.

(B) Absent an effective waiver, Dealer cannot propose a full strict foreclosure if Tim has paid at least 50% of the cash price of the car.

(C) Dealer must send its proposal of a full strict foreclosure to Robert.

(D) Dealer's proposal of a full strict foreclosure is binding on Tim only if he expressly consents to the proposal.

163. Two years ago, Dealer sold a grand piano on credit to the ZinnMark Resort for use at various functions. Dealer retained an enforceable security interest in the piano to secure its purchase price. Dealer perfected its security interest by filing a financing statement soon after the sale.

A few months ago, following a downturn in the economy, the Resort began defaulting on its material contracts, including its contract with Dealer. Dealer repossessed the piano, with the Resort's consent, three weeks ago.

Dealer intends to sell the piano, either to a private buyer or at a public auction. Once it makes a final decision on how to proceed, it will send a disposition notice to the Resort.

To be effective under Article 9, the notice must

(A) be sent to, but need not be received by, the Resort.

(B) be written, and cannot be electronic or oral.

(C) be sent at least ten days before the earliest time of disposition.

(D) be notarized, if the unpaid secured debt exceeds $5,000.

164. Should Dealer request a UCC search report against the Resort and the piano before it sells the piano?

ANSWER:

165. Dealer has decided to sell the piano to a private buyer. To be effective under Article 9, Dealer's disposition notice should

   (A) remind the Resort that it remains liable for any deficiency remaining after the sale.

   (B) inform the Resort that it is entitled to an accounting of the unpaid debt.

   (C) state the date on which Dealer will sell the piano to the private buyer.

   (D) remind the Resort that it can redeem the piano prior to the date of sale.

166. Assume, instead, that Dealer decided to sell the piano at a public auction. It gave timely notice to the Resort of the proposed disposition that satisfied all statutory requirements. Immediately prior to the auction, the Resort owed $12,000 to Dealer. Following the auction, which yielded a sales price of $8,000, Dealer initiated a deficiency action for $4,000. The Resort responded with convincing proof that several aspects of the auction were not commercially reasonable. Furthermore, the Resort's expert testified that the piano had a fair market value of $9,500 at disposition (but offered no evidence on what could be obtained at a commercially reasonable sale). Dealer responded with proof that, even if all aspects of the sale had been commercially reasonable, the piano would not have sold for more than $8,300.

   Based on this evidence, the court should enter a deficiency judgment against the Resort for

   (A) $0.

   (B) $2,500.

   (C) $3,700.

   (D) $4,000.

167. Henry has a security agreement granting to him a security interest in all presently owned and after-acquired inventory and equipment, authenticated by an entity that signed as "Q Corp." Henry has filed with the appropriate filing office an otherwise valid financing statement listing "Q Corp." as the debtor.

   Q Corp. owes Henry $20,000 and is in default. With the aid of a sheriff acting under a writ of replevin, Henry repossesses Q Corp.'s inventory and equipment. He then schedules a public auction of the goods for next week. He does no advertising and sends no notice to Q Corp. or anyone else.

   One day before the scheduled auction, Henry meets with Beth, who produces a valid security agreement authenticated by "Q Corporation, Inc." It is signed by the same individuals who signed Henry's security agreement. Beth's security agreement includes a warranty provision stating that "Q Corporation, Inc." is the legal name of the entity and "Q Corp." is its trade name. Beth has filed her financing statement in the same office where Henry filed, and Beth's filing bears an earlier filing date. Finally, Beth tells Henry that "Q Corporation, Inc." has defaulted on a $15,000 loan she has made to that company. She asks Henry to turn over to her all collateral that he intends to sell at the auction.

Confused and surprised, Henry asks Beth to leave, after telling her that he does not believe that her security interest is valid. Henry holds the sale the next day and sells the goods for $10,000 to Sarah, who knows nothing of the discussions between Henry and Beth.

Assume that "Q Corp." and "Q Corporation, Inc." are just different names for the same legal entity, and that the appropriate filing office lists the entity's legal name as "Q Corporation, Inc." Assume further that a search for filings against "Q Corporation, Inc." will not disclose any filings made against "Q Corp."

After the sale,

(A) Beth may sue Q Corporation, Inc., to recover no more than $5,000, and she may sue Sarah to recover the inventory and equipment.

(B) Beth may sue Q Corporation, Inc., to recover $15,000, and she may sue Sarah to recover the inventory and equipment (subject to a maximum recovery of $15,000).

(C) Beth may sue Henry for the $10,000 sale proceeds on a theory of conversion, and then she may proceed against Q Corporation, Inc., for any deficiency remaining.

(D) Beth may sue Q Corporation, Inc., to recover $15,000, may sue Henry for the $10,000 sale proceeds on a theory of conversion, and may also sue Sarah to recover the inventory and equipment (subject to a maximum recovery of $15,000).

168. On March 1, Remington Farms sold a horse to Simon Webster for $100,000. Simon delivered a $35,000 cashier's check to Remington Farms, which agreed to finance the $65,000 balance. Remington Farms retained an enforceable security interest in the horse to secure repayment of Simon's purchase obligations, but Remington Farms never filed a financing statement. Simon and his family use the horse for recreational pleasure.

On July 1, Simon granted an enforceable security interest in the horse to First Bank to secure a $15,000 personal loan made the same day. First Bank perfected its security interest by filing a financing statement that day with the proper official. Simon's sister, Rachel, guaranteed repayment of the $15,000 loan.

On August 15, Simon granted an enforceable security interest in the horse to Second Bank to secure a $10,000 personal loan made the same day. Second Bank perfected its security interest by filing a financing statement that day with the proper official.

For reasons beyond his control, Simon defaulted on the loan from First Bank on September 1. Shortly thereafter, First Bank seized the horse with Simon's consent.

First Bank intends to sell the horse at a public sale. Remington Farms has provided First Bank with written notice of its security interest, but Second Bank has not. First Bank has ordered, and received, a UCC search report reflecting all financing statements filed against

Simon and the horse through September 15.

In order to comply with the requirements of Article 9, First Bank must send its notice of sale to

(A) Simon.

(B) Simon and Rachel.

(C) Simon and Remington Farms.

(D) Simon, Remington Farms, and Second Bank.

169. After sending proper notice to the required party (or parties), First Bank sells the horse for $65,000 at a public sale (all aspects of which are commercially reasonable). First Bank has received a timely written demand for proceeds from Remington Farms but no demand from Second Bank. At the time of the sale, Simon owes $50,000 to Remington Farms, $10,000 to First Bank, and $8,000 to Second Bank.

After deducting $10,000 to satisfy its own debt, to whom should First Bank distribute the remaining $55,000? You may assume that there are no costs of repossession or sale.

ANSWER:

170. Karen recently filed a Chapter 7 bankruptcy petition. BigBank holds a perfected purchase-money security interest in her 2011 Lexus sport utility vehicle to secure an unpaid debt of $38,000. Appraisers and on-line services estimate the fair market value of the vehicle as low as $36,500 and as high as $39,000. BigBank intends immediately to file a motion to lift the automatic stay, hoping that it can take possession of the vehicle and conduct a nonjudicial foreclosure as permitted by Article 9.

With respect to any motion to seek relief from stay that BigBank files,

(A) Karen has the burden of proof on the issues of adequate protection and her equity in the vehicle.

(B) BigBank has the burden of proof on the issues of adequate protection and Karen's equity in the vehicle.

(C) Karen has the burden of proof on the issue of her equity in the vehicle, and BigBank has the burden of proof on the issue of adequate protection.

(D) BigBank has the burden of proof on the issue of Karen's equity in the vehicle, and Karen has the burden of proof on the issue of adequate protection.

171. Henry borrowed $1 million from Yost Bank. The loan agreement provides that Henry will use the loan proceeds in his business, Hank's Socks LLC. Henry secures the loan with a security interest in all of his deposit accounts held at Yost Bank (they do this because the state in which Henry resides does not recognize common law liens in deposit accounts). Beset by bad business, Hank's Socks files a Chapter 11 bankruptcy petition; Henry also files a Chapter 11 bankruptcy petition. Henry's lawyers make a mistake in noticing creditors in Henry's case. Although they listed Yost Bank as a creditor in Hank's Socks's bankruptcy, they neglected to do so in Henry's. As a result, Yost Bank receives notice of Hank's Socks's bankruptcy only. One week after the two filings, Yost Bank applies all of the funds in Henry's deposit accounts to its outstanding loan to Henry. Henry finds this out when he is buying groceries, and his debit card is declined. Incensed, he immediately calls Yost Bank, tells it of his filing and demands that it credit his account with its previous balance. Yost Bank's representative simply hangs up the phone and does nothing.

In Henry's action for violation of the automatic stay, a well-informed court will most likely

(A) rule in Henry's favor, since consumer deposit accounts are outside the scope of Article 9.

(B) rule in Yost Bank's favor because they did not receive proper notice and thus did not violate any stay of which it was aware.

(C) rule in Henry's favor and award damages for Henry's losses because the stay of 11 U.S.C. § 362(a) is automatic, and is effective without notice.

(D) rule in Henry's favor and award damages incurred from and after Henry's phone call caused by Yost Bank's refusal to restore Henry's deposit account to its previous balance.

172. On July 1, Bank made a $150,000 loan to Clinic, repayment of which was secured by an enforceable security interest in all of Clinic's equipment, whether then owned or thereafter acquired. Bank perfected its interest on July 7 by filing a proper financing statement with the appropriate authority.

On August 1, MedCo sold a $100,000 kidney dialysis machine on credit to Clinic under a retail installment contract. MedCo retained an enforceable security interest in the machine. MedCo delivered the machine to Clinic on August 9 and filed a proper financing statement in the proper place on August 25.

On December 1, Clinic filed a Chapter 7 bankruptcy petition. As of that date, Clinic owed $120,000 to Bank and $80,000 to MedCo (all loan repayments on both loans were made outside the preference period). As of December 1, Clinic's equipment had a fair market value of $140,000 (which included $90,000 attributable to the kidney dialysis machine sold to Clinic by MedCo).

If the bankruptcy trustee cannot set aside or otherwise avoid the two creditors' security interests, which of the following statements best states their respective claims to Clinic's equipment?

(A) Bank has a $60,000 secured claim and a $60,000 unsecured claim, and MedCo has an $80,000 secured claim.

(B) Bank has a $90,000 secured claim and a $30,000 unsecured claim, and MedCo has a $50,000 secured claim and a $30,000 unsecured claim.

(C) Bank has a $120,000 secured claim and MedCo has an $80,000 secured claim.

(D) Bank has a $120,000 secured claim, and MedCo has a $20,000 secured claim and a $60,000 unsecured claim.

173. On June 1, Dealer sold a freezer on credit to Restaurant Corp. Under terms of the contract executed by both parties on that date, Dealer retained an enforceable security interest in the freezer to secure repayment of the purchase price. Dealer delivered the freezer to Restaurant on June 10. Dealer filed a proper financing statement with the appropriate official on June 18. Unknown to Dealer, Restaurant had filed a Chapter 7 bankruptcy petition on June 12.

Which statement is true?

(A) Dealer's interest in the freezer was automatically perfected as a purchase-money security interest.

(B) The freezer may be "exempt property" in the bankruptcy, and thus not subject to Dealer's security interest.

(C)   Dealer did not violate the automatic stay by filing a post-petition financing statement.

(D)   By filing its petition under Chapter 7, Restaurant is seeking reorganization.

174. Bank made a $2 million loan to Debtor on February 1. To secure repayment of the loan, Bank obtained an enforceable and perfected security interest in Debtor's inventory and accounts. The security agreement, also dated February 1, included an after-acquired property clause. Bank filed a proper financing statement with the appropriate official on February 10.

Debtor filed a Chapter 11 bankruptcy petition on July 1. On that date, Debtor owed $1 million to Bank. On August 1, Debtor still owed $1 million to Bank. Information on Debtor's inventory and accounts as of that date follows:

Inventory:	
Existed as of July 1	$300,000
Purchased after July 1 with cash received from:	
accounts existing as of July 1	$100,000
accounts generated after July 1	$50,000
sale on July 15 of Google stock purchased last year	$50,000
Total Value of Inventory	$500,000
Accounts:	
Existed as of July 1	$250,000
Generated after July 1 from credit sales of:	
inventory existing as of July 1	$100,000
inventory acquired after July 1	$50,000
equipment donated to Debtor last year	$50,000
Total Value of Accounts	$450,000

Ignoring voidable preference or fraudulent conveyance concerns, Bank can claim a perfected security interest in collateral worth

(A) $550,000.

(B) $750,000.

(C) $750,000–$850,000.

(D) $800,000–$900,000.

175. The "strong arm clause" permits the bankruptcy trustee to avoid

(A)   an unperfected security interest.

(B)   a property transfer made by the debtor "with actual intent to hinder, delay, or defraud" a creditor.

(C)   a property transfer made by the debtor who "received less than a reasonably equivalent value in exchange for such transfer."

(D)   a judicial lien that impairs an exemption.

176. Debtor, a Delaware corporation, filed a Chapter 11 bankruptcy petition on September 13. Under which of the following situations is Secured Party most vulnerable to an attack by the bankruptcy trustee under 11 U.S.C. § 544(a), the "strong arm clause"?

(A)   Secured Party's security interest in Debtor's equipment (located at a Delaware plant) attached on February 1, and Secured Party filed a financing statement covering equipment with the appropriate Delaware official on February 7. On May 1, Debtor closed the Delaware plant and relocated the equipment to an Illinois plant. Secured Party never refiled a financing statement in Illinois.

(B)   Secured Party's security interest in Debtor's investment property (a stock certificate held by Debtor in a safety deposit box in Atlanta) attached on July 2. None of Secured Party's then-existing financing statements covered this type of collateral, and so on July 6 Secured Party filed its financing statement with the appropriate Georgia official.

(C)   Secured Party's purchase-money security interest in Debtor's inventory (located in Texas) attached on September 8; on that date there is no financing statement covering such inventory. Secured Party never filed a financing statement in Texas, and did not file a financing statement with the appropriate Delaware official until three days after the petition date.

(D)   Secured Party's security interest in Debtor's bank account (maintained with Secured Party) attached on July 20; Secured Party took no action to perfect its security interest.

177. Sally gives her daughter a birthday gift of a new car on her daughter's sixteenth birthday. Two weeks later, when one of Sally's judgment creditors seeks to levy execution on the car to satisfy that creditor's judgment,

(A)   Sally's daughter will retain possession of the car so long as it is titled in her name.

(B)   the judgment creditor will prevail if he can show that Sally is not generally paying her debts as they become due, and Sally does not offer any additional evidence at trial.

(C)   Sally's daughter will retain possession of the car if she (the daughter) can prove that she is solvent.

(D)   the judgment creditor will prevail only if Sally did not file a financing statement against her daughter describing the car as collateral.

178. Fred is the sole owner of all of the common stock issued by Gadgets, Inc., a Delaware corporation ("GI"). GI is a family business physically located in Kentucky that Fred incorporated for tax reasons several years ago. GI's general manager, Alice, knows that Fred wants to retire, and that Fred has no sons or daughters who want to continue the business. Alice approaches Fred and offers to buy the business for $350,000. Fred agrees, and Alice and Fred agree that the purchase price will be paid by a downpayment of $50,000 at the closing on March 1, and then by the payment of four equal installments of $75,000 on each July 1 following the sale. Alice will sign a note to evidence the deferred portion of the purchase price.

Fred also wants collateral for the note. To accommodate his desires, at the closing, simultaneously with the transfer of the stock in GI from Fred to Alice, Alice (as the new GI chairperson of the board and president) will sign a security agreement on behalf of GI under which GI will grant an interest in "all inventory, accounts, equipment, general intangibles, instruments, investment securities, and deposit accounts, in each case whether now owned or hereafter acquired." The security agreement will secure the note and all of Fred's enforcement costs under the security agreement.

The closing goes as planned, and Fred files an accurate and complete financing statement with the Delaware Secretary of State that describes the collateral as "all assets."

Running the business, however, does not go as planned. It is a disaster. Alice tries to raise new equity capital, but she cannot do so. She tries to borrow money but is told that the presence of Fred's senior security interest makes any loan to GI too risky. Both Alice and GI file a Chapter 7 bankruptcy petition on June 30.

Fred claims a security interest in all of GI's assets to secure the unpaid portion of the note. You represent GI's trustee in bankruptcy.

Your best option to obtain any recovery for GI's numerous unsecured creditors is

(A) do nothing; Fred is right and should get all the assets.

(B) bring an action against Fred alleging that the grant of the security interest in the assets of the business was an avoidable preference.

(C) bring an action against Fred alleging that the grant of the security interest in the assets of the business was a fraudulent transfer.

(D) bring an action against Fred alleging that the grant of the security interest in the assets of the business was both an avoidable preference and a fraudulent transfer.

179. Darren Debtor, a lifelong resident of Carson City, Nevada, runs a printing business. On June 1, Darren entered into negotiations with First Bank for a loan of $5,000,000. When Darren signed the letter of intent for the loan, First Bank had Darren sign the following: "I authorize First Bank to file an 'all assets' financing statement with the Nevada Secretary of State." First Bank then filed an otherwise accurate and complete financing statement with the Nevada Secretary of State naming Darren as the debtor and describing the collateral as "all assets." On June 15, Darren signed a security agreement granting a security interest to First Bank. The collateral description in the security agreement is stated as "all equipment." The security agreement described the secured obligation as "that certain loan in the amount of $5,000,000 made by First Bank to Darren Debtor, all obligations under this security agreement (including all attorneys' fees), and all advances made by First Bank to Darren Debtor hereafter."

After the security agreement is signed, First Bank lends Darren $5,000,000. First Bank does not amend its financing statement.

On July 1, as anticipated in the security agreement with First Bank, Darren purchased a new printing press for $1,000,000, using a portion of the $5,000,000 loan proceeds. On August 15, Darren sells some surplus ink and paper to Seraph Printing, Inc. ("SPI"), another printing business. SPI gives Darren a check for the purchase price of $5,000. On September 30, Darren sells a used printing press to SPI for $500,000, with SPI giving

Darren a check for $100,000, and its written promise to pay the balance by December 1.

Darren defaulted under the security agreement on October 1 and filed a Chapter 11 bankruptcy petition on October 15. It is now October 16. No purchases or sales of any of Darren's property other than completed printing jobs occurred between June 15 and October 15 except as stated above. Darren has not cashed, and still holds, the $5,000 and the $100,000 checks from SPI.

If the bankruptcy court determines that the value of all collateral in which First Bank has a perfected security interest is $6,000,000, the amount of First Bank's secured claim in bankruptcy is

(A) less than $5,000,000.

(B) $5,000,000.

(C) $5,000,000 plus any of First Bank's attorneys' fees, but in no event more than $6,000,000.

(D) $6,000,000.

180. If the bankruptcy court determines that the value of all collateral in which First Bank has a perfected security interest is $4,000,000, the amount of First Bank's secured claim in bankruptcy is

(A) less than $5,000,000.

(B) $5,000,000.

(C) $5,000,000 plus any of First Bank's attorneys' fees, but in no event more than $6,000,000.

(D) $6,000,000.

181. Larry owns all of the membership interests in Larry's LLC, a restaurant. Diablo Bank has lent Larry's LLC $1 million, and has a perfected and enforceable security interest in all of its equipment and inventory. It does not have a security interest in any intangible, and thus does not have a security interest in any of Larry's LLC's accounts or bank accounts. Larry owns the land on which the restaurant operates, and leases it to Larry's LLC at a market rate.

Larry's LLC owes over $250,000 to its unsecured creditors. Its total assets are probably worth no more than $1 million. Many of the unsecured creditors are in the process of obtaining judgments against Larry's LLC.

Larry devises the following plan, with the assistance of Diablo. Larry will incorporate Larry, Inc. On Friday, Larry's LLC will acknowledge default, and Diablo will foreclose on all of its collateral at Larry's LLC. Diablo will sell the collateral at a UCC foreclosure sale (to which Larry will consent in all respects, after acknowledging default) to Larry's, Inc. Larry's, Inc. will borrow the necessary money from Diablo, who will then take a security interest in all of Larry, Inc.'s personal property (Larry will also contribute $500 to Larry's, Inc., which will be sufficient to make it just barely solvent). Larry will terminate the lease with Larry's LLC, and re-lease the property to Larry, Inc. on the same terms. The transfers are made right after Larry closes the restaurant on Friday night.

The result is that when Larry unlocks the doors on Saturday morning, he will be doing so for Larry, Inc., and not Larry's LLC. To the public, nothing will have changed. The creditors of Larry's LLC, however, will have only an assetless shell against which to pursue their claims.

Larry, Inc. has no better luck than Larry's LLC. Eighteen months later, Larry files bankruptcy for Larry, Inc.

Without consideration of any state law successor liability theories, does Diablo have anything to fear from Larry, Inc.'s bankruptcy trustee?

(A)   No, because more than one year has passed since the transaction.

(B)   No, because Diablo did not intend to defraud any of Larry's LLC's creditors.

(C)   No, because Larry's, Inc. was solvent after the transaction.

(D)   Yes, if Larry and Diablo intended to hinder or delay the creditors of Larry's LLC through the transaction with Diablo.

182. Debtor borrowed $100,000 from Bank on June 1. To secure repayment of the loan, Debtor granted to Bank a security interest in its current and future equipment. The security agreement was executed on June 1. On June 4, Bank filed a proper financing statement against Debtor's equipment with the appropriate filing officer. On June 8, Debtor used its own funds to buy a new piece of equipment (the "Item") from Seller, who placed a "sold" sticker on the Item. At Debtor's request, Seller did not deliver and install the Item at Debtor's office until June 12.

Debtor fell on hard times and filed a bankruptcy petition in late August. The bankruptcy trustee has challenged Bank's property interest in the Item as a voidable preference.

Under applicable bankruptcy law, the "transfer" took place on

   (A) June 1.

   (B) June 4.

   (C) June 8.

   (D) June 12.

183. On March 1, Kirk borrowed $5,000 from a co-worker, Robert. Kirk executed an unsecured promissory note with a maturity date of June 30. Kirk was unable to pay the note at maturity and requested a six-month extension. Robert agreed, provided that Angela (Kirk's sister) guarantee repayment of the loan and Elliott (Kirk's brother) collateralize the loan with a security interest in his investment portfolio. Angela obliged by executing a guaranty on July 10. Elliott obliged by creating an enforceable security interest in the investment portfolio on July 12. Robert perfected the security interest on July 25.

Alas, Kirk's financial situation did not improve, and he filed a Chapter 7 bankruptcy petition on October 15. On that date, he owed $4,500 to Robert. Angela had paid $500 to Robert on the debt just three days before the bankruptcy petition was filed.

Evidence reveals that Kirk has been insolvent for five months, and his unsecured creditors will not be paid in full in the bankruptcy.

Ignoring any possible defenses, the bankruptcy trustee can attack as voidable preferences

   (A) neither the $500 payment nor the security interest.

   (B) the $500 payment and the security interest.

   (C) the $500 payment but not the security interest.

(D)   the security interest but not the $500 payment.

184.   In a voidable preference action, the bankruptcy trustee

(A)   enjoys an irrebuttable presumption of insolvency during the ninety-day preference period.

(B)   bears the burden of proving non-avoidability of the transfer under any exception found in 11 U.S.C. § 547(c).

(C)   can never prove that a security interest transfer was made for antecedent debt if the security interest is perfected within thirty days of attachment.

(D)   cannot recover loan repayments from a non-insider creditor that were received by that creditor outside the ninety-day preference period, even if the one-year preference period applies (e.g., when the debt is guaranteed by an insider).

185.   Which of the following voidable preference exceptions preserves only payment transfers?

(A)   The "substantially contemporaneous exchange" exception.

(B)   The "ordinary course of business" exception.

(C)   The "enabling loan" exception.

(D)   The "floating lien" exception.

186.   Bank loaned $2 million to Debtor on July 16. To secure repayment of the loan, Bank obtained a non-purchase-money security interest in Debtor's existing and future inventory under a security agreement executed by Debtor at the time of the loan. Bank filed a proper financing statement in the right place on July 18. Debtor filed a bankruptcy petition on October 1. Debtor had not repaid any of the loan, and its inventory (which turns over every fifteen days) had the following value on the stated dates:

July 1	$2.1 million
July 16	$1.7 million
August 1	$1.6 million
August 16	$1.5 million
September 1	$1.5 million
September 16	$1.6 million
October 1	$1.8 million

The bankruptcy trustee has attacked Bank's security interest in each item of inventory as a voidable preference and has proven all elements of its case under Bankruptcy Code § 547(b).

Under the "floating lien" exception, Bank can preserve its security interest in inventory worth

(A) $1.5 million.

(B) $1.6 million.

(C) $1.7 million.

(D) $1.8 million.

187. Susan borrows $5,000 from Friendly Bank on January 1. She also signs a valid security agreement granting Friendly a security interest in her existing television set, an 85", flat-screen wonder. She uses the loan funds to take a trip to Bermuda. Friendly Bank does not file any financing statement.

Susan defaults on her loan on May 1, and Friendly accelerates the debt. Friendly sends one of its collection agents to Susan's house on May 15 to repossess the television set. Susan allows the person to come into her house to take the set. She does not object to the repossession in any way.

The next day, on May 16, Friendly forecloses upon the television set by selling it to one of its tellers for $2,500, which is the fair market value of the used set.

On May 17, Susan files a Chapter 7 bankruptcy petition. Susan's trustee in bankruptcy demands that Friendly Bank give the trustee the $2,500 proceeds of sale.

Friendly Bank

(A) can keep the $2,500.

(B) must pay the trustee the $2,500 because the trustee has the status of a lien creditor under state law.

(C) must pay the trustee the $2,500 because Friendly's repossession of the television set was a preference.

(D) must pay the trustee the $2,500 because it breached the peace by entering Susan's house to repossess the set.

188. Which of the following situations creates a voidable preference? (Assume that unsecured claims will not be paid in full and no creditor is an insider.)

(A) On May 1, Debtor borrows $1,000 from Lender. The loan is unsecured. Debtor's brother repays the loan on June 1. Prior to that time, Debtor did not owe her brother anything. Debtor files a bankruptcy petition on July 1.

(B) On June 1, Debtor buys a piece of equipment for $100,000 from Dealer. Debtor makes a $20,000 cash payment and finances the $80,000 balance with Dealer, who retains a security interest in the equipment. Dealer files its financing statement against the equipment on June 8. Debtor makes a $35,000 loan repayment to Dealer on July 15 and files a bankruptcy petition on August 7. At all relevant times the equipment had a value of at least $80,000.

(C) On April 1, Debtor borrows $50,000 from Bank. The loan is unsecured. Debtor repays the loan on May 1 and files a bankruptcy petition on August 15.

(D) On February 1, Debtor borrowed $10,000 from Finance Company. The loan is unsecured. On February 5, after Debtor releases a poor earnings report, Finance Company insists on collateral. On February 8, Debtor granted to Finance Company a security interest in its existing inventory and equipment (which at all relevant times had a value of at least $20,000). Finance Company filed its financing statement on February 9. Debtor filed a bankruptcy petition on April 25.

189. Soup Bowls, Inc. borrowed $100,000 from Ladle Bank. It is secured by Soup Bowls' accounts receivable. There was nothing remarkable about the loan. Ladle is known, however, for its quick collection practices. Six months after the loan is made, Soup Bowls is two days late with its monthly $5,000 payment. Ladle sends its burliest collector out to Soup Bowls. He is nothing but polite and soft-spoken, but does request the payment due. The scrawny accounts payable clerk, intimidated by the mere size of the collector, pays the amount owing with a regular company check. Soup Bowls files a Chapter 11 bankruptcy petition the next day; its account receivable are only $20,000, and have only been $20,000 for the last month.

When the bankruptcy trustee sues to recover the $5,000 payment as preferential, the most likely outcome is

(A) the trustee will lose, because Ladle was secured.

(B) the trustee will win, because the accounts payable clerk was forced to make the payment.

(C) the trustee will lose, because all Ladle collected was what it was owed.

(D) the trustee will win, because Ladle's quick collection procedures are not within industry standards.

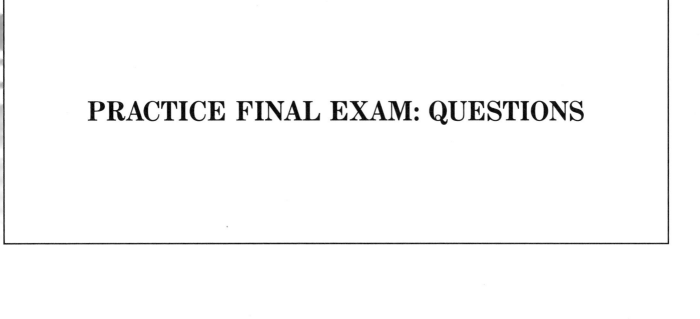

PRACTICE FINAL EXAM: QUESTIONS

This "practice final exam" consists of approximately sixty questions (a fourth of which are short-answer questions). Neither of us would dare give this as an actual final exam, nor do we expect you to be able to complete this practice final exam in three hours. Our best guess is that you can complete the final exam in five hours, which assumes that you actually write answers to the short-answer questions. (Alternatively, if you forego the short-answer questions, we believe you can complete all of the multiple choice questions in three hours.) If you want to take the practice final exam in two discrete (and similar) blocks of time, we suggest that you break somewhere around Question 224. The questions in the first block of time will test your knowledge of Topics 2 through 8 (Definitions, Attachment, Perfection, Proceeds, Fixtures, and Priority Disputes Between Secured Parties). The questions in the second block of time will test your knowledge of Topics 8 through 10 (Priority Disputes Between Secured Parties, Secured Parties and Buyers of Collateral, and Secured Parties and Lien Creditors) and Topics 12 through 14 (Default and Bankruptcy).

190. In which of the following transactions can the secured creditor most likely claim a purchase-money security interest?

   (A) On August 1, Karen Chavez borrows $4,000 from her uncle and buys a new plasma screen, high-definition, television. The dealer delivers and installs the TV three days later. On August 15, Karen borrows $4,000 from SmallBank and uses the money to repay the unsecured loan from her uncle. SmallBank secures repayment of its loan by taking an enforceable security interest in the TV.

   (B) Bill Baxter buys 200 shares of capital stock of Dreyfus Corp. on credit, as permitted by his brokerage agreement with Josephson Investments, Inc. Under that agreement, the 200 shares secure repayment of the loan.

   (C) Esther Johnson buys a new snowmobile from Winterpark Motors, which retains an enforceable security interest in the snowmobile to secure its unpaid purchase price. Winterpark Motors erroneously attempts to perfect its security interest by filing a financing statement (rather than complying with the applicable certificate-of-title statute).

   (D) Gordon Smith borrows $25,000 from Friendly Finance to purchase a comic book collection at an upcoming estate sale. To secure repayment of the loan, Gordon grants to Friendly Finance a security interest in the collection. Friendly Finance wires the $25,000 into Gordon's bank account. Three weeks later, at the estate sale, Gordon purchases the comic book collection with a $25,000 check drawn on that bank account.

191. Lender is making a $1 million secured loan to BAMCO. The parties have agreed that the collateral will include all of BAMCO's assets, including a large savings account maintained with Prosperity Bank.

   Lender will have "control" of the savings account

(A) if BAMCO executes a written security agreement that reasonably identifies the account.

(B) if the three parties execute a written agreement under which Lender has the right to liquidate the account without BAMCO's interference, and BAMCO retains the ability to withdraw funds from the account as long as the account balance never falls below $25,000.

(C) if BAMCO and Lender have agreed in writing that Lender can liquidate the account without BAMCO's interference and BAMCO cannot withdraw any funds from the account without BAMCO's prior written consent.

(D) automatically if Lender is a "bank" as defined by the UCC.

192. On July 1, Bank executed a binding commitment to lend up to $750,000 to Clinic in one or more advances. On July 6, Bank (with Clinic's permission) filed its financing statement against Clinic's equipment. On July 8, Clinic requested the initial advance of $200,000. On July 11, Clinic executed a written security agreement granting to Bank a security interest in Clinic's existing and after-acquired equipment to secure repayment of the loan. Bank funded the $200,000 advance on July 14.

Bank's security interest will attach to an X-Ray machine, acquired by Clinic on July 9, on

(A) July 8.

(B) July 9.

(C) July 11.

(D) July 14.

193. Bank's security interest will attach to an MRI machine, acquired by Clinic on July 12, on

(A) July 6.

(B) July 11.

(C) July 12.

(D) July 14.

194. As a general rule, a written security agreement need not include a real estate description. An exception exists, though, if the security interest covers

(A) consumer goods that are, or will become, "fixtures."

(B) timber to be cut.

(C) minerals that have not yet been, but will be, extracted from the ground.

(D) inventory and equipment that the debtor keeps in more than one state.

195. Lauren borrowed $13,000 from her parents on January 15, 2010, to purchase a new piano from

Dealer that same day. Lauren plays the piano for personal enjoyment and intends to start her twin boys on piano lessons in a year or so.

On July 20, 2010, Lauren borrowed $13,000 from Finance Company and used the money to repay the unsecured loan to her parents. At the time of the loan, Lauren executed a written security agreement that created an enforceable security interest in the piano in favor of Finance Company.

A year later, Lauren's husband lost his job. The family struggled financially for several months before filing a bankruptcy petition in October 2011.

The bankruptcy trustee ordered a UCC search report against Lauren and her husband. The report revealed no filings against any member of the family.

What advice do you have for the trustee?

ANSWER:

196. Lender should file a financing statement against Debtor in Illinois if

   (A) Debtor is a general partnership that provides food services at professional sports stadiums in many states; the collateral will be limited to revenues generated by Debtor for services performed at Chicago venues.

   (B) Debtor is a Texas corporation with its chief executive office, and all of its tangible property, located in Chicago.

   (C) Debtor is a Michigan resident who, as a sole proprietor, operates a business in Chicago, and the collateral is limited to Debtor's business assets.

   (D) Debtor is a Chicago resident who will offer, as collateral, a rare comic book collection that he keeps in his parents' vault in Richmond, Virginia.

197. MegaCorp is a Delaware corporation. MegaCorp has two wholly owned-subsidiaries, Alpha Corporation (an Arizona corporation) and Omega Corporation (a New Mexico corporation). MegaCorp's ownership of the two subsidiaries is evidenced by stock certificates issued by the subsidiaries to — and in the name of — MegaCorp. MegaCorp keeps the stock certificates at its chief executive office in Salt Lake City, Utah.

To secure repayment of a $20 million loan, MegaCorp has granted an enforceable security interest in its Alpha and Omega stock certificates to Zion Finance. Zion Finance intends to perfect its security interest by filing a financing statement.

Zion Finance should file its financing statement in

   (A) Delaware.

   (B) Arizona (against the Alpha stock certificates) and New Mexico (against the Omega stock certificates).

   (C) Utah.

(D) Utah, and, if different, states in which Alpha and Omega maintain their respective chief executive offices.

198. Today is March 1, 2011. Canyon Bank is negotiating the terms of a $25 million loan to Arizona Healthcare, Inc. ("AHI"), an Arizona corporation that operates several clinics in the Phoenix and Tucson metropolitan areas. The parties contemplate that the loan will be secured by a security interest in AHI's current and future accounts and equipment.

Last week Canyon Bank received a UCC search report against "Arizona Healthcare, Inc." The search report does not disclose any filings against AHI.

But there are two filings unknown to Canyon Bank.

First, in August 2010, Dealer filed a financing statement against AHI to perfect its PMSI in an MRI machine. The filing officer, however, erroneously recorded the filing against "Arizona Health Corp." — a completely different entity.

Second, on February 1, 2009, Integrity Finance filed a financing statement against "Phoenix Healthcare, Inc." to perfect its security interest in all current and future equipment owned by Phoenix Healthcare, Inc. ("PHI"). Later that year, PHI expanded its operations from Phoenix to Tucson, and — effective September 1, 2009 — PHI changed its legal name to "Arizona Healthcare, Inc." (the same entity that is borrowing $25 million from Canyon Bank). Integrity Finance has always known of the name change but has taken no filing action in response.

As of today (March 1, 2011), what is the perfected status of security interests held by Dealer and Integrity Finance?

(A) Both creditors are unperfected.

(B) Dealer's PMSI in the MRI machine is perfected by its filing, but Integrity Finance is no longer perfected by its filing.

(C) Dealer's PMSI in the MRI machine remains perfected by its filing, and Integrity Finance remains perfected by its filing — but only in equipment acquired by PHI-AHI prior to the name change.

(D) Dealer's PMSI in the MRI machine remains perfected by its filing, and Integrity Finance remains perfected by its filing — but only in equipment acquired by PHI-AHI prior to the name change and within a few months thereafter.

199. Wallace & Bradford, a general partnership, is a law firm located in New York City. Meredith, a Connecticut resident, is one of the firm's partners. She wants to use her partnership interest as collateral for a $500,000 loan from Gotham Bank. Her other partners have consented. Gotham Bank has reviewed the partnership agreement, which does not prohibit the transaction and nowhere mentions the Uniform Commercial Code generally, or any UCC Article specifically.

Using Article 9 terminology, the collateral is

(A) an account.

(B) a general intangible.

(C) investment property.

(D) a contract right.

200. To perfect its security interest in Meredith's partnership interest in the law firm, Gotham Bank should

(A) file a financing statement, naming the law firm as the debtor, in New York.

(B) file a financing statement, naming Meredith as the debtor, in New York.

(C) file a financing statement, naming Meredith as the debtor, in Connecticut.

(D) take possession of the law firm's partnership agreement.

201. Foxx Furniture operates three furniture stores in Atlanta. Last year it borrowed $5 million from Peachtree Bank. The loan is secured by an enforceable security interest in Foxx Furniture's current and after-acquired inventory and accounts. Peachtree Bank filed its financing statement with the appropriate filing office within days after funding the loan.

Two months ago, Foxx Furniture sold two sofas and three bookcases to an entity in exchange for a new photocopier and $1,000 cash. Three days later, Foxx Furniture took the cash and bought a new refrigerator for the employee lounge.

Assuming that Peachtree Bank can satisfy any tracing burden, it has (as of today)

(A) a perfected security interest in the photocopier and the refrigerator.

(B) a perfected security interest in the photocopier and an unperfected security interest in the refrigerator.

(C) an unperfected security interest in the photocopier and the refrigerator.

(D) an unperfected security interest in the photocopier and no security interest in the refrigerator.

202. Lender has a perfected security interest in Debtor's inventory and accounts. Contrary to the terms of the security agreement, Debtor deposited cash proceeds in a bank account in June that contained deposits of non-proceeds. Evidence reveals the following activity during June:

- the opening balance on June 1 was $7,000 ($3,000 of which is proceeds)
- Debtor deposited cash proceeds into the account as follows:

    $6,000 on June 8

    $4,000 on June 22

- Debtor deposited non-proceeds into the account as follows:

    $5,000 on June 15

    $2,000 on June 26

- Debtor made the following withdrawals from the account:

  $5,000 on June 6

  $2,000 on June 18

  $6,000 on June 24

As of June 30, the lowest intermediate balance rule, Lender can claim a security interest in

(A) $8,000.

(B) $9,000.

(C) $11,000.

(D) $12,000.

203. Bamco manufactures bicycles and sells them to retailers throughout the country. In February, it sold 100 bikes to The Bike Barn ("TBN"), an Arizona corporation that sells bikes to the public through its retail stores in Nevada, Idaho, and Arizona (its main office is in Las Vegas, Nevada, which is where all corporate records are kept, where all executives have their office, and where all major corporate decisions are made). The parties agreed that TBN would pay for the 100 bikes no later than July 31. At the time of purchase, TBN executed a negotiable promissory note for the price. The note described each of the 100 bikes and also stated: "Bamco reserves title in all bikes sold to secure payment of the purchase price." Bamco filed its financing statement against TBN and the bikes with the Secretary of State of Arizona in February. At TBN's direction, Bamco shipped the bikes to TBN's stores in Nevada, Idaho, and Arizona later that month.

In late June, TBN filed a bankruptcy petition, still owing Bamco approximately $21,000. After investigation, it appears that sixty of the bikes remain unsold at TBN's retail stores. Of the remaining forty bikes, TBN has checks from customers for ten of them (three sold more than twenty days before the petition date, and seven within twenty days before the petition date). TBN also is owed $1,000 from Happy Trails, Inc., a Delaware corporation, which bought five of the bikes on unsecured credit from TBN on May 25. There is no trace of what happened to the remaining twenty-five bikes.

TBN's trustee in bankruptcy can use the strong-arm clause to successfully challenge Bamco's security interest in

(A) all sixty bikes.

(B) all bikes located at TBN's retail stores in Idaho only.

(C) all bikes located at TBN's retail stores in Idaho and Nevada only.

(D) none of the sixty bikes.

204. TNB's trustee in bankruptcy can use the strong-arm clause to successfully challenge Bamco's security interest in

(A) none of the ten checks, nor in the $1,000 debt from Happy Trails, Inc.

(B) the three oldest checks, but not the seven recent checks and not the $1,000 debt from Happy Trails, Inc.

(C) all ten checks, but not the $1,000 debt from Happy Trails, Inc.

(D) all ten checks and the $1,000 debt from Happy Trails, Inc.

205. Gwen earns her living by giving piano lessons at a studio that she operates near her home in Boulder, Colorado. In January, Gwen purchased a new Yamaha grand piano for her studio from Dealer on credit. Dealer retained and perfected its PMSI in the piano by filing a financing statement in Colorado.

In March, Gwen married a law professor from the University of Colorado. She did not change her legal name.

In April, Gwen's husband accepted an offer to join the law faculty at Notre Dame University, so Gwen and her husband moved in July to South Bend, Indiana, where Gwen opened a new music studio and began giving piano lessons. Despite Gwen's musical talents and savvy marketing endeavors, she did not enjoy much financial success. So in late December, two days before Christmas, she closed the studio and sold the Yamaha grand piano to the music school at Notre Dame University for a $15,000 cashier's check, which she then indorsed over to Seller three days later when she visited Seller's store and purchased baby furniture for her soon-to-be-born twins.

Dealer has

(A) no security interest in the baby furniture.

(B) an unperfected security interest in the baby furniture.

(C) a perfected security interest in the baby furniture for twenty days following the purchase date, but thereafter the security interest becomes unperfected.

(D) a perfected security interest in the baby furniture for twenty days following the purchase date, and perfection will not lapse immediately thereafter.

206. Assume, instead, that within two weeks after her marriage (to Buzz Markell), Gwen changed her legal name from "Gwen Zinnecker" to "Gwen Markell." The happy couple remained in Colorado and did not move to Indiana. She did close her studio in December and sold the Yamaha grand piano to the music school at the University of Colorado for a $15,000 cashier's check, which she then indorsed over to Seller three days later when she visited Seller's store and purchased baby furniture for her soon-to-be-born twins.

Discuss whether, under these revised facts, Dealer has a security interest in the baby furniture and (if so) the perfected status of that security interest.

ANSWER:

207. Briefly state four differences between a standard financing statement and a fixture filing.

ANSWER:

208. Meredith bought her first home in March of this year. Fidelity Finance financed the purchase and holds the mortgage on the home, "all fixtures now or hereafter affixed thereto," and the underlying real estate. The mortgage (which is not a construction mortgage) was filed in the appropriate real property records in March.

On October 1, Meredith purchased a chandelier for her home on credit from ZinnCo Lighting, which retained an enforceable security interest in the chandelier as of that date. ZinnCo installed the chandelier (a "fixture" under applicable law, and not readily removable) at Meredith's home on October 18.

ZinnCo's security interest in the chandelier

(A) is not automatically perfected.

(B) is automatically perfected, but only until the chandelier becomes a fixture, at which time automatic perfection ceases.

(C) enjoys priority over the competing claim asserted by Fidelity Finance in December, but only if ZinnCo filed a proper fixture filing no later than twenty days after ZinnCo acquired rights in the chandelier.

(D) enjoys priority over the competing claim asserted by Fidelity Finance in December if ZinnCo filed a proper fixture filing on November 5.

209. Assume, instead, that ZinnCo's priority dispute is not with Fidelity Finance, but with Buzz Norton. Buzz won a recent tort lawsuit against Meredith and obtained a lien on Meredith's residence (and fixtures thereto) on October 10. ZinnCo has never filed a standard financing statement or a fixture filing.

Who will win this priority dispute in the chandelier?

ANSWER:

210. In February, Jennifer bought a hot tub on credit from Dealer. Dealer installed the hot tub at Jennifer's residence later that month and retained an enforceable security interest in the hot tub to secure repayment of its purchase price. Dealer filed a standard financing statement, proper in all respects, with the appropriate central filing official.

In May, Jennifer borrowed $3,000 from her parents. To secure repayment of the loan, she granted to her parents an enforceable security interest in various assets, including the hot tub. A week after making the loan, her parents filed a proper fixture filing against the hot tub in the appropriate real estate records.

In August, Jennifer used the equity in her residence to borrow $15,000 from Bank. To secure repayment of the loan, Jennifer executed a mortgage in favor of Bank (the mortgage is not a "construction mortgage"). The collateral description included not only the land and the house, but all fixtures thereto. Bank properly recorded its mortgage in the appropriate real estate records.

By December, Jennifer had fallen on hard financial times and had defaulted on her obligations. Soon thereafter, a priority dispute in the hot tub arose among Dealer, Jennifer's parents, and Bank. The parties have stipulated that the hot tub is a "fixture" under applicable law and not readily removable from the house.

The court should conclude that

(A) Jennifer's parents have priority over Dealer and Bank.

(B) Bank has priority over Dealer and Jennifer's parents.

(C) Dealer has priority over Jennifer's parents, but not Bank.

(D) Bank and Jennifer's parents have priority over Dealer.

211. In January, Lauren Eastman Jefferson (a resident of San Francisco) opened a photography studio that she operated as a sole proprietorship under the name "Snapshots and Memories." She borrowed $100,000 from Lender for general business purposes. To secure the loan, Lauren granted an enforceable security interest in all of her business equipment. The security agreement included an after-acquired property clause. That same month, Lender filed a financing statement in California against the equipment, naming the debtor as "Lauren Eastman Jefferson."

At the suggestion of her lawyer and financial advisor (and following her divorce from Tom Jefferson), Lauren incorporated her photography business as "Eastman Photography" under California law on June 1. Without Lender's approval, Lauren transferred all of her business equipment to the new corporate entity, which became a "new debtor" under applicable law by assuming all of Lauren's business debts (including her obligations under the security agreement with Lender). Lender discovered the asset transfer but never filed a financing statement against the corporate entity.

On August 15, Eastman Photography borrowed $200,000 from Bank, using its equipment as collateral. Bank perfected its enforceable security interest by filing its financing statement in California on August 18. The security agreement included an after-acquired property clause.

On December 15, Bank filed a declaratory action against Lender to resolve a priority dispute in the equipment of Eastman Photography, including the following:

Item #1 (acquired by Lauren on March 1; transferred to Eastman Photography on June 10)

Item #2 (acquired by Lauren Photography on September 15)

Item #3 (acquired by Lauren Photography on November 1)

As of December 15, Lender's security interest is

(A) perfected in all three Items.

(B) perfected in Items #1 and #2 only.

    (C) perfected in Item #1 only.

    (D) unperfected in all three Items.

212. Would your analysis change if Lauren had incorporated her business under Delaware law (and, accordingly, Bank had filed its financing statement in Delaware)?

ANSWER:

213. As of December 15 (under the original facts), Lender has priority in

    (A) none of the Items.

    (B) Item #1 only.

    (C) Items #1 and #2 only.

    (D) Items #1, #2, and #3.

214. Would your analysis change if Lauren had incorporated her business under Delaware law (and, accordingly, Bank had filed its financing statement in Delaware)?

ANSWER:

215. First Bank obtained an enforceable security interest in Debtor's current and after-acquired inventory in January 2007. First Bank filed its financing statement on January 10, 2007.

Second Bank obtained an enforceable security interest in Debtor's current and after-acquired accounts in August 2008. Second Bank filed its financing statement the same month. Second Bank had knowledge of First Bank's security interest and financing statement.

In March 2013, Second Bank filed a motion, seeking a declaratory judgment on the priority of its security interest in Debtor's accounts (all of which are traceable as proceeds of inventory dispositions in the ordinary course of Debtor's business within the last fifteen months). Evidence reveals that First Bank filed its continuation statement on July 5, 2011, and Second Bank has not filed a continuation statement.

The trial judge should rule that

    (A) First Bank has priority, although Second Bank's security interest is perfected.

    (B) First Bank has priority because Second Bank's security interest is unperfected.

    (C) Second Bank has priority, although First Bank's security interest is perfected.

    (D) Second Bank has priority because First Bank's security interest is unperfected.

216. On October 1, John obtained an enforceable security interest in 250 shares of Waldorf capital stock, evidenced by a single certificate that is owned and held by Sharon. John perfected his security interest by filing a financing statement on October 7.

On November 1, Heather obtained an enforceable security interest in the same Waldorf shares. Heather perfected her security interest by taking delivery of the stock certificate on November 3.

On December 1, Sharon defaulted on both loans, triggering a priority dispute over the Waldorf shares.

Which statement is true?

(A) John will win the priority dispute because he perfected his security interest before Heather took delivery of the stock certificate.

(B) Heather will win the priority dispute, whether or not the stock certificate is in blank form or registered form.

(C) John will win the priority dispute if the stock certificate was issued to Sharon in registered form and has not been indorsed by Sharon or registered in Heather's name by Waldorf.

(D) Heather will win the priority dispute because when she took delivery of the certificate she perfected her security interest by control.

217. Cooperstown Bank made a $90,000 loan to The Card Shop (a Delaware corporation) in January. The loan was secured by a security interest in The Card Shop's inventory of baseball cards, and the security agreement included an after-acquired property clause. Cooperstown Bank promptly filed its financing statement.

The Card Shop changed its name to "Home Run Collectibles" on March 20. Bank knew of the name change, but took no action in response.

Doubleday Finance made a $45,000 loan to Home Run Collectibles in August. The loan was secured by a security interest in the borrower's inventory of baseball cards, and the security agreement included an after-acquired property clause. Doubleday Finance promptly filed its financing statement. Doubleday Finance was unaware of Cooperstown Bank's loan and security interest; the UCC search report that Doubleday Finance ordered against "Home Run Collectibles" did not disclose any filings.

Home Run Collectibles defaulted on both loans in December. A priority dispute in three rare baseball cards has erupted. Evidence reveals that the debtor used its own funds to acquire Card #1 on June 5, Card #2 on July 25, and Card #3 on October 1.

As of December 20, Cooperstown Bank has

(A) a perfected security interest in Cards #1 and #2 only, but priority in none of the three Cards.

(B) a perfected security interest in Card #1 only, and priority in that Card only.

(C) an unperfected security interest in all three Cards, and priority in none of the three Cards.

(D) no security interest in any of the three Cards, and priority in none of the three Cards.

218. BizMax sells and leases office equipment to commercial and consumer customers. Its current and after-acquired inventory is encumbered by an enforceable security interest in favor of Fidelity Bank, which filed its financing statement against the collateral just days after BizMax authenticated the security agreement last year.

Two weeks ago, BizMax leased a photocopier to a law firm. The lease described the photocopier and obligated the firm to pay $400 each month for three years.

Last week BizMax sold and delivered the lease to CommCorp, an entity in the business of buying commercial paper (including leases). Before buying the lease, CommCorp ordered a UCC search report against BizMax and discovered Fidelity Bank's filing.

If a priority dispute in the lease erupts during its term, then

(A) Article 9 will not resolve the dispute because its scope does not include sales of lease contracts.

(B) Fidelity Bank will win the dispute because the perfected status of its interest in the photocopier extends to the lease as a "proceed."

(C) Fidelity Bank will win the dispute, but only if the dispute is resolved within twenty days after the lease becomes enforceable.

(D) CommCorp will win the dispute, notwithstanding Fidelity Bank's perfected status.

219. In 2010, Texas National Bank ("TNB") made a $1 million loan to Barnaby's Bookstores, Inc., a corporation that operates three bookstores in the San Francisco area. To secure repayment of the loan, TNB obtained an enforceable security interest in the borrower's inventory, accounts, and equipment. TNB filed its financing statement against the collateral soon after funding the loan. An after-acquired property clause appeared in the collateral description found in both the security agreement and the financing statement.

In June 2011, Barnaby's Bookstores purchased three photocopiers on credit from Dealer. Dealer retained an enforceable security interest in the photocopiers, which it delivered and installed on June 5. Dealer filed its financing statement on June 23. Being prudent, Dealer had ordered a UCC search report that revealed TNB's filing. Nevertheless, Dealer never notified TNB of its security interest in the photocopiers.

In August 2012, ZinnMark Press sold 300 hardback copies of the national bestseller, "My Life on the Bench," an autobiography penned by Judge Atticus Holmes. ZinnMark shipped the books from its Denver distribution center and delivered them to Barnaby's Bookstores on August 19. ZinnMark retained an enforceable security interest in the book shipment and filed its financing statement against the collateral on August 13. On August 11, ZinnMark sent a written notice of its security interest in the books to TNB; the contents of the notice satisfied the statutory requirements of UCC Article 9. TNB received the notice on August 17.

After Barnaby's Bookstores defaulted on its material contracts in November 2012, a priority dispute arose (i) between TNB and Dealer in the three photocopiers and (ii) between TNB and ZinnMark Press in the unsold Holmes books.

TNB has priority in

(A) the photocopiers and the unsold Holmes books.

(B) the photocopiers but not the unsold Holmes books.

(C) the unsold Holmes books but not the photocopiers.

(D) neither the photocopiers nor the Holmes books.

220. Evidence reveals that Barnaby's Bookstores sold one of the photocopiers two weeks ago to Tim, an employee, creating proceeds that remain identifiable.

In a priority dispute between TNB and Dealer over these proceeds,

(A) TNB will win if Tim charged the purchase to his credit card.

(B) TNB will win if Tim paid for the photocopier by swiping his debit card.

(C) TNB will win if Tim paid for the photocopier with his personal check.

(D) Dealer will win if Tim paid for the photocopier with a cashier's check.

221. Evidence reveals that Barnaby's Bookstores sold fifty of the Holmes books last week to the Bay Area Law School, creating proceeds that remain identifiable, if tangible, and are in the possession of Barnaby's Bookstores.

In a priority dispute between TNB and ZinnMark Press over these proceeds,

(A) ZinnMark will win if the Law School executed a promissory note, promising to pay for its purchase in ninety days.

(B) ZinnMark will win if the Law School paid for the purchase by swiping its debit card.

(C) TNB will win if the Law School paid cash at the time of purchase.

(D) TNB will win if the Law School paid for the purchase with a teller's check.

222. Three years ago, Dealer sold a grand piano on credit to Timmy Zee, a law professor who plays the piano for personal enjoyment and relaxation. Dealer retained an enforceable security interest in the piano but never filed a financing statement.

A few months ago, without Dealer's consent, Timmy Zee sold the piano to First Church on credit. Timmy Zee retained an enforceable security interest in the piano to secure the purchase obligation. Timmy Zee filed a financing statement against First Church and the piano within two weeks after First Church came to his home and took the piano to its worship center.

Last week Dealer discovered that Timmy Zee had sold the piano. Dealer has asked a mediator to resolve its priority dispute with First Church. Timmy Zee says "not so fast. I have a PMSI that enjoys superpriority."

The mediator should resolve the three claims in the order of

(A) Timmy Zee, then First Church, then Dealer.

    (B) First Church, then Dealer, then Timmy Zee.

    (C) Dealer, then Timmy Zee, then First Church.

    (D) Timmy Zee, then Dealer, then First Church.

223. MolarCorp is a Texas corporation that operates a dental clinic in Dallas.

In 2009, First Bank made a $500,000 loan to MolarCorp, secured by an enforceable security interest in all of MolarCorp's current and future equipment. First Bank filed its financing statement against MolarCorp and its equipment on the day of the loan.

In March 2010, MolarCorp bought a new imaging machine on credit from Dealer for $75,000. With First Bank's consent, MolarCorp used its existing imaging machine as a trade-in, which Dealer valued at $25,000. Dealer financed the $50,000 balance, retaining an enforceable security interest in the new machine. Dealer delivered the machine to MolarCorp on March 23 and filed its financing statement on April 10.

In December 2011, MolarCorp defaulted on its obligations to both First Bank and Dealer, having paid only $5,000 to the former and $15,000 to the latter for the new imaging machine.

A liquidator has sold the imaging machine for $45,000. After subtracting its $5,000 fee, how should the liquidator distribute the remaining $40,000 between First Bank and Dealer?

ANSWER:

224. Assume that Dealer accepted MolarCorp's imaging machine as a $25,000 trade-in, but refused to finance the $50,000 balance itself. So MolarCorp borrowed $50,000 from its principal shareholder, Willie Floss, and remitted those funds to Dealer. To secure repayment of the $50,000 loan, MolarCorp authenticated a security agreement that granted to Willie Floss an enforceable security interest in the new imaging machine. Willie Floss filed his financing statement within a month after Dealer delivered the new imaging machine to MolarCorp.

Later, MolarCorp defaulted on its obligations to both First Bank and Willie Floss, having paid only $5,000 to the former and $15,000 to the latter for the new imaging machine.

A liquidator has sold the imaging machine for $45,000. After subtracting its $5,000 fee, how should the liquidator distribute the remaining $40,000 between First Bank and Willie Floss?

ANSWER:

225. Dealer sells a school bus to Smallville Independent School District ("SISD") on credit on February 15 for $20,000. Dealer retains an enforceable security interest in the bus, which Dealer perfects that month by complying with state certificate-of-title laws.

SISD has all of the seats in the bus replaced in July by BusCo at a cost of $8,000. SISD takes delivery of the serviced bus on August 12. To secure repayment for the purchase and installation cost, BusCo obtains and perfects a security interest in the seats by filing a financing statement on August 29.

Later, SISD defaults on its obligations to Dealer and BusCo. The bus is sold for $11,000 (of which

$3,500 is attributable to the seats).

How should the sales proceeds be distributed?

ANSWER:

226. Bruce buys a wall tapestry on credit from Gilmore Artworks for $8,000 on April 20. Gilmore Artworks retains an enforceable security interest in the tapestry and perfects its interest by filing a financing statement within two weeks after the sale.

A few days later, Bruce contracts with Framed Again! to make a frame, at a cost of $2,000, for the tapestry. Framed Again! makes the frame, affixes it to the tapestry, and returns the finished product to Bruce on May 23. Framed Again! retains a security interest in the frame and perfects its interest by filing a financing statement on June 15.

Last week, Bruce filed a bankruptcy petition, still owing $7,500 to Gilmore Artworks and $1,500 to Framed Again! The trustee has sold the framed tapestry (which had been hanging in Bruce's office) for $6,500 (of which $1,000 is attributable to the frame). The trustee should distribute

(A) nothing to Framed Again! and $6,500 to Gilmore Artworks.

(B) $1,000 to Framed Again! and $5,500 to Gilmore Artworks.

(C) $1,100 to Framed Again! and $5,400 to Gilmore Artworks.

(D) $1,500 to Framed Again! and $5,000 to Gilmore Artworks.

227. BAM, Inc., is a Nevada corporation that operates three fitness centers in the Las Vegas area.

In 2009, Fitness Finance made a $250,000 loan to BAM, secured by an enforceable security interest in all of BAM's inventory, equipment, and accounts. Fitness Finance filed a financing statement on July 20, 2009, the date on which BAM authenticated a security agreement (which included an after-acquired property clause).

On August 1, 2010, BAM bought seven UniFlex machines (an all-in-one stairmaster, elliptical, and treadmill device) for its fitness centers, at a cost of $25,000. It financed the purchase with an unsecured loan from its majority shareholder, Brenda Mahan, evidenced by a negotiable promissory note, payable in one year.

On September 1, 2010, BAM borrowed $25,000 from Muscles Bank and used the money to repay Brenda's loan. Muscles Bank secured repayment of its loan by taking an enforceable security interest in the seven UniFlex machines. Muscles Bank perfected its security interest by filing a financing statement.

In June 2011, BAM defaulted on its material contracts, triggering a priority dispute between Fitness Finance and Muscles Bank over the seven UniFlex machines.

The dispute should be resolved in favor of

(A) Muscles Bank, because it has a PMSI that enjoys superpriority.

(B) Muscles Bank, if it filed its financing statement no later than when its security interest attached.

(C) Muscles Bank, if it filed its financing statement no later than twenty days after its security interest attached.

(D) Fitness Finance, because its filing date is earlier than Muscles Bank's filing date.

228. Bruce visits Integrity Motors to purchase a used Camaro. He pays the $10,000 purchase price by check and drives the Camaro off the lot. During negotiations, Integrity Motors assured Bruce that it would mail the "pink slip" (industry jargon for the certificate of title) to him.

Unknown to Bruce, the certificate of title shows Lauren as the registered owner, and reflects AutoFinance as the "first lienholder" (which, under the local certificate of title statute, effectively perfects AutoFinance's security interest in the vehicle). Integrity Motors had paid $8,500 to Lauren for the car, and Lauren had then indorsed the certificate of title in all appropriate places so as to effect a transfer of title to the Camaro to Integrity Motors.

Also unknown to Bruce, Beta Bank finances the vehicle inventory of Integrity Motors and has an enforceable security interest in all current and future vehicles. Beta Bank did not record its security interest on any certificates of title, instead opting to file a single financing statement with the appropriate official.

AutoFinance has discovered that the Camaro has been sold twice (by Lauren, and then by Integrity Motors). Lauren's sale triggered a default under her security agreement with AutoFinance, to whom she still owes nearly $10,000. Lauren did not forward to AutoFinance any of the $8,500 she received from Integrity Motors, which is in default under its contract with Beta Bank.

In a replevin action for the Camaro among AutoFinance, Beta Bank, and Bruce,

(A) Bruce will prevail because he bought the car in the ordinary course of business.

(B) Beta Bank will prevail because it had a perfected security interest in all cars in Integrity Bank's vehicle inventory.

(C) AutoFinance will prevail because its name was noted on the certificate of title.

(D) Beta Bank will prevail because Lauren did not turn over to AutoFinance the sales price that Integrity Motors paid to Lauren.

229. On February 1, BAMCO sold a lawn tractor on credit to Joe Smith, an Atlanta resident, for use in Joe's lawncare business (a sole proprietorship). BAMCO retained a security interest in the tractor to secure payment of the unpaid purchase price and filed a financing statement in Georgia on February 4. (The tractor is not subject to any certificate-of-title law.)

In April, Joe moved his family and lawncare business (including the tractor) to Birmingham, Alabama.

In May, Joe sold the tractor to his neighbor, Billy, for personal use. Billy is unaware of the transaction between BAMCO and Joe.

BAMCO soon discovers Joe's relocation and sale; both actions violated the terms of Joe's security agreement. BAMCO then brings a conversion action against Billy for the tractor. BAMCO has never filed any papers in Alabama.

If the lawsuit is resolved as of July 15, then

(A) BAMCO will win the dispute, because Joe's sale violated the terms of BAMCO's security agreement.

(B) Billy will win the dispute, because he is a buyer in the ordinary course of business.

(C) Billy will win the dispute, because he is using the tractor as a consumer good.

(D) Billy will win the dispute, because BAMCO's security interest was unperfected when Billy bought the tractor.

230. Assume that the conversion lawsuit is resolved as of September 10.

Who will win the lawsuit under these revised facts?

ANSWER:

231. Assume that the conversion lawsuit is resolved as of September 10, and BAMCO filed a financing statement in Alabama against Joe and the tractor on June 15.

Who will win the lawsuit under these revised facts?

ANSWER:

232. Assume that Joe never moved to Alabama, he sold the tractor to Billy (a relative living in Birmingham) in May, BAMCO never filed any papers in Alabama, and BAMCO's conversion lawsuit is resolved fifteen months after Billy's purchase.

Who will win the lawsuit under these revised facts?

ANSWER:

233. Meredith, an astronaut, borrowed $8,000 from Knight Finance and used the funds to purchase a chess set for personal use and display in her home. Meredith authenticated a security agreement, granting to Knight Finance an enforceable security interest in the chess set. Knight Finance did not file any financing statement.

Two weeks later (and without the knowledge or consent of Knight Finance), Meredith sold the chess set to a merchant (for its inventory) for $10,000.

Meredith promptly deposited the $10,000 into her checking account at Bishop Bank. Three days later, Meredith drew a check on this account for $12,000 to purchase a rare comic book.

Six weeks have passed since Meredith sold the chess set to the collector. Knight Finance has discovered the unauthorized sale. Evidence reveals that Meredith's checking account had a $5,000 balance immediately before she deposited the $10,000. Following the deposit, the account balance has been as low as $0 and as high as $18,000. The current balance is $13,000. The merchant still holds the chess set, and Meredith still owns the rare comic book. And Meredith filed a bankruptcy petition this morning.

In a priority dispute with the bankruptcy trustee (who will stipulate that the facts raise no voidable preferences), Knight Finance can assert a superior interest in

(A)   the chess set, the comic book, and up to $10,000 in Meredith's checking account.

(B)   the chess set and the comic book, but not any part of Meredith's checking account.

(C)   the chess set, but not the comic book or any part of Meredith's checking account.

(D)   neither the chess set, the comic book, nor any part of Meredith's checking account.

234.   ZinnCo is a Delaware corporation that operates a retail outlet in Las Vegas, from which it sells pool tables and related items. Nevada Bank has an enforceable security interest in ZinnCo's current and after-acquired inventory. The security agreement authenticated by the parties is silent on when ZinnCo's buyers may take free of Nevada Bank's security interest. Nevada Bank perfected its security interest by filing a financing statement in Delaware.

Last Monday, Hannah visited ZinnCo's store and signed a contract to purchase a pool table for her home and family pleasure. The price was set at $4,000 (which is $500 less than the purchase price of the same pool table model offered for sale by one of ZinnCo's local competitors). In an effort to avoid an additional $200 delivery charge, Hannah agreed to return to the store on Thursday with a truck and her three athletic sons, at which time she would tender a $4,000 cashier's check as payment. ZinnCo did not set aside or mark any specific pool table for Hannah (and the contract she signed did not identify the pool table by serial number or any other unique identifying mark). Hannah was not aware of ZinnCo's relationship with Nevada Bank.

When Hannah returned on Thursday, she found the store closed, and the front doors chained and padlocked. A well-dressed woman approached Hannah and displayed identification as "Erin Merrick — ASSET LIQUIDATORS." Erin explained that ZinnCo had been in default on its secured loans from Nevada Bank in recent months, and Nevada Bank had retained her services to seize the store and its inventory the previous day. (You may assume that Erin is telling the truth, and the lockdown and seizure did not breach the peace or violate any law.)

In the inevitable priority dispute between Nevada Bank and Hannah over the pool table,

(A)   Hannah has a superior right of possession, because she was a buyer in the ordinary course of ZinnCo's business.

(B)   Nevada Bank has a superior right of possession, because Hannah did not take immediate possession of the pool table.

(C) Hannah has a superior right of possession, because she was a good faith purchaser for value.

(D) Nevada Bank has a superior right of possession because Hannah had not paid any of the purchase price prior to the lockdown and seizure.

235. On June 1, Bank took and perfected a security interest in Borrower's current and future equipment. Bank advanced $35,000 on the same day. The security agreement included a future advance clause but did not obligate Bank to fund any additional advances.

On June 15, BAM Corporation became a "lien creditor" under UCC Article 9. Its lien (for $90,000) encumbered Borrower's equipment.

Later, Bank funded the following advances to Borrower: $15,000 (June 20); $20,000 (July 8); $35,000 (July 25); and $10,000 (August 5). Bank discovered BAM's lien on July 15, and a priority dispute arose soon thereafter.

With everyone's consent, the sheriff sold Borrower's equipment for $130,000 on August 10. Borrower still owes $115,000 to Bank and $90,000 to BAM.

The sheriff should distribute

(A) $115,000 to Bank and $15,000 to BAM.

(B) $105,000 to Bank and $25,000 to BAM.

(C) $70,000 to Bank and $60,000 to BAM.

(D) $50,000 to Bank and $80,000 to BAM.

236. How should the sheriff distribute the $130,000 if Borrower's security agreement obligated Bank to loan up to $150,000 in one or more advances?

ANSWER:

237. First Bank obtained an enforceable security interest in Debtor's current and after-acquired inventory in August 2007. First Bank filed its financing statement on August 10, 2007.

Ima Victum, an involuntary tort creditor, obtained a monetary judgment against Debtor in February 2012 and a judgment lien on Debtor's current and future inventory in July 2012.

Second Bank obtained an enforceable security interest in Debtor's current and after-acquired inventory in September 2012. Before funding its secured loan, Second Bank had ordered a search report that revealed First Bank's original filing and a continuation statement filed on February 5, 2012.

In December 2012, First Bank seeks a judicial resolution of the priority dispute among the three creditors in Debtor's inventory.

Which statement is true?

(A) First Bank enjoys priority over Ima and Second Bank.

(B) First Bank enjoys priority over Second Bank, but not Ima.

(C) Second Bank enjoys priority over First Bank and Ima.

(D) Ima enjoys priority over Second Bank, but not First Bank.

238. For many years, Fidelity Finance has made secured loans only to businesses. But in an effort to expand its customer base, Fidelity has decided to make secured loans to consumers. Fidelity realistically expects some of its consumer debtors to default, after which Fidelity may sell, lease, or otherwise dispose of the collateral at a nonjudicial foreclosure. Fidelity knows that Article 9 normally requires the secured party to send notice of the disposition to the debtor and perhaps other parties. Fidelity intends to use its existing standard form of notice for businesses as a model for its "consumer goods" disposition notice.

In doing so, Fidelity must amend its existing form to mention

(A) the debtor's right to attend any public disposition and purchase the collateral.

(B) the debtor's liability for any deficiency remaining after the foreclosure.

(C) a description of the default.

(D) the debtor's right to insist on a strict foreclosure.

239. Two years ago, ZinnCorp borrowed $1 million from BankOne. ZinnCorp is the parent company of BAMCO. To secure repayment of its $1 million loan to ZinnCorp, BankOne obtained and timely perfected an enforceable security interest in BAMCO's major asset (the "Asset") worth $3 million if unencumbered by any liens or security interests.

A year ago, BAMCO borrowed $500,000 from BankTwo, which timely perfected an enforceable security interest in the Asset.

Six months ago, BAMCO borrowed $250,000 from BankThree, which timely perfected an enforceable security interest in the Asset.

Three months ago, ZinnCorp and BAMCO defaulted on their respective loans from BankOne, BankTwo, and BankThree.

With BAMCO's consent, BankTwo has taken possession of the Asset. It intends to sell the Asset either to a private buyer or at a public auction.

Article 9 requires BankTwo to send its disposition notice to

(A) ZinnCorp, BAMCO, BankOne, and BankThree.

(B) BAMCO, BankOne, and BankThree only.

(C) ZinnCorp, BAMCO, and BankOne only.

(D) BankOne and BankThree only.

240. After complying with the statutory notice requirements of Article 9, BankTwo conducted a

commercially reasonable foreclosure sale of the Asset. Buyer purchased the Asset for $2 million (its fair market value at that time, if unencumbered). At the time of sale, ZinnCorp owed $500,000 to BankOne, and BAMCO owed $400,000 to BankTwo and $300,000 to BankThree.

How should the sale proceeds of $2 million be allocated among the parties?

ANSWER:

241. What effect does the foreclosure sale have on the various property interests in the Asset?

ANSWER:

242. Did Buyer pay too much for the Asset?

ANSWER:

243. Dealer is in the business of selling home entertainment systems. Historically, Dealer has extended unsecured credit to about a third of its customers (the remaining customers pay with cash or a credit card). But given the recent downturn in the economy and the increased number of bankruptcies, Dealer has decided that any credit sales over $1,000 must be secured. Dealer is aware that Article 9 permits a secured party to dispose of collateral after default, and that every aspect of the disposition must be "commercially reasonable."

Which statement regarding the quoted phrase is true?

(A) Dealer can waive its duty to dispose of collateral in a "commercially reasonable" manner by agreement with its customers, but only in a transaction other than a consumer transaction.

(B) Dealer can waive its duty to dispose of collateral in a "commercially reasonable" manner by agreement with its customers, but only if the waiver is unambiguous and conspicuous and the agreement is authenticated by the customer after default.

(C) Dealer and its customers can determine, by agreement, standards of "commercially reasonable" behavior, but those standards cannot be unreasonable.

(D) Dealer and its customers can determine, by agreement, standards of "commercially reasonable" behavior, but those standards cannot be manifestly unreasonable.

244. Otto's Autos is in the business of selling new and used cars. A few customers pay with cash, but most take advantage of Otto's secured financing. With its eye on the possibility of post-default repossession, Otto's standard form of security agreement includes the following provision: *"Debtor agrees that Secured Party may, without notice to Debtor, repossess the Vehicle from Debtor's residential premises, place of employment, or any other location where the Vehicle may be found at any time without damage to any*

surrounding property."

Following the default of one of its customers, Keith (who had authenticated the standard form of security agreement), Otto's Autos employed Towtruck Tim, an independent contractor, to repossess Keith's vehicle. Towtruck Tim went to Keith's home in the middle of the night and determined, by looking through a window, that the vehicle was in the garage. Finding the garage door unlocked, Towtruck Tim opened the garage door, removed the vehicle, closed the garage door, and towed the vehicle away. Towtruck Tim was on Keith's property less than five minutes and neither the neighbors nor Keith heard any noise throughout the repossession.

Keith discovered the repossession in the morning. Being a litigious sort, Keith quickly initiated an action against Otto's Autos and Towtruck Tim for breaching the peace, seeking compensatory and punitive damages.

With respect to the lawsuit,

(A)   Otto's Autos will be liable for any breach of the peace, for which both compensatory and punitive damages may be awarded.

(B)   neither Otto's Autos nor Towtruck Tim will be liable for breaching the peace because of the provision, quoted above, in the security agreement authenticated by Keith.

(C)   neither Otto's Autos nor Towtruck Tim will be liable for breaching the peace because Towtruck Tim was on Keith's premises for such a brief period of time, during which neighborhood tranquility remained undisturbed.

(D)   Otto's Autos will not be liable for any breach of the peace because Towtruck Tim, an independent contractor, actually repossessed the vehicle.

245.   Harold is the president of Hal's Coaches, Inc. ("HCI"). HCI borrowed $1 million from Rapacious Bank two years ago, and Rapacious took a valid and properly perfected security interest in all of HCI's accounts to secure the loan (the security agreement describes the collateral simply as "all accounts" without any other qualifying language). HCI recently filed a Chapter 11 bankruptcy petition. It still owes Rapacious $1 million.

Rapacious seeks relief from the stay and a prohibition against the use of cash collateral. Rapacious will likely

(A)   lose, because Rapacious did not use an after-acquired property clause when describing the collateral.

(B)   win, if the accounts total less than $1 million.

(C)   lose, if the accounts are necessary for an effective reorganization, and if HCI offers a replacement lien in its post-petition accounts.

(D)   win, unless HCI agrees to continue to make its monthly payments until the loan is paid in full.

246.   Sally bought a car for her daughter's personal use. She financed it with Drive Bank, giving

it a valid and perfected security interest in the car to secure the deferred portion of the purchase price. Both Sally and her daughter sign the note for the car; the car, however, remains titled in Sally's name only.

Sally's daughter files a Chapter 13 bankruptcy petition, and files a plan under which Drive Bank will be paid over the five-year life of the plan, well beyond the three-year maturity of the note.

Drive Bank may

(A) repossess the car so long as it complies with Article 9.

(B) telephone Sally to demand payment.

(C) commence a state court action for replevin on the car.

(D) take none of these actions.

247. An undersecured creditor in bankruptcy is entitled to a distribution

(A) that includes post-petition interest, but not attorneys' fees.

(B) that includes post-petition interest and attorneys' fees.

(C) equal to the value of its collateral as of the time the case commenced.

(D) equal to the value of its collateral as of the time the case commenced, plus a distribution on its deficiency.

248. DHI is a Chapter 11 debtor. It has proposed a plan which it will be able to confirm if it can either obtain BigBank's consent or provide appropriate treatment of BigBank's claim in its plan of reorganization. BigBank made a loan to finance some highly complicated equipment for DHI. DHI was to "take out" and repay BigBank with a larger loan it was to obtain to finance all of its business; that loan never materialized. BigBank's loan, which is in the amount of $5 million, matured and was fully due and payable one month before DHI commenced its bankruptcy case. BigBank's loan bears an interest rate of 12% per annum; the market rate for such loans is now 6%. Also, the equipment which secures BigBank's loan is worth $7.5 million.

BigBank will never consent to any plan by DHI. DHI's plan calls for repayment of BigBank's loan over a five-year period, on a fully amortizing basis, at 6% interest. DHI's projections show that it can make these payments easily.

If BigBank objects, then most likely the bankruptcy court

(A) will not confirm the plan unless the interest rate is changed to 12%.

(B) will not confirm the plan unless DHI increases the claim to the value of the collateral, or $7.5 million.

(C) will not confirm the plan unless the plan is changed to pay BigBank in cash, with interest from its original maturity date.

(D) will confirm the plan.

249. LargeBanc lent $5 million to David Debtor. Both signed a security agreement granting a valid security interest in David's existing Renoir painting, which is worth $2.5 million. LargeBanc takes possession of the painting.

On June 1, David makes a $2 million payment to LargeBanc. On July 1, David files a Chapter 7 bankruptcy petition.

When the bankruptcy trustee sues LargeBanc to recover the $2 million payment as a preference, then most likely

(A) LargeBanc will prevail since it has possession of the painting.

(B) LargeBank will lose unless it can show that David was solvent on June 1.

(C) LargeBanc will lose unless the trustee can show that David was insolvent on June 1.

(D) LargeBanc will prevail since the painting was worth more than the amount of the payment.

250. Now assume that LargeBanc does not take possession of the painting and files no financing statement. All other facts are the same.

When the bankruptcy trustee sues LargeBanc to recover the $2 million payment as a preference, then most likely

(A) LargeBanc will prevail since it did not need to take possession or file a financing statement as the painting was a consumer good.

(B) LargeBanc will lose unless it can show that David was solvent on June 1.

(C) LargeBanc will lose unless the trustee can show that David was insolvent on June 1.

(D) LargeBanc will prevail if the trustee has filed and fully prosecuted an action under the "Strong Arm" provisions of 11 U.S.C. § 544.

ANSWERS

1. **Answer (D) is correct.** Section 9-109 is the scope provision of Article 9. Section 9-109(a) states that Article 9 applies to "(3) a sale of accounts, chattel paper, payment intangibles, or promissory notes." Credit card receivables are "accounts" under section 9-102(a)(2)(vii), **making Answer (A) an incorrect answer.** Automobile lease contracts are examples of "chattel paper" under section 9-102(a)(11) (i.e., a record that evidences a monetary obligation [the periodic lease payments] and a lease in specific goods [one or more automobiles]), **making Answer (B) an incorrect answer.** Sales of promissory notes also fall within the language of section 9-109(a)(3), even if the notes themselves are secured by real estate or other examples of non-Article 9 collateral. *See* § 9-109(b), 9-109(d)(11), 9-109 cmt. 7. Therefore, **Answer (C) is incorrect.** Computer software diskettes can indeed serve as Article 9 collateral, but the mere sale of the diskettes, without additional details of the transaction (Cash? Unsecured credit? Secured credit?), does not by itself trigger application of Article 9, **making Answer (D) the correct answer.**

2. **Answer (A) is correct.** The scope provision of Article 9 is section 9-109. Subsection (a) states: "Except as otherwise provided in subsections (c) and (d), this article applies to: (1) a transaction . . . that creates a security interest in personal property or fixtures by contract." As a general rule, then, Article 9 applies to any voluntary transaction in which the collateral is not real estate (unless the real estate qualifies as a fixture). Under this general rule, Article 9 covers all three items, each an example of "personal property."

    The Dalmatian is a "good" under section 9-102(a)(44) as a "movable" object (and notice that clause (iii) even picks up *unborn* young of animals). Therefore, Article 9 will cover the parents' interest in the dog.

    The automobile also is a good (again, a movable item). Because the automobile is already serving as collateral for repayment of other debt, using it to secure new debt may trigger a contractual breach under the other agreement or create a priority dispute between the other creditor and Grace's parents. But the pre-existing security interest does not preclude Grace from using the automobile as collateral in a transaction that triggers Article 9.

    The right held by Grace to a federal income tax refund is an example of a "payment intangible" and a "general intangible" under sections 9-102(a)(61) and 9-102(a)(42), respectively. The IRS may challenge the amount of the claim, and tracing the claim (or, more likely, its proceeds) after the IRS mails a refund check to Grace, or deposits the refund directly into Grace's bank account, may pose a challenge. But these concerns do not prevent the federal income tax refund from serving as Article 9 collateral.

    In summary, then, all three items may serve as Article 9 collateral. Therefore, because only Answer (A) lists all three items of property as Article 9 collateral, **Answer (A) is correct and Answers (B), (C), and (D) are incorrect.**

3. **Answer B is correct.** All of the items are examples of personal property (anything other

than real estate). So perhaps Article 9 covers all three assets. Observe, however, that section 9-109(a) is subject to exclusions found in subsections (c) and (d). Subsection (c)(1) states that Article 9 "does not apply to the extent that . . . a statute, regulation, or treaty of the United States preempts" Article 9. Federal law has created a national filing registry when airplanes (or engines, propellers, or some other aircraft parts) serve as collateral. (In effect, then, filing a traditional financing statement where the debtor is located will not perfect a security interest in the airplane.) But federal law does not prohibit a debtor from using its airplane as collateral. Article 9, then, does cover the airplane to the extent that federal law does not preempt Article 9.

The other two items of collateral raise concerns under subsection (d), which expressly excludes certain types of property from the scope of Article 9. Subsection (d)(8) excludes any transfer by BizCorp of its rights as beneficiary under a life insurance policy. Therefore, Article 9 will not apply to BizCorp's rights under the life insurance policy. (Those rights may be used as collateral, but the parties must comply with law other than Article 9. The parties should consult with the insurance company and follow its instructions on how to effectively assign BizCorp's rights as beneficiary to MidBank.)

Section 9-109(d)(12) excludes tort claims, other than "commercial tort claims." The term is defined in section 9-102(a)(13) and picks up BizCorp's claim because BizCorp is an organization (defined in Article 1 as a party other than a human). So Article 9 will bring the patent infringement claim within its scope.

In summary, then, Article 9 will apply to the airplane and the patent infringement claim, so **Answer (B) is the correct answer. Answer (A) is incorrect** because it fails to include the airplane. **Answer (C) is incorrect** for two reasons: it erroneously mentions the life insurance policy, and it fails to mention the patent infringement claim. **Answer (D) is incorrect** because it includes the life insurance policy.

4.   No. Ingrid is correct that Article 9 does not cover the assignment of her claim against her employer for wages. § 9-109(d)(3). As that claim is periodically paid, however, it ceases to exist. The claim has been replaced with a paycheck, which Ingrid has deposited into her bank account. It is that asset (the bank account, a "deposit account" under section 9-102(a)(29)) in which Matt believes he has an Article 9 security interest. Article 9 does indeed apply to a deposit account, unless the creditor's interest arises in a "consumer transaction" (*see* § 9-109(d)(13)). The transaction between Ingrid and Matt is a "consumer transaction" under section 9-102(a)(26) because Ingrid used the $600 to pay personal debts and the bank account is her personal bank account. Therefore, Article 9 does not cover Matt's interest in Ingrid's personal bank account, and he will have to look to other bodies of law to determine the scope (if any) of his interest in the deposit account and what rights and remedies he may enjoy.

5.   **Answer (C) is correct.** Section 9-109(a)(1) states that Article 9 applies to "a transaction, regardless of its form, that creates a security interest in personal property or fixtures by contract." This question focuses attention on two requirements. First, the property interest must arise contractually (consensually). Second, the property interest must be in personal property or fixtures (and not real estate).

Answer (C) is correct because the dealer's interest in the car (personal property) arises contractually. The contract is labeled "Promissory Note" and not "Security Agreement," but the statutory language quoted above reveals that substance trumps form. The contract includes "title retention" language, which effectively gives the dealer a "security interest" in the vehicle. *See* § 1-201(b)(35) (stating, in the penultimate sentence of the definition of "security interest," that "[t]he retention or reservation of title by a seller of goods notwithstanding shipment or delivery to the buyer under section 2-401 is limited in effect to a reservation of a 'security interest' "). Because the dealer's interest in the car is a "security interest" that arises contractually, Article 9 applies and **Answer (C) is correct.**

Boats and investment property can both serve as collateral under Article 9. But the county assessor's interest in the boat arises statutorily, and the neighbor's interest in the investment property is created by judicial process. Neither creditor's interest in the personal property arises contractually, so Article 9 does not apply and therefore **Answers (A) and (B) are incorrect.**

Unlike the county assessor and the dealer, the bank has a property interest that arises contractually. But the property interest is in Norman's residence, which is real estate (rather than personal property). Therefore, Article 9 does not apply and **Answer (D) is incorrect.**

6.   **Answer (D) is the correct answer.** Section 9-102(a)(2) defines an "account" as "a right to payment of a monetary obligation . . . (vii) arising out of the use of a credit or charge card or information contained on or for use with the card." A later sentence in the definition warns that an "account" does not include "rights to payment evidenced by chattel paper or an instrument." Grace did sign a writing, which should prompt you to consider whether the exclusionary language applies. Observe, though, that the definitions of "chattel paper" (§ 9-102(a)(11)) and "instrument" (§ 9-102(a)(47)) both exclude "writings that evidence a right to payment arising out of the use of a credit or charge card." Therefore, **Answers (A) and (B) are incorrect.**

      The credit card receivable also is not a "payment intangible." That term is defined in section 9-102(a)(61) as a subset of "general intangible," a term that is defined in section 9-102(a)(42). A "general intangible" is the catch-all, or residual, classification of collateral that cannot otherwise be classified as some other type of collateral (observe that the definition "means any personal property . . . *other than*") (emphasis added). Because the credit card receivable is an "account," it cannot be a "general intangible" (or the subset "payment intangible"). Perhaps rephrased, the terms "account" and "payment intangible" are mutually exclusive, and if the collateral can be the former, it will not be the latter. Therefore, **Answer (C) is incorrect and Answer (D) is correct.**

7.   **Answer (A) is the correct answer.** Section 9-102(a)(23) defines "consumer goods" as "goods that are used or bought for use primarily for personal, family, or household purposes." A "good," defined in section 9-102(a)(44), is something that is moveable when the security interest becomes enforceable. Of the four possibilities, only the wedding album and the photocopier are "goods." The certificate of deposit is either an "instrument" or a "deposit account" (with the choice explained in section 9-102 cmt. 12), **making Answer (B) an incorrect answer.** An income tax refund claim is an example of a "general intangible" (because the claim falls within no other collateral classification label), so **Answer (D) is incorrect.**

      To be a "consumer good," the asset must be used by the consumer debtor *primarily* for personal, family, or household reasons. John uses the photocopier for equal purposes, neither of which is primary. If John used the photocopier more than 50% of the time for personal reasons, the photocopier would be a "consumer good." But because John's personal use is not dominant, or primary, the photocopier is deemed "equipment" — the residual classification of "goods." *See* § 9-102(a)(33) (defining "equipment" in the negative). Therefore, **Answer (C) is incorrect.** Nothing in the problem suggests that John's wedding album is used for any purpose other than to provide sentimental and personal memories, so the album falls within the definition of "consumer good," **making Answer (A) the correct answer.**

8.   **Answer (C) is the correct answer.** "Investment property" is defined in section 9-102(a)(49)

and includes "a security, whether certificated or uncertificated, security entitlement, [and] securities account." The terms "certificated security," "securities account," "security entitlement," and "uncertificated security" are defined in UCC Article 8. Typical examples of investment property are stocks, bonds, and mutual fund shares that are traded on the securities exchanges. Answer (C) describes shares of capital stock. As noted above, investment property need not be evidenced by a tangible certificate, so the absence of a certificate is not fatal. And the fact that the market value is considerably less than the original purchase price is irrelevant, a red herring. Without getting bogged down in the intricate definitions of Article 8, it appears that the shares may be an "uncertificated security" (if John purchased the shares directly from BizCorp) or perhaps a "securities entitlement" (if the shares were purchased at John's request by his broker, who manages John's investment portfolio). Both an "uncertificated security" and a "security entitlement" are examples of "investment property," so **Answer (C) is the correct answer.**

Many investors purchase certificates of deposit as an investment. The annual rate of return may not be high, but many investors take comfort in knowing that the investment may be covered by FDIC insurance. Even so, certificates of deposit are not "investment property" as defined by Article 9, but instead are either "instruments" or "deposit accounts" (see section 9-102 cmt. 12 for further discussion). Therefore, **Answer (A) is incorrect.**

Many individuals buy antiques, figurines, baseball cards, stamps, coins, and other collectibles as an "investment," hopeful that the market value of the items will increase with the passage of time. Perhaps those hopes come true. But the collector's motive, even if investment-driven and realized, does not convert these "goods" into "investment property" as defined by Article 9. Therefore, **Answer (B) is incorrect.**

As with collectibles, a party may buy real estate as an investment. John's annual revenue stream suggests that he has made a wise investment. But Article 9 does not apply to real estate collateral (*see* § 9-109(d)(11)), so John's condominium in a resort location cannot be "investment property," at least within the meaning of Article 9. **Answer (D), then, is incorrect.**

9.   **Answer (D) is the correct answer.** Article 9 defines "general intangible" in a negative manner ("any personal property . . . other than"), making it the catch-all classification for collateral that does not fall within any of the other Article 9 classifications. A payment right arising from a winning lottery ticket is an "account" under section 9-102(a)(2)(viii), unless the claim is evidenced by a writing that falls within the definition of "chattel paper" or "instrument." But each of those three terms are excluded from the definition of "general intangible." For this reason, **Answer (D) is the correct answer** (because the question asks you to identify which asset is *not* a "general intangible").

A payment right that represents a debtor's obligation to repay borrowed funds might appear to be an "account." But that term expressly excludes from its definition "rights to payment for money or funds advanced or sold." *See* § 9-102(a)(2) (clause (vi) of last sentence). So John's claim against his brother is not an "account." And because John's claim arises from an oral (rather than a written) agreement, the claim cannot be "chattel paper" or an "instrument." By default, then, the claim falls within the definition of "payment intangible," a term defined in section 9-102(a)(61). Because "payment intangibles" by definition are "general intangibles," **Answer (A) is an incorrect answer.**

A domain name does not fall within any other collateral classification, making it a "general intangible" and **Answer (B) an incorrect answer.**

Patents, trademarks, and copyrights also are examples of "general intangibles." *See* § 9-102 cmt. 5.d. Therefore, **Answer (C) is incorrect.**

10. **Answer (B) is the correct answer.** Article 9 defines "registered organization" in section 9-102(a)(70) as "an organization organized solely under the law of a single State . . . and as to which the State . . . must maintain a public record showing the organization to have been organized." Examples include a limited partnership (Answer (A)), a limited liability company (Answer (C)), and a corporation (Answer (D)). *See* § 9-102 cmt. 11 (second paragraph). The fact that the entity may be delinquent in paying its property taxes (Answer C)) or in bankruptcy proceedings (Answer (D)) is irrelevant, the proverbial "red herring." So **Answers (A), (C), and (D) are incorrect,** as the question asks you to identify which entity is *not* a registered organization. A sole proprietorship, even one that has complied with any "d/b/a" filing requirements, is not a registered organization (the law does not sever a proprietor's personal identity from the business identity), so **Answer (B) is the correct answer.**

Also be aware that a general partnership is *not* a registered organization.

11. **Answer (D) is the correct answer.** Section 9-102(a)(9) defines "cash proceeds" as "proceeds that are money, checks, deposit accounts, or the like." The term "proceeds" includes "whatever is acquired upon the sale . . . of collateral." § 9-102(a)(64)(A). BizCorp acquired a "proceed" when it sold the unit of inventory to Jessalyn. That proceed will be a "cash proceed" if Jessalyn purchased the item by paying with money, a check, etc. In Answer (A), Jessalyn paid with her personal check, and in Answer (C) she paid with a cashier's check. Checks (whether issued by the drawer to BizCorp, or to Jessalyn and then indorsed to BizCorp) are "cash proceeds." Therefore, **Answers (A) and (C) are incorrect** because the question asks you to identify a proceed that is *not* a "cash proceed." If Jessalyn pays by using her debit card, she is sending an electronic message that will debit her bank account and credit BizCorp's bank account. Because of the near-instantaneous form of payment (much like cash), payment with a debit card creates a "cash proceed" (under the "or the like" language of the definition prior to, or in a "deposit account" after, the electronic entry) and **Answer (B) is incorrect.** Payment by a credit card, however, whether a traditional bank card or a merchant card, creates an "account" under section 9-102(a)(2)(vii). An "account" is not a "cash proceed," so **Answer (D) is the correct answer.** (Do not reach a contrary result by confusing "deposit accounts" and "accounts.")

Why is the classification important? Perhaps the most important reason is found in section 9-315(d)(2), which automatically extends the temporary twenty-day perfection period applicable to proceeds if those proceeds are "identifiable cash proceeds." No such automatic extension applies to noncash proceeds.

12. **Answer (A) is the correct answer.** Section 9-102(a)(3) defines "account debtor" as "a person obligated on an account, chattel paper, or general intangible" but does not include a person "obligated to pay a negotiable instrument." The question tests your ability to review Allison's obligation and determine whether that obligation is an account, chattel paper, a general intangible, or a negotiable instrument (a term defined in UCC Article 3).

Answer (A) states that the promissory note (along with a check, a common form of instrument) is negotiable. The note is unsecured, which prevents it from being chattel paper.

Answer (A), then, is correct because the question asks you to identify an obligation on which Allison will *not* be an "account debtor," and that term excludes obligations evidenced by a negotiable instrument.

Answer (B) is incorrect because the sales contract is chattel paper. The contract evidences not only Allison's monetary obligation but also creates a security interest in the computer. *See* § 9-102(a)(11) (defining "chattel paper"). Therefore, Allison is an "account debtor."

Answers (C) and (D) are incorrect because both answers describe an "account" under section 9-102(a)(2)(i). One concern might be that the obligation could be evidenced by a writing that qualifies as chattel paper or an instrument. But Answer (C) refers to an oral agreement, so it remains an "account." And Answer (D) refers to a *non-negotiable* writing, so the writing will not be an "instrument" under section 9-102(a)(47) and the obligation is *unsecured*, so the writing cannot be "chattel paper" under section 9-102(a)(11). Because Answers (C) and (D) describe an "account," Allison is an "account debtor" and **both answers are incorrect.**

13.   **Answer (A) is the correct answer.** Section 9-109(a)(4) states that Article 9 applies to a "consignment." That term is defined in section 9-102(a)(20) in a manner that requires the transaction to meet several requirements. This question tests your knowledge of some of those requirements.

Answer (B) is incorrect because the bikes are used by Maggie primarily for personal and family purposes, making them "consumer goods" under section 9-102(a)(23). The definition of "consignment" excludes goods that are "consumer goods immediately before delivery." *See* § 9-102(a)(20)(B). Therefore, Maggie's delivery of the bikes to a dealer for resale is not a "consignment" as defined by Article 9, **making Answer (B) incorrect.**

Answer (C) is incorrect because the seller is an auction house, and the definition of "consignment" excludes transactions in which goods are delivered to a merchant who is an auctioneer. *See* § 9-102(a)(20)(A)(ii).

The definition of "consignment" also excludes transactions in which goods are delivered to a merchant who is "generally known by its creditors to be substantially engaged in selling the goods of others." *See* § 9-102(a)(20)(A)(iii). A merchant with the name of "Joe's Consignment Shoppe" should give its creditors the knowledge that the merchant is substantially engaged in the business of selling third-party goods. Therefore, ZinnCo's delivery of the photocopiers to Joe's Consignment Shoppe will not be a "consignment" as defined by Article 9, **making Answer (D) incorrect.**

Answer (A), then, is the correct answer. The piano is not a consumer good because Annie is a professional musician, making the piano "equipment" under section 9-102(a)(33). The piano has a value that far exceeds the threshold amount of $1,000 under section 9-102(a)(20)(B). There are no facts that suggest that the dealer is an auctioneer or known by its creditors to be substantially engaged in selling the goods of other parties. The limited facts, then, suggest that Annie's delivery of the piano to the dealer for resale may indeed be a "consignment," **making Answer (A) the correct answer.**

14.   **Answer (B) is the correct answer.** A party will be a "debtor" if it falls within one of the three classifications found in section 9-102(a)(28). BAMCO is a "debtor" under subsection (B) if it is a seller of accounts. BAMCO also is a "debtor" under subsection (C) if it is a consignee (the merchant to whom goods are delivered for resale). BAMCO is such a party in **Answer**

(A) and Answer (D), respectively. Therefore, **those two answers are incorrect**, as the question asks you to identify a transaction in which BAMCO is *not* a "debtor."

Section 9-102(a)(28)(A) states that a "debtor" is "a person having an interest, other than a security interest or other lien, in the collateral, whether or not the person is an obligor." BAMCO is a "debtor" under this definition if it acquires (with or without knowledge) an asset that is encumbered with a security interest previously granted by BAMCO's seller to a third party. (Security interests in non-inventory usually survive the disposition. *See generally* §§ 9-201(a), 9-315(a)(1).) BAMCO has acquired such an asset in **Answer (C)**, **making BAMCO a "debtor" and the answer incorrect.** On the other hand, BAMCO is not the owner of the assets serving as collateral in Answer (B). Instead, the collateral is owned by BAMCO's two subsidiaries, making each of them a "debtor." BAMCO may be the "borrower" and an "obligor" as those terms are generally understood or defined, but BAMCO's lack of a property interest in the collateral means that BAMCO is not a "debtor," **making Answer (B) the correct answer.** For an additional illustration of this last point, see section 9-102 cmt. 2.a. (Example 3).

15. Section 9-104(a) provides three ways in which Lender can achieve "control" of Debtor's deposit account maintained with Bank. The first option, which gives "control" to a secured party that is also the financial institution that maintains the account, is not available to Lender because a third party — Bank — maintains the deposit account. The second option is available to Lender, though. It requires Lender, Debtor, and Bank to authenticate a record in which Bank agrees to honor Lender's instructions to liquidate the deposit account without Debtor's further consent. The third option permits Lender to obtain "control" if it becomes Bank's "customer" on the deposit account. Section 9-102(b) incorporates the definition of "customer" found in section 4-104(a)(5), which defines the term, in part, as "a person having an account with a bank." Under this definition, Lender could become Bank's "customer" (and thereby achieve "control") if the account records at Bank are revised in a manner that names Lender as the owner (or perhaps co-owner with Debtor) of the deposit account.

Appreciate that Lender can achieve "control" even if Debtor "retains the right to direct the disposition of funds from the deposit account." *See* § 9-104(b). (Lender obviously should seriously consider under what conditions, if any, Debtor may access the account.)

Why does "control" matter? You will find an explanation in section 9-104 cmt. 2.

16. **Answer (B) is the correct answer.** Section 9-102(a)(44) defines "goods" as "all things that are movable when a security interest attaches."

The definition continues and expressly includes fixtures. Therefore, a chandelier — even one that has become a fixture — is a "good." **Answer (A), then, is incorrect** (the question asks you to identify an asset that is *not* a "good").

A twenty-dollar bill is movable (otherwise it has little utility!). But the last sentence of the definition of "goods" expressly excludes "money" (defined in section 1-201 in a manner that will include U.S. coins and currency). Therefore, the $20 bill is not a "good," **making Answer (B) the correct answer.**

As mentioned in a previous "answer," a person sometimes buys baseball cards, rare books, glassware, and other collectibles for investment reasons. But the investment purpose will not convert these "goods" into "investment property" as defined by Article 9. The rare postage stamps are "goods," and **Answer (C) is incorrect.**

The last sentence of the definition excludes from the definition of "goods" any "oil, gas, or other minerals before extraction." This means that these minerals are goods *after* extraction. Therefore, gas in a plastic container used by a homeowner to fuel various implements is a "good." Accordingly, **Answer (D) is incorrect.**

17. (Perhaps this question is a bit unfair, especially if you have not studied UCC Article 3 in a "payment systems" course (which went by the moniker "Bills and Notes" or "Commercial Paper" when your co-authors attended law school). So do not panic if this question raises a topic that is completely foreign to you. Just skip it and move on to the next question. One of your co-authors regularly teaches a "payment systems" course and yielded to the strong temptation to include a rather basic question on the topic of "negotiable instruments." The question does raise important "real world" issues, as debt instruments are bought and sold in large quantities all the time.)

Answer (B) is the correct answer for the reasons that follow.

Whether the writing is a "negotiable instrument" will be dictated by whether the writing satisfies the numerous requirements found in UCC Article 3, particularly section 3-104(a). Section 3-104(a)(2) requires the writing to evidence a debt that is "payable on demand or at a definite time." The quoted language is further discussed in section 3-108. Subsection (a) states that the debt is "payable on demand" if the writing "does not state any time of payment." Therefore, the blank line (presumably intended to capture a payment date) does not prevent the language in Answer (A) from being a "negotiable instrument," so **Answer (A) is incorrect** (the question asks you to identify language that will *not* create a "negotiable instrument"). Answer (D) does provide a specific payment date — May 15, 2015 — but it then includes a proviso that creates the possibility of an earlier (but unknown) payment date if an unemployment contingency is triggered. This is an example of an "acceleration clause," which does not prevent the promise from being payable at a definite time or otherwise remove the writing from the definition of "negotiable instrument." *See* § 3-108(b)(ii). So **Answer (D) is incorrect.**

Answer (C) also contains a blank line, presumably intended to provide the name of the person to be paid (the "payee"). Section 3-104(a)(1) requires the writing to be "payable to bearer or to order," the so-called magical words of negotiability. As stated in section 3-109(a)(2), a writing that "does not state a payee" is payable to bearer. The blank line, then, does not preclude the writing from being a "negotiable instrument," and **Answer (C) is incorrect.**

This leads to the conclusion that **Answer (B) is the correct answer.** Why? Observe in Answers (A) and (D) that Meredith is promising to pay $15,000 "to the order of ZinnCo," whereas in Answer (B) she is promising to pay the same amount "to ZinnCo." This slight difference in language — the presence or absence of "order of" — is of paramount importance. As noted in the previous paragraph, the promise must be "payable to bearer or to order." The language in Answer (B) names ZinnCo as payee, so the promise is not payable to bearer. *See* § 3-109(a). Under subsection (b), the promise is payable to order only if the word "order" precedes or follows "ZinnCo" (e.g., "to the order of ZinnCo" or "to ZinnCo or its order"). The writing in Answer (B) fails to include the "order" language. Meredith's promise probably is enforceable, but the writing is not a "negotiable instrument" and Article 3 will not apply. For this reason, **Answer (B) is the correct answer.**

18. **Answer (B) is the correct answer.** Section 9-102(a)(48) defines "inventory" as "goods, other than farm products." The term "farm products" is defined in section 9-102(a)(34) and will include grape clusters, at least while they remain on the vines. At some point, the grapes will be picked and then used by the debtor in manufacturing its prize-winning beverages. Sometime after the grapes are picked they will become "inventory." But prior to severance from the vines, the grape clusters will be "farm products" (and, therefore, not "inventory"). Thus, **Answer (B) is the correct answer.**

Section 9-102(a)(48)(A) defines "inventory" to include goods leased by the debtor as lessor. Therefore, vehicles leased by the debtor to customers at an airport site are "inventory," **making Answer (A) incorrect** (the question asks you to identify assets that are *not* "inventory").

Section 9-102(a)(48)(D) defines "inventory" to include "raw materials . . . or materials used or consumed in a business." This language would pick up cooking oil used by a debtor in the restaurant business. Therefore, **Answer (C) is incorrect.**

Section 9-102(a)(48)(B) defines "inventory" to include goods held by the debtor for sale (the common understanding of the term). Therefore, board games in the hands of a toy company are inventory, and a customer's primary use of the board games is irrelevant, a red herring. For this reason, **Answer (D) is incorrect.**

19. **Answer (C) is the correct answer.** Section 9-102(a)(52)(A) defines "lien creditor" to include "a creditor that has acquired a lien on the property involved by attachment, levy, or the like." Perhaps rephrased, a "lien creditor" acquires its property interest pursuant to judicial process, rather than by contract or statute. **Answer (C) is correct** because the tort victim has a property interest that arises from a court-issued writ (rather than by contract or statute).

Answer (A) is incorrect. A purchase-money creditor does not become a "lien creditor" if it fails to take the steps necessary to achieve superpriority. The PMSI arose contractually, and the absence of perfection or priority will not convert the consensual interest into a judicial lien. (The creditor also does not lose its purchase-money status, a common misunderstanding.)

Answer (B) is incorrect because the lender's interest in the real estate is arising contractually, not by judicial process.

Answer (D) is incorrect because the mechanic's lien on the vehicle arises statutorily, rather than by judicial process.

Appreciate that the definition of "lien creditor" expressly includes the bankruptcy trustee. *See* § 9-102(a)(52)(C). We will have more to say on this point in our bankruptcy questions and answers.

20. **Answer (D) is the correct answer.** Section 9-102(a)(61) defines "payment intangible" as "a general intangible under which the account debtor's principal obligation is a monetary obligation." But because a "general intangible" is defined as the catch-all, or residual, category of personal property, a "payment intangible" cannot be a monetary obligation that is an account, chattel paper, or an instrument. Answer (D) is the only answer in which the monetary obligation is not one of those three types of collateral, **making Answer (D) the**

correct answer.

A credit card receivable is an "account" under section 9-102(a)(2)(vii), so it cannot be a "payment intangible." Therefore, **Answer (A) is incorrect.**

A right to payment arising from the lease or license of property (where the debtor is the lessor or the licensor) also creates an "account" under section 9-102(a)(2)(i), unless it is evidenced by a writing that is "chattel paper" or an "instrument" (see clause (i) of last sentence of section 9-102(a)(2)). The payment claims in Answer (B) and Answer (C), then, are an account, chattel paper, or an instrument. The payment claims cannot be anything else, including a "payment intangible." For these reasons, **Answer (B) and Answer (C) are incorrect.**

A claim for the return of a cash deposit made as part of an unsuccessful ticket request does not fall within the definition of "account." The last sentence of section 9-102(a)(2) excludes from the definition "(vi) rights to payment for money or funds advanced . . . other than rights arising out of the use of a credit or charge card." (Observe that if the deposit had been charged against the debtor's credit card, then the claim for a refund would be an "account.") Nor is the claim for the return of the cash deposit likely to be evidenced by "chattel paper" or an "instrument." Instead, the obligation of the ticket issuer to refund the cash deposit has created a "payment intangible" in favor of the debtor. Therefore, **Answer (D) is the correct answer.**

21.   **Answer (B) is the correct answer.** Vehicle sales can certainly give the seller the status of "secured party." But this buyer executed an *unsecured* promissory note, and the seller's possession of the certificate of title is ineffective to convert the vehicle into collateral and the sale into a secured transaction. The vehicle seller is not a "secured party," so **Answer (B) is correct** (as the question asks you to identify an answer in which ZinnCo is *not* a "secured party").

ZinnCo is a "secured party" in Answer (A). The lease contracts are chattel paper in the hands of Dealer under section 9-102(a)(11) (writings that evidence monetary obligations of various customers, and the writings are leases of specific office equipment). ZinnCo is purchasing this chattel paper from Dealer. A purchaser of chattel paper is a "secured party" under section 9-102(a)(72)(D). Therefore, **Answer (A) is incorrect.**

ZinnCo is a "secured party" in Answer (C). A contract that reserves title in favor of the seller until the buyer has honored all of its payment obligations creates a security interest in favor of the seller. *See* § 1-201(b)(35) (penultimate sentence of definition of "security interest"). A person "in whose favor a security interest is created" is a "secured party" under section 9-102(a)(72)(A). Therefore, **Answer (C) is incorrect.**

ZinnCo also is a "secured party" in Answer (D). The parties understand that the baseball card will serve as collateral. The understanding is oral, rather than written. But because ZinnCo has taken possession of the card, the oral understanding is sufficient to create an enforceable security interest in the card. *See* § 9-203(b)(3)(B) (permitting oral security agreements if the secured party possesses the collateral). If ZinnCo returns the card to the customer (e.g., when the account balance falls below $300), then ZinnCo loses its security interest in the card. But while ZinnCo possesses the card it has an enforceable security interest in the card, and during such time ZinnCo is a "secured party," **making Answer (D) an incorrect answer.**

22.   The stock certificate is a "certificated security" under Article 8 and, therefore, a form of "investment property" under section 9-102(a)(49). Section 9-106(a) states that a person has "control of a certificated security . . . as provided in Section 8-106." Because the facts indicate that the stock certificate is registered in Debtor's name, section 8-106(b) applies. Lender must satisfy two requirements. First, Lender must take "delivery" of the certificate as that term is defined in section 8-301(a) (e.g., the Lender, or a third party who satisfies specific requirements, takes possession of the certificate). Second, Debtor must endorse the certificate (either to Lender, or in blank), or the certificate must be registered by the issuer in Lender's name (upon either issuance of a new certificate to Lender or registration of transfer by Debtor to Lender). The goal is to put Lender in a position "where it can have the securities sold, without further action by the owner." *See* § 8-106 cmt. 1 (last sentence).

Why should Lender strive to achieve "control" of the stock certificate? The reason is found in section 9-338(1): a security interest in investment property that is perfected by control enjoys priority over a competing security interest that is not perfected by control (e.g., perfected merely by filing), regardless of the timing of the creation or the perfection of the competing security interest.

23.   **Answer (A) is the correct answer.** Section 9-601(a) states in part: "After default, a secured party has the rights provided in this part [Part Six of UCC Article 9; §§ 9-601 through 9-628] and, except as otherwise provided in Section 9-602, those provided by agreement of the parties." This provision, then, stresses the importance of knowing the meaning of "default." Logical places to look for a definition include sections 9-102 and 9-601 of Article 9 and section 1-201 of Article 1. But those searches will be in vain because Article 9 "leaves to the agreement of the parties the circumstances giving rise to a default." § 9-601 cmt. 3. Therefore, **Answer (A) is the correct answer and Answers (B), (C), and (D) are incorrect** (although these last three answers do provide examples of matters that the parties should consider when drafting the definition).

24.   **Answer (B) is the correct answer.** Section 9-102(a)(1) defines "accession" as "goods that are physically united with other goods in such a manner that the identity of the original goods is not lost." Mixing food ingredients (e.g., flour, water, eggs, etc.) together destroys their identity, which is replaced with a finished product (e.g., a cake). This is an example of "commingled goods" (*see* § 9-336), rather than "accessions" (see section 9-335 for further discussion). Therefore, because the question asks you to identify the example of non-accessions, **Answer (B) is the correct answer.** The other three examples illustrate the physical union of goods which retain some identity after the union, making them "accessions." Therefore, **Answers (A), (C), and (D) are incorrect answers.**

25.   **Answer (C) is the correct answer.** Although an oversimplification, investment property purchased directly from the issuer is a "certificated security" (if certificated) or an "uncertificated security" (if uncertificated), and investment property purchased through and held by a broker for its customer is a "security entitlement" (with the broker being a "securities intermediary"). If the collateral consists of every investment in the customer's broker-managed portfolio, the collateral consists of a "securities account" and one or more "security entitlements." If the collateral consists of some, but not all, investments in the broker-managed account, the collateral consists of one or more "security entitlements" but is not a "securities account." See Article 8 for definitions of these terms. Based on the foregoing, Erin's broker — Marbury Madison Group — is a "securities intermediary,"

making Answer (C) the correct answer.

Answer (A) is incorrect because certificated securities can be in registered form (issued in the name of the purchaser) or bearer form (issued in blank or to "bearer").

Answer (B) is incorrect because Erin purchased the mutual fund shares directly from the issuer, making them "uncertificated securities." If Erin's broker had purchased the mutual fund shares as part of her broker-managed portfolio, then the mutual fund shares would represent a "security entitlement."

Answer (D) is incorrect because the ZeeMart shares are part of Erin's broker-managed portfolio, making them a "security entitlement" rather than an "uncertificated security."

26. **Answer (D) is the correct answer.** Under section 9-103(a) and (b), a secured party can hold a purchase-money security interest only in goods (or software integrated into the goods). The book (notwithstanding its placement in a safety deposit box at the bank), the bottle of champagne (notwithstanding its location in a foreign country), and the motorcycle (notwithstanding the application of a certificate-of-title statute) are all goods under section 9-102(a)(44), so **Answers (A), (B), and (C) are incorrect**, since the question asks you to identify the asset in which a creditor *cannot* claim a purchase-money security interest. The shares of common stock purchased on "margin" (i.e., credit extended, based on the value of the purchaser's other investments in the portfolio) are an example of "investment property" under section 9-102(a)(49). And under section 9-102(a)(2)(44), "goods" excludes "investment property." Therefore, because a secured party may not obtain a purchase-money security interest in a non-software asset that is not a "good," **Answer (D) is the correct answer.**

27. **Answer (D) is the correct answer.** Section 9-203(b)(3)(A) requires the parties to include only two pieces of information in the written security agreement: the debtor's authentication (see section 9-102(a)(7), defining "authenticate" to include a signature), and a description of the collateral. All four possible answers address the necessity of including one or more specific details of the secured debt. That information may be important, useful, or material, but Article 9 does not require the inclusion of any payment particulars in the security agreement. Therefore, **Answer (D) is correct** (no such information is required) and **Answers (A), (B), and (C)** — each of which suggest such information is or may be required — **are incorrect.**

A company that must comply with certain SEC reporting requirements may include details of its material debt in those reports (which may be available to the public).

28. **Answer (B) is the correct answer.** For attachment, section 9-203(b)(3)(A) requires the debtor, and only the debtor, to authenticate (e.g., sign) the security agreement. Therefore, only ZinnCorp must sign the security agreement, **making Answer (B) the correct answer.** **Answer (A) is incorrect** because it erroneously suggests that BigBank must also always execute the security agreement. **Answers (C) and (D)** (both nonsense answers) **are incorrect** because they erroneously suggest that BigBank must also execute the security agreement if specific conditions exist. BigBank, as the secured party, *may* authenticate the security agreement (particularly if the agreement obligates BigBank to take, or refrain from taking, certain action), but authentication by the secured party is not necessary for attachment.

29. **Answer (C) is the correct answer.** Section 9-203(b)(3)(A) states that a written security agreement must provide "a description of the collateral." That statute offers no other guidance on the quoted language. Guidance, though, is found elsewhere. Section 9-108 ("Sufficiency of Description") offers the general rule that the collateral description is "sufficient . . . if it reasonably identifies what is described." Therefore, **Answer (C) is correct** because it adopts the "reasonably identifies" standard, and **Answers (A), (B), and (D) are incorrect** because they adopt some other erroneous standard.

Answer (D) suggests that the parties must utilize Article 9's defined terms, such as "inventory" and "equipment." Section 9-108(b)(3) *permits* the parties to use those terms (with few exceptions), but the statute *does not require* the parties to do so, offering another reason why **Answer (D) is incorrect.**

30. **Answer (A) is the correct answer.** Section 9-108(a) states that a collateral description is sufficient if it "reasonably identifies what is described." Section 9-108(b) gives examples of reasonable identification, permitting descriptions by type of collateral, "except as otherwise provided in subsection (e)." Subsection (e) states: "A description only by type of collateral defined in [the Uniform Commercial Code] is an insufficient description of: (1) a commercial

tort claim[.]" Thus, **Answer (A) is the correct answer.** (The limitation does not apply to investment property, deposit accounts, or payment intangibles, so **Answers (B), (C), and (D) are incorrect answers.**) The policy is explained in cmt. 5: "Subsection (e) requires greater specificity of description in order to prevent debtors from inadvertently encumbering certain property." Comment 5 also notes that a description such as "all tort claims arising out of the explosion of debtor's factory" would be acceptable, "even if the exact amount of the claim, the theory on which it may be based, and the identity of the tortfeasor(s) are not described. (Indeed, those facts may not be known at the time.)"

31.   **Answer (A) is the correct answer.** Section 9-204(a) approves the use of an after-acquired property clause, which negates any need for the parties to negotiate or authenticate a security agreement every time that the debtor buys more inventory or equipment, generates new accounts, etc. The statute does not expressly state the date to which the "after" in "after-acquired property clause" refers. But the general understanding is that the "after" refers to any time after the moment when the debtor executes, or otherwise authenticates, the security agreement. That understanding makes sense, given that the clause cannot exist apart from the security agreement itself. Section 9-204 cmt. 4 also supports that understanding. Therefore, **Answer (A) is correct** because it refers to the date on which ZinnCorp authenticates the security agreement. **Answers (B), (C), and (D) are incorrect** because they refer to some other date.

32.   **Answer (B) is the correct answer.** As a general rule, Article 9 permits the use of after-acquired property clauses under section 9-204(a). But subsection (a) is subject to subsection (b). Subsection (b) states two situations in which the after-acquired property clause is ineffective. First, the clause will not encumber consumer goods acquired more than ten days after the secured party has given value (inapplicable to this question). And second, the clause will not encumber a commercial tort claim. Therefore, **Answer (B) is the correct answer** because a patent infringement claim is an example of a "commercial tort claim" (defined in section 9-102(a)(13)). (The limitations do not apply to copyrights, electronic chattel paper, or motor vehicles, so **Answers (A), (C), and (D) are incorrect.**) The effect of this exception is to require the parties to amend the original security agreement or authenticate another security agreement if they want the collateral package to include commercial tort claims that arise after ZinnCorp authenticates the initial security agreement.

Section 9-204 cmt. 4 discusses this exception but does not state a reason for it. Perhaps the unique nature of the asset and its nontraditional use as collateral justify the exclusion as an attempt to avoid inadvertent use of the claim as collateral. This explanation seems plausible in light of section 9-108(e)(1), which requires the security agreement to describe a commercial tort claim with particularity.

33.   **Answer (A) is the best answer.** Section 9-203(b)(3)(B) permits oral security agreements, but only if the secured party has possession of the collateral (and the collateral cannot be a certificated security, inapplicable in this question).

The secured party cannot take possession of collateral unless the collateral has a tangible quality. Computer equipment is tangible, so it is possible that BigBank could take possession of it. Therefore, an oral security agreement can create an enforceable security interest in ZinnCorp's computer equipment. For this reason, **Answer (C) is incorrect** (the question asks you to identify the collateral that *cannot* be encumbered under an oral security agreement).

Promissory notes executed by customers have a tangible quality. They could be "instruments" or "chattel paper" as those terms are defined in section 9-102(a)(47) and (11), respectively. If so, then an oral security agreement would suffice, **making Answer (B) incorrect.** Perhaps, though, the written promissory notes fail to satisfy one or more of the technical requirements of those two defined terms, in which case the writings are "accounts" as defined in section 9-102(a)(2). Accounts are not tangible (even when evidenced by a writing), and an oral security agreement will not be effective to create an enforceable security interest in them. Therefore, **Answer (B) could be correct.** Ultimately, the correct or incorrect nature of Answer (B) turns on examining the written notes themselves and determining whether the notes are instruments, chattel paper, or accounts. Because **Answer (B) requires additional information,** it is not the best answer (assuming, of course, that another answer provides certainty for its correctness).

A corporate bank account does not have a tangible quality. But section 9-203(b)(3)(D) may permit an oral security agreement if such an agreement can give BigBank "control" of the corporate bank account (a "deposit account" as defined in section 9-102(a)(29)). Section 9-104(a) describes three ways in which a secured party can take "control" of a deposit account. The first option is automatic if the secured party is the bank where the debtor maintains the deposit account. The facts do not mention where ZinnCorp maintains the corporate bank account. If ZinnCorp maintains the deposit account with BigBank, then BigBank has automatic control of (and an enforceable security interest in) the deposit account — even though its security agreement is oral. If ZinnCorp maintains the account with a third party, then BigBank can achieve "control" by taking the necessary action under the other two options, which more than likely will require written documentation. Ultimately, then,

Answer (D) may be correct or incorrect. Additional information is required, **precluding Answer (D) from being the best answer.**

Patents are an example of a "general intangible" as defined in section 9-102(a)(42). *See* § 9-102 cmt. 5.d. (giving, as an example of a general intangible, "various categories of intellectual property"). BigBank cannot take possession of a general intangible. Therefore, an oral agreement cannot create an enforceable security interest in ZinnCorp's patents. No other information is required to reach this conclusion, making **Answer (A) the best answer.**

34.   Oliver's parents will have an enforceable security interest in the kitchen table and chairs, and the bedroom furniture; they will not have an enforceable security interest in the washer/dryer.

As a general rule, Article 9 permits a debtor to grant a security interest in collateral that the debtor acquires after it authenticates the security agreement, by including in the agreement an after-acquired property clause. *See* § 9-204(a). But in an effort to discourage a creditor's predatory practices, Article 9 renders ineffective an after-acquired property clause that attempts to encumber consumer goods acquired by the debtor more than ten days after the creditor has given value. *See* § 9-204(a), (b).

Oliver's household furnishings are consumer goods as defined in section 9-102(a)(23) (goods that Oliver has acquired primarily for a personal, family, or household purpose). His parents made the $5,000 loan on June 1, so the after-acquired property clause will not encumber furnishings that Oliver acquired after June 11 (notice that the ten-day period commences when Oliver's parents give value, not when Oliver authenticates the security agreement).

The first two purchases on June 2 and June 9 are within the ten-day period, so the parents will have an enforceable security interest in the kitchen table and chairs, and the bedroom furniture. The third purchase on June 18 is outside the ten-day period, so the parents will not have an enforceable security interest in the washer/dryer.

(Observe that Oliver's parents, as purchase-money creditors, are not engaged in any predatory practice. What might they have done differently? They should not have advanced the funds in a single advance to Oliver prior to the purchases. Instead, they should have extended credit as Oliver made his purchases.)

35. Because the security agreement failed to include a future advance clause, Hoover Finance will have a secured claim no greater than the initial loan of $1 million. The security agreement did include an after-acquired property clause, so the value of the collateral is $1.95 million. Therefore, Hoover Finance has a secured claim of $1 million (and the collateral securing that claim is $1.95 million). Hoover Finance also has an unsecured claim of $550,000 (the sum of the April and August advances). The surplus collateral value of $950,000 does *not* secure Hoover Finance's two unsecured loans.

36. The security agreement included a future advance clause, so Hoover Finance might have a secured claim equal to the sum of all advances: $1.55 million. But the security agreement failed to include an after-acquired property clause, so the collateral is limited to the equipment owned by GEC on the date of the agreement: $1.2 million. Therefore, Hoover Finance has a secured claim of $1.2 million, and an unsecured claim of $350,000. Hoover Finance has no security interest in the road grader or the bulldozer acquired by GEC in May and June, respectively.

37. **Answer (D) is the correct answer.** As Bruce has given value of $2,500, and Tim has rights in the baseball card collection, Bruce will have an enforceable security interest in the collection under section 9-203 if one of the four "security agreement" conditions of section 9-203(b)(3) is met. The third and fourth options (section 9-203(b)(3)(C) and (D)) are inapplicable because the baseball card collection is not a deposit account, electronic chattel paper, investment property, or a letter-of-credit right, and the first option (section 9-203(b)(3)(A)) is not met because the parties are relying on an oral agreement rather than an authenticated agreement. The parties can rely on an oral security agreement under section 9-203(b)(3)(B) if the baseball card collection "is in the possession of the secured party under Section 9-313." **This eliminates Answer (A)**, which suggests a blanket prohibition on oral security agreements. **It also eliminates Answer (B)**, a nonsense answer, which includes conditions not found in the statute.

The only difference between Answers (C) and (D) is that the former requires Bruce (and only Bruce) to take possession, whereas the latter permits Bruce — or an independent third party — to take possession. Section 9-203(b)(3)(B) states that the "secured party" must take possession, suggesting Answer (C), rather than Answer (D), is correct. But the statute also cross-references section 9-313, which indicates (in cmt. 3) that the secured party can appoint an agent (other than the debtor or a person too closely connected with or controlled by the debtor) to take possession of the collateral. Therefore, the oral understanding between Tim and Bruce will create an enforceable security interest in the baseball card collection if Bruce — or an appropriate third party — takes possession of the collection. For this reason,

Answer (D) is correct and Answer (C) is incorrect.

We offer two additional comments. First, if Tim and Bruce decide that a third party will possess the collection but Bruce is worried that a court might conclude that the third party lacks independence (or fails to qualify as an "agent"), Bruce should consider making that risk irrelevant by insisting that Tim authenticate a written security agreement that reasonably identifies the baseball card collection. Second, a third party cannot be forced into acting as Bruce's agent, and Bruce would be wise to obtain an authenticated acknowledgment from any third-party possessor. *See* § 9-313 and cmts. 3 and 4.

38. **Answer (D) is the correct answer.** Article 9 permits a debtor to offer a deposit account as collateral, subject to the notable exception found in section 9-109(d)(13): the transaction cannot be a "consumer transaction." (The policy for the exception is probably rooted in a concern that most humans need unfettered access to a deposit account to buy food and clothing, to pay bills, and to otherwise function in society on a daily basis.) Section 9-102(a)(26) defines "consumer transaction" in a manner that requires the consumer debtor to (i) incur the secured debt primarily for a personal, family, or household reason *and* (ii) hold or acquire the collateral primarily for a personal, family, or household reason. Tim is using the loan proceeds for a business purpose in Answer (D), so the transaction contemplated by Answer (D) is not a "consumer transaction." In the absence of a "consumer transaction," the prohibition found in section 9-109(d)(13) does not apply. Even so, the oral understanding must satisfy one of the four "security agreement" options of section 9-203(b)(3). Because Tim maintains his personal checking account (a "deposit account" under section 9-102(a)(29)) with the Credit Union (a "bank" under section 9-102(a)(8)), which is the secured party, the Credit Union has "control" of the checking account under section 9-104(a)(1). Because the Credit Union has control of Tim's checking account, their oral understanding suffices as the security agreement under section 9-203(b)(3)(D). Therefore, the Credit Union has an enforceable security interest in Tim's checking account if Tim uses the loan proceeds for a business purpose (regardless of the primary use of the checking account itself), making **Answer (D) the correct answer.**

Answer (A) is incorrect because Article 9 does not always require a written security agreement when the collateral is a deposit account. As noted in the preceding paragraph, an oral understanding can suffice in certain situations.

Answer (B) is incorrect because Article 9 permits a deposit account to serve as collateral if the transaction is *not* a consumer transaction. *See* § 9-109(d)(13).

Answer (C) is incorrect because section 9-203(b)(3) nowhere conditions the effectiveness of an oral security agreement on the type of debtor or the amount of secured debt.

39. **Answer (B) is the correct answer.** The collateral description turns on the *debtor's* use. The use of the debtor's *customers* is irrelevant. The debtor is BizCorp. In its hands, the musical instruments are inventory under section 9-102(a)(48)(B) (goods held for sale). Therefore, **Answer (B) is correct.** It is irrelevant that BizCorp sells the musical instruments to customers who may use them as equipment or consumer goods. Therefore, **Answer (C) is incorrect.**

The inventory is "goods," but "goods" is a much broader term. *See* § 9-102(a)(44). For example, describing the collateral as "goods" would include BizCorp's equipment as collateral, perhaps an unintended result. Therefore, **Answer (D) is incorrect.**

A piano, a guitar, a trombone, etc. are all examples of an "instrument" as that term is used in everyday conversation. But "instrument" has a completely different meaning under Article 9, most often referring to promissory notes and checks (and certainly not musical instruments). *See* § 9-102(a)(47). For this reason, **Answer (A) is incorrect.**

40. **Answer (A) is the correct answer.** Unlike the filing rules under former Article 9, the current version of Article 9 adopts a "single filing" rule for non-fixtures. The place to search, then, will be the same place to file. Section 9-301(1) states that MegaBank, the secured party, should file its financing statement in the jurisdiction where Friendly Furniture Corp., the debtor, is located. Friendly is a corporation, so it is a "registered organization" under section 9-102(a)(70). Under section 9-307(e), a registered organization is located in its state of incorporation. Friendly is chartered under California law, so MegaBank will file — and need only search — in California. Therefore, **Answer (A) is the correct answer.** MegaBank need not search in Nevada or Arizona, **making Answer (B) incorrect.** The location of a debtor's chief executive office may be relevant if the debtor is not a registered organization (*see* § 9-307(b)(3)), but Friendly is a registered organization, so **Answer (C) is incorrect.** Also, the location of a corporate debtor's operations is irrelevant when the debtor is a registered organization, **making Answer (D) incorrect.**

MegaBank is taking a security interest in Friendly's equipment. Equipment can be a "fixture" as that term is defined in section 9-102(a)(41). If MegaBank is concerned about possible priority disputes with Friendly's real estate creditors, it should file (and, therefore, also search) for fixture filings, which are recorded in the county where the relevant real estate is located. *See* §§ 9-501(a)(1), 9-334. For this reason, MegaBank may wish to search the county records in counties where Friendly has physical operations in California, Nevada, and Arizona. But the facts of this problem focus attention on non-fixture encumbrances.

41. **Answer (D) is the correct answer.** Section 9-523 addresses search inquiries. Subsection (c) obligates the filing officer to provide particular information, and subsection (e) requires the filing officer to respond "not later than two business days after the filing office receives the request." In this question, the filing officer received the lawyer's request on Wednesday, July 22. Therefore, the filing officer must communicate the results of its search to the lawyer no later than two business days later, or Friday, July 24. For this reason, **Answer (D) is correct**, and the other suggested dates, all erroneous, **make Answers (A), (B), and (C) incorrect.**

42. **Answer (B) is the correct answer.** A searcher wants timely information. Information that is stale exposes the searcher to the risk that another creditor has filed (or may file) a financing statement after the date of the report (which may prevent the searcher, who has yet to file, from enjoying priority). Section 9-523(c) addresses this concern by requiring the filing office to provide a report that is current as of a date "not . . . earlier than three business days before the filing office receives the request." In this question, the filing officer received the lawyer's request on Wednesday, July 22, so the search report must provide information through a date no earlier than three business days before that date, or Friday, July 17. For this reason, **Answer (B) is correct**, and the other suggested dates, all erroneous, **make Answers (A), (C), and (D) incorrect.**

43. **Answer (D) is the correct answer.** Sometimes filings are innocently recorded against the wrong entity (this could result, for example, if the preparer used an incorrect name, which happened to be the name of a third party). And sometimes filings are intentionally, but fraudulently, filed against a particular party. Section 9-518 addresses inaccurate or wrongfully filed financing statements and permits the affected party to file a "correction statement." The statement must cross-reference the filing number of the filing to which it relates, state that it is being filed as a correction statement, and offer an explanation of the problem. The affected party can file the correction statement unilaterally, **making Answer (D) the correct answer and Answer (B) an incorrect answer.** The correction statement need not be executed or otherwise authenticated by a different party (such as the party whose name is reflected as "debtor" on the earlier filing), **making Answer (C) an incorrect answer.** And the affected party does not file a "termination statement" (a filing addressed by section 9-513 and reserved for a different matter), **making Answer (A) an incorrect answer.**

Friendly's general counsel should note that a correction statement does not remove the other filings from the public records or otherwise terminate their effectiveness. *See* § 9-518(c). It merely permits the general counsel to explain the alleged problem in the public records. As noted in section 9-518 cmt. 3, though, the general counsel may resort to other law for further redress as needed.

44. **Answer (D) is the correct answer.** After-acquired property clauses (and future advance clauses) permitted by section 9-204 should be written into the security agreement, but need not be referenced in the financing statement. *See* §§ 9-204 cmt. 7; 9-502 cmt. 2 (last paragraph). Therefore, **Answer (D) is the correct answer.**

Section 9-501 permits a secured party to perfect its security interest in fixtures by filing its financing statement centrally (subsection (a)(2)), rather than locally (subsection (a)(1)). Therefore **Answer (A) is incorrect.** As you may discover later, however, a secured party that relies on a central, rather than a local, filing may not enjoy priority in fixtures if the competing claimant is a real estate creditor. *See generally* § 9-334 (sometimes awarding priority to a secured party that has timely filed a "fixture filing," which — under section 9-501(a)(1) — is filed locally in the county where the affected real estate is located, rather than centrally).

The secured party may file its financing statement before the debtor authenticates the security agreement. *See* § 9-502(d). So **Answer (B) is incorrect.** This act (sometimes referred to as "pre-filing") cannot perfect a security interest prior to its attachment. *See* § 9-308(a). Also, the debtor must authorize any pre-filing, which may raise concerns if the parties are squabbling over what will serve as collateral or the debtor has yet to authenticate the security agreement. *See* §§ 9-509(a) (requiring the debtor to authorize any filing), 9-509(b) (providing such authorization through the debtor's authentication of the security agreement).

As noted in the preceding paragraph, Friendly (the debtor) must *authorize* the financing statement. But in an effort to accommodate electronic filing, the current version of Article 9 departs from the predecessor statute and no longer requires Friendly, as the debtor, to sign, execute, or otherwise *authenticate* the financing statement. *See* § 9-502 cmt. 3. Therefore, **Answer (C) is incorrect.**

45. **Answer (A) is the correct answer.** Section 9-502(a) requires a financing statement to

include the names of both parties (or, if applicable, the secured party's agent). Therefore, **Answer (A) is correct.** The same statute also requires the financing statement to include a collateral description. Unlike the description that must be found in the security agreement, the description in the financing statement can be supergeneric, such as "all assets" or "all of the debtor's personal property." *See* § 9-504 and cmt. 2. Therefore **Answer (C) is incorrect.** Neither the security agreement nor the financing statement needs to describe the secured debt (and the parties may have legitimate reasons for not disclosing the terms in the public records), so **Answer (B) is incorrect.** And, as previously noted, MegaBank must file its financing statement against Friendly, a corporation and a registered organization, only in the state of Friendly's incorporation (California), rather than in any (or every) state in which it has a physical presence. *See* §§ 9-301(1), 9-307(e). For this reason, **Answer (D) is incorrect.**

46. A filing officer does not have unfettered discretion when deciding whether to accept or reject a financing statement. Section 9-520(a) says that a "filing officer shall refuse to accept a record for filing for a reason set forth in Section 9-516(b) and may refuse to accept a record for filing only for a reason set forth in Section 9-516(b)." Some of those reasons include the following: the filing fails to include a mailing address for MegaBank or Friendly (*see* § 9-516(b)(4), (5)(A)), the filing fails to mention that Friendly is a corporation chartered under California law (*see* § 9-516(b)(5)(C)(i), (ii)), and the filing fails to provide Friendly's organizational identification number (or mentions that Friendly has no such number) (*see* § 9-516(b)(5)(C)(iii)).

The foregoing comments are responsive to the question posed. But the following four remarks provide additional insight on this matter. First, the rejection rules generally focus attention on the complete omission of information, rather than the inclusion of incorrect information. Second, notwithstanding the filing officer's mandate to reject a filing for a *proper* reason, section 9-520(c) says that if the filing officer accepts such a filing, then the filing is "effective" (if it otherwise meets the requirements of section 9-502(a)). Third, section 9-516(d) states that if the filing officer rejects a filing for an *improper* reason, then the rejected filing "is effective as a filed record except as against a purchaser of the collateral which gives value in reasonable reliance upon the absence of the record from the files." And fourth, whenever the filing officer rejects (properly or wrongfully) a filing, the officer must timely communicate the rejection to the filing party (who hopefully will take prompt corrective action). *See* § 9-520(b).

47. **Answer (A) is the correct answer.** As noted in the preceding answer, section 9-520(b) requires the filing officer to timely communicate its rejection to the filing party, specifically "in no event more than two business days after the filing office receives the record." As noted in the facts to the previous question, the filing officer received MegaBank's filing on Wednesday, August 12. Therefore, the officer must communicate its decision to MegaBank no later than Friday, August 14, **making Answer (A) the correct answer.** The other dates are all erroneous, **making Answers (B), (C), and (D) incorrect.**

48. **Answer (C) is the correct answer.** As a general rule, a financing statement will perfect a security interest in all collateral. There are notable exceptions, however. These include: collateral, such as an airplane or a ship, that is subject to federal registration (*see* § 9-311(a)(1)), vehicles that are not held by the debtor as inventory and are otherwise subject to certificate-of-title laws (*see* § 9-311(a)(2), (d)), deposit accounts and letter-of-credit rights,

which require "control" (*see* § 9-312(b)(1), (2)), and money, which requires possession by the creditor (*see* § 9-312(b)(3)). Friendly's fleet of delivery trucks will be equipment, rather than inventory. So MegaBank must comply with applicable certificate-of-title laws to obtain perfection; its financing statement will not suffice. Therefore, **Answer (C) is the correct answer.**

A security interest in investment property (whether or not subject to federal or state regulatory oversight) may be perfected by filing. *See* § 9-312(a). Therefore, **Answer (A) is incorrect** (because the question asks you to identify collateral in which a security interest *cannot* be perfected by filing).

As noted in the first paragraph above, a security interest in a bank account (a "deposit account" under Article 9 terminology) can be perfected only by control. *See* § 9-312(b)(1). The statutory language does not turn on the presence or absence of FDIC insurance coverage. Therefore, **Answer (B) is incorrect.** (The secured party may rely on a financing statement to perfect a security interest in a deposit account on a "proceeds" theory, but the call of the question asks you to ignore this argument.)

A domain name is an example of a "general intangible" as defined in section 9-102(a)(42). As a general rule (and no exception applies in this instance), a filing will perfect a security interest in general intangibles. Therefore, MegaBank's filing will perfect its security interest in Friendly's domain name, **making Answer (D) an incorrect answer.**

49.   **Answer (C) is the correct answer.** Credit card receivables are an example of an "account" under section 9-102(a)(2)(vii). Sometimes a writing is produced at the close of the transaction, but that writing cannot be an "instrument" or "chattel paper" as those terms are defined in section 9-102(a)(47) and (11), respectively (see "The term does not include" language in each definition). Therefore, MegaBank cannot perfect its security interest in the receivables by possessing any writing, leaving its financing statement as the sole method of perfection. For this reason, **Answer (C) is the correct answer.**

Article 9 does not apply to the assignment of a beneficiary's payment rights under a life insurance policy. *See* § 9-109(d)(8). Therefore, MegaBank's filing will not perfect any property interest that it can claim in Friendly's rights under the policy, **making Answer (A) an incorrect answer.**

Cash (paper money and coins, *but not checks*) is "money" under section 1-201(b)(24) (incorporated by reference into Article 9 via section 9-102(c)). A secured party can perfect a security interest in money only by taking possession of it. Filing will not suffice. *See* § 9-312(b)(3). Therefore, **Answer (B) is incorrect.**

The lease contracts, which most likely evidence the lessee's monetary obligation and describe the furniture being leased, are "chattel paper" as defined in section 9-102(a)(11). A security interest in chattel paper can indeed be perfected by filing. *See* § 9-312(a). But filing is not the exclusive method. MegaBank also can perfect its security interest by taking possession of the contracts. *See* § 9-313(a). Therefore, **Answer (D) is incorrect.**

50.   **Answer (B) is the correct answer.** Subject to rare exceptions (which are inapplicable to our questions), a financing statement is effective for five years. *See* § 9-515(a). The effectiveness of the original filing (usually a UCC-1 form) can be extended for an additional five-year period by the timely filing of a continuation statement (usually a UCC-3 form, with the "continuation" box checked). To be timely, the continuation statement must be filed "within

six months before the expiration of the five-year period." The filing officer recorded MegaBank's financing statement on August 12, 2010, so the filing is effective for the five-year period thereafter (concluding in mid-August 2015). The preceding six-month period runs from mid-February 2015 through mid-August 2015, so the correct answer must be a date that falls within that period. The date of March 6, 2015, is such a date, so **Answer (B) is correct.** Filing dates in 2016 are too late, so **Answers (C) and (D) are incorrect.** The filing period for continuation statements does not turn on the amount of principal outstanding on any particular date, so **Answer (A) is incorrect.**

51.   **Answer (D) is the correct answer.** A continuation statement that is not filed within the six-month period provided by section 9-515 "is ineffective." *See* § 9-510(c). This is so, even though the "notice" function is served by the original filing and the tardy continuation statement. Therefore, **Answer (A) is incorrect.** Nor does Article 9 provide any "grace period" for continuation statements filed outside the six-month window, no matter how close to the window the filing falls. Therefore, **Answer (B) is incorrect.**

Because MegaBank has not timely filed its continuation statement, the effectiveness of MegaBank's original filing has lapsed. *See* § 9-515(c). This leaves MegaBank unperfected (absent perfection by a non-filing method, such as possession or control) prospectively. MegaBank can (and, upon discovering its error, should immediately) file a new financing statement. While that new filing will cure its unperfected status prospectively, it will not provide MegaBank with continuous and uninterrupted perfection. The lapse of the original filing has created a period of time (even if only brief) during which MegaBank is unperfected, and MegaBank can take no filing action that will yield a retroactive cure. Therefore, **Answer (C) is incorrect and Answer (D) is correct.**

The risk, then, for MegaBank is that it may now find itself losing a priority dispute with a creditor who was a junior creditor that now has moved ahead of MegaBank following the lapse of MegaBank's original filing.

52.   Once the transaction has concluded and Friendly has honored all of its payment and other obligations, MegaBank can, on its own volition, file a termination statement (usually a UCC-3 form with the "termination" box checked). Section 9-513(c) is phrased, however, in a manner that permits MegaBank to remain passive until it receives from Friendly an authenticated demand for a termination statement. Within twenty days following its receipt of Friendly's demand, MegaBank must file a termination statement or, alternatively, prepare and send the termination statement to Friendly (who presumably will file it). If MegaBank breaches its duty to timely respond, section 9-509 permits Friendly to unilaterally file a termination statement (which must indicate why Friendly, rather than MegaBank, is filing the statement). Section 9-625(b) permits Friendly to recover damages caused by MegaBank's breach (e.g., Friendly's "inability to obtain, or increased costs of, alternative financing" triggered by the delay in filing the termination statement and the resulting questionable cloud on Friendly's assets). Furthermore, section 9-625(e)(4) imposes an automatic statutory penalty of $500 for MegaBank's breach, whether or not the breach caused loss or harm to Friendly.

(Appreciate that if the debtor is a consumer and the collateral includes consumer goods, then the secured party cannot remain passive and wait for the debtor's request for a termination statement. Instead, the secured party must timely take the lead in preparing and filing the termination statement itself. *See* § 9-513(a), (b).)

53. **Answer (B) is the correct answer.** The only instance in which a secured party should file its financing statement at the county level (rather than in the state's central filing office) is if the financing statement will serve as a fixture filing. *See* § 9-501(a). Alex is offering both personal and business assets as collateral. Alex intends to use the loan proceeds to open a restaurant. Presumably, then, some of the business assets will include restaurant equipment. Some of that equipment may be affixed to the walls and floors in such a manner that it becomes a "fixture" as that term is defined in section 9-102(a)(41). Therefore, Essex Financing should file a fixture filing (at the county level) to better protect itself against competing claims (in the fixtures) asserted by Alex's real estate creditors. For this reason, **Answer (B) is the correct answer.**

Answer (A) is incorrect because the nature of the debtor (human v. entity) does not dictate the filing office.

Answer (C) is incorrect because neither the marital status of a human debtor nor the property laws of the state in which the human debtor resides dictate the filing office.

Answer (D) is incorrect because a security interest in Alex's personal automobile cannot be perfected by filing (in any office). Instead, Essex Financing must comply with relevant certificate-of-title laws in order to perfect its security interest in the vehicle.

54. No, the filing is sufficient to perfect security interests claimed by BigBank (and MidBank and SmallBank). To be effective, a financing statement must provide "the name of the secured party or a representative of the secured party." § 9-502(a)(2). The filing identifies MegaBank as a representative ("AS AGENT"). Even so, BigBank and its fellow syndicate members may be concerned that the filing fails to identify for whom MegaBank is acting as agent. This concern is addressed in section 9-503(d), which states: "Failure to indicate the representative capacity of a secured party or representative of a secured party does not affect the sufficiency of a financing statement." Further discussion (including an example similar to the fact pattern posed in the question) is found in section 9-503 cmt. 3, and indicates that each syndicate bank is protected by the filing, whether or not specifically identified as "secured party" on the filing (and even if the words "AS AGENT" fail to accompany MegaBank's name).

55. **Answer (D) is the correct answer.** The initial issue is to identify whether Robert Zimmer or RWZ Consulting is the debtor. (Unlike the situation where Zimmer operates the business as a sole proprietorship and the law treats the two as the same legal entity, Zimmer in this problem has incorporated his business and created a separate legal entity.) The computer system is serving as collateral. Zimmer bought the computer system, but the facts state that he did so as an agent (e.g., executive officer) of the consulting service. Therefore RWZ Consulting is the debtor, **eliminating Answer (A) and Answer (B)** (both of which erroneously suggest that Zimmer himself is the debtor). Under section 9-301(1), BCC should file its financing statement in the jurisdiction where the debtor is located. The debtor, RWZ Consulting, is a corporation chartered under Delaware law. A corporation is an example of a "registered organization" as defined in section 9-102(a)(70). Section 9-307(e) states that a registered organization is located in the state of its incorporation. RWZ Consulting, then, is located in Delaware, and the central filing office in that state is where BCC should file its financing statement. For this reason, **Answer (D) is the correct answer. Answer (C) is incorrect** because the location of a corporate debtor's operations does not dictate the filing office.

56. Section 9-309 provides a list of situations in which a security interest is automatically perfected at the moment of attachment. Perhaps the best known example appears first on the list: a PMSI in consumer goods (excluding vehicles subject to certificate-of-title laws). BCC has a PMSI in the computer system because it provided seller financing for the object serving as collateral. *See* § 9-103(a), (b)(1). But the computer system is being used by the debtor — RWZ Consulting — as equipment in its business. It is not being used primarily for personal, family, or household purposes, so it is not a "consumer good" as defined in section 9-102(a)(23). (The foregoing conclusion remains true even if Zimmer operates his business as a sole proprietorship and he uses the computer at least 50% of the time for business purposes.) Therefore, notwithstanding the purchase-money nature of its security interest, BCC cannot rely on automatic perfection, but instead must perfect its PMSI by other means (in this instance, filing).

57. A contract in which a seller retains title to goods sold on credit until the buyer has fulfilled all payment obligations creates, under the UCC, a security interest in the seller's favor in those goods. *See* §§ 1-201(b)(35), 2-401(1). BizCorp's contracts, then, are "chattel paper" as defined in section 9-102(a)(11) because they evidence both the buyer's monetary obligation and a security interest in the goods being purchased by the buyer.

The first proposed transaction is nothing more than a traditional secured transaction: BizCorp is offering the contracts as collateral to secure a loan. Lender can perfect its security interest in the contracts — chattel paper — by filing a financing statement in the appropriate office (*see* § 9-312(a)) or, alternatively, by taking possession of the contracts (*see* § 9-313(a)).

The second proposed transaction — in which BizCorp will *sell* the contracts to Lender for a discounted price — is not a traditional secured transaction. Nevertheless, Article 9 does apply to certain sales transactions, including the sale of chattel paper. *See* §§ 9-109(a)(3) and cmt. 4; 9-102(a)(28)(B) (defining "debtor" to include BizCorp as the seller of chattel paper), 9-102(a)(72)(D) (defining "secured party" to include Lender as the buyer of chattel paper). Lender should take the same action mentioned above to perfect its property interest: file a financing statement, or take possession of the contracts.

58. The analysis would change in two respects. First, because the negotiable promissory notes are unsecured, they are no longer "chattel paper." Instead, they are "promissory notes" and "instruments" as those terms are defined in section 9-102(a)(65) and (47), respectively. Second, Lender's property interest in the promissory notes that it *purchases* from BizCorp is automatically perfected. *See* § 9-309(4). Other than these two modifications, the previous analysis remains unchanged.

59. **Answer (B) is the correct answer.** A security interest becomes perfected "if it has attached and all of the applicable requirements for perfection [e.g., filing a financing statement] . . . have been satisfied. A security interest is perfected when it attaches if the applicable requirements are satisfied before the security interest attaches." § 9-308(a). So Bank's security interest became perfected upon filing, if the interest had previously attached; but Bank's security interest became perfected on attachment, if filing had previously occurred. Under section 9-203(a) and (b), Bank's interest attached on August 7. The security agreement was in place on August 1. Debtor acquired rights in the computer system as early as August 3, when it purchased the system. And Bank gave value under section 1-204(1) as early as August 7 when it entered into a binding commitment to make a loan. The date on

which the last of those three events occurred — August 7 — is the date of attachment. As Bank had previously filed its financing statement on August 4, attachment and perfection occurred simultaneously on August 7, **making Answer (B) the correct answer.**

Answer (A) is incorrect because the filing date of August 4 cannot be the perfection date of a security interest that does not attach until a later date (in this case, August 7).

Answer (C) is incorrect because BizCorp acquired rights in the computer system on the purchase date of August 3. BizCorp need not take possession of the system as a predicate to acquiring rights in the system.

Bank did indeed give value on August 12 when it funded the $100,000 loan request. But Bank also gave value on the earlier date of August 7, when it contractually agreed to make the loan. Therefore, **Answer (D) is incorrect.**

60. Never. Bank cannot perfect a security interest that never attaches. TBN authenticated a security agreement that described the collateral as "equipment." But TBN is a retail bookseller, and it will hold the shipment of children's books for sale in its ordinary course of business, making them "inventory" under section 9-102(a)(48)(B). Bank's security interest is limited to the collateral description in the security agreement, which does not include "inventory" or any other language that would reasonably identify these books. Therefore, Bank has no security interest in the shipment. And absent attachment, perfection is a moot point.

61. **Answer (B) is the correct answer.** Section 9-301 provides rules that "determine the law governing perfection," but those rules are subject to sections 9-303 through 9-306. Because the collateral is investment property, one of the referenced sections — section 9-305 — applies. Section 9-305(a) provides general rules governing perfection, but subsection (a) is subject to subsection (c). And subsection (c) states: "The local law of the jurisdiction in which the debtor is located governs . . . perfection of a security interest in investment property by filing." Under section 9-307(b)(1), a debtor who is an individual is located at her principal residence. Because Maria is a Dallas resident, Texas law governs perfection by filing and is the state in which SmallBank should file its financing statement. SmallBank will not file a fixture filing — the only filing that is recorded in the county records. So **Answer (A) and Answer (D) are incorrect.** Instead SmallBank will file a standard financing statement with the central filing office in Texas. *See* § 9-501(a). Therefore, **Answer (B) is the correct answer.** The law under which an investment is created, the law under which her brokerage manager is organized, and the law that governs Maria's investment contracts are all irrelevant and have no bearing on where SmallBank should file its financing statement. Therefore, **Answer (C) and Answer (D) are incorrect.**

62. SmallBank should file a financing statement against Arturo in the central filing office of New York. SmallBank's security interest survives the unauthorized disposition. *See* § 9-315(a)(1). Arturo has become a "debtor" as defined in section 9-102(a)(28)(A). As a general rule, SmallBank's filing against Maria remains effective to perfect its security interest in the shares of stock now owned by Arturo. *See* § 9-507(a). But an exception to this general rule arises because Arturo lives in New York, rather than in Texas (where SmallBank filed its financing statement). Section 9-316(a)(3) addresses this change in jurisdiction (from Texas to New York) by continuing the effectiveness of SmallBank's original filing for one year from

the date on which Maria sold the shares to her father. In order to avoid any lapse in perfection, section 9-316(b) requires SmallBank to file a financing statement against Arturo in New York before that one-year period expires.

(Observe that the one-year grace period is not absolute. It can be shorter if the five-year period of the filing's effectiveness will conclude within that one-year period. *See* § 9-316(a)(1).)

63.   SmallBank should file a financing statement against Maria in the central filing office of New Mexico. Appreciate that Maria's creditors may be misled because SmallBank's filing (in Texas) will not be discovered by a search against Maria where she is now "located" — New Mexico. Section 9-316(a)(2) addresses this change in jurisdiction (from Texas to New Mexico) by continuing the effectiveness of SmallBank's original filing for four months from the date on which Maria relocated from Texas to New Mexico. In order to avoid any lapse in perfection, section 9-316(b) requires SmallBank to file a financing statement against Maria in New Mexico before that four-month period expires.

(Observe, again, that the four-month grace period is not absolute. It can be shorter if the five-year period of the filing's effectiveness will conclude within that four-month period. *See* § 9-316(a)(1).)

64.   The statement, taken as a whole, is false (because part of it is false). If BAMCO is a corporation, then it also is a "registered organization" as defined in section 9-102(a)(70). Section 9-301(1) informs VegasBank that it should file its financing statement where BAMCO is "located." Under section 9-307(e), a debtor that is a registered organization is located in the state of its creation. If BAMCO is a Delaware corporation, then VegasBank should file its financing statement in the central filing office of Delaware. The location of BAMCO's business operations, chief executive office, books and records, and collateral is irrelevant. VegasBank needs to file only one financing statement, in only one place: Delaware. The statement erroneously suggests that VegasBank must file in multiple jurisdictions, making the statement false.

65.   The statement, taken as a whole, is false (because part of it is false). If BAMCO is a general partnership, then it is *not* a "registered organization" as defined in section 9-102(a)(70). *See* § 9-102 cmt. 11. As noted earlier, section 9-301(1) informs VegasBank that it should file its financing statement where BAMCO is "located." Under section 9-307(e), a debtor that is an organization (other than a registered organization) with multiple locations is deemed located at its chief executive office. BAMCO's chief executive office is in Las Vegas, so VegasBank should file its financing statement in the central filing office of Nevada. The location of collateral is irrelevant. VegasBank needs to file only one financing statement, in only one place: Nevada. The statement erroneously suggests that VegasBank must file in multiple jurisdictions, making the statement false.

66.   The statement is true. As noted earlier, section 9-301(1) informs VegasBank that it should file its financing statement where BAMCO is "located." If BAMCO is a corporation, then it also is a registered organization. A registered organization is located in the state of its formation. BAMCO can move its chief executive office from Las Vegas (Nevada) to Denver (Colorado), without re-incorporating or otherwise changing its "location" under Article 9. Therefore, the original filing (presumably in the state under which BAMCO is incorporated) remains

effective for the duration of its five-year term (and thereafter, if timely continued), and BAMCO's relocation of its chief executive office from Nevada to Colorado imposes no filing duty on VegasBank.

(Observe, though, that a debtor's relocation of its chief executive office to a different state can have adverse consequences if the debtor is *not* a registered organization. *See* § 9-316(a)(2), (b) (giving the secured party a four-month grace period in which to refile in the new state when a debtor changes its location to a new jurisdiction).)

67.   **Answer (B) is the correct answer.** The collateral is a certificated security, a form of "investment property" under section 9-102(a)(49). Section 9-313(a) permits Bank to perfect its security interest in a certificated security by taking "delivery" of the certificate under section 8-301. Bank has taken "delivery" under that section because it has taken possession of the certificate. Therefore Bank is perfected, **making Answer (B) the correct answer.** (Because the certificate is issued in Meredith's name, the absence of her indorsement may prevent Bank from having "control" of the shares under section 8-106(b), but the indorsement is not necessary for "delivery" and perfection.)

Bank has a perfected security interest in Tom's boat if Bank has a PMSI and the boat is a consumer good. *See* § 9-309(1). The facts state that Bank holds a PMSI in the boat. The boat is a consumer good under section 9-102(a)(23) if Tom uses the boat *primarily* for personal, family, or household purposes. He uses the boat equally for personal and business purposes, so neither purpose is primary (more than 50%). Therefore, the boat is not a consumer good. Instead, it is "equipment" as defined in section 9-102(a)(33) (a good that is not a consumer good, inventory, or a farm product). Bank cannot claim automatic perfection of its PMSI in equipment, so the absence of a financing statement leaves Bank unperfected. Therefore, **Answer (A) is incorrect.**

Normally, Bank must comply with certificate-of-title laws in order to perfect its security interest in a debtor's motor vehicles. An exception exists under section 9-311(d) if the motor vehicles are "inventory held for sale or lease by a person or leased by that person as lessor and that person is in the business of selling goods of that kind," in which case Bank can perfect its security interest in the motor vehicles by filing a financing statement. Zippy Rental Agency falls within the first half of the quoted language. But Zippy is in the business of leasing, rather than selling, its motor vehicles. Perhaps it is true that Zippy typically sells a motor vehicle when it reaches a certain mileage or age. Even so, these ultimate sales do not convert Zippy into an entity "in the business of selling goods of that kind." *See* § 9-311 cmt. 4 (second paragraph). Because the filing exception does not apply, Bank can perfect its security interest in Zippy's fleet of vehicles only by complying with certificate-of-title laws. It has failed to do so, leaving it unperfected, and **making Answer (C) an incorrect answer.**

The only method by which Bank can perfect a security interest in BizCorp's deposit accounts is by control. *See* § 9-312(b)(1). A financing statement is ineffective, and BizCorp is unperfected. It is true that control is automatic if the debtor maintains the deposit accounts with the secured party. *See* § 9-104(a)(1). But in this transaction, BizCorp maintains the deposit accounts not with Bank, but with other financial institutions. For these reasons, **Answer (D) is an incorrect answer.**

68.   **Answer (A) is the correct answer.** Section 9-109(c)(1) states that Article 9 "does not apply to the extent that . . . a statute, regulation, or treaty of the United States preempts this article." Therefore, the secured party must be concerned that federal law may require it to

record its security interest in a debtor's registered copyrights, trademarks, and patents with the applicable national registry. Under existing case law, a secured party must record its security interest in a debtor's registered copyrights in the national registry (**making Answers (B) and (D) incorrect answers**), but may perfect its security interest in a debtor's registered patents and registered trademarks by filing a financing statement in the appropriate state filing office (**making Answer (A) the correct answer** and **making Answer (C) an incomplete and incorrect answer**). The leading cases in this area are *In re Peregrine Entertainment, Ltd.*, 116 B.R. 194 (C.D. Cal. 1990) (copyrights); *Trimarchi & Personal Dating Servs. v. Together Development Corp.*, 255 B.R. 606 (D. Mass. 2000) (trademarks); and *Moldo v. Matsco, Inc. (In re Cybernetic Services, Inc.)*, 252 F.3d 1039 (9th Cir. 2001) (patents).

69. **Answer (C) is the best answer.** A search against the debtor's current legal name of "ZinnCo," using the filing office's standard search logic, is not likely to reveal the earlier filing against "BAM Corp." Therefore, under section 9-506(c), the debtor's name change has caused Bank's financing statement to become seriously misleading. Nevertheless, the filing against "BAM Corp." remains effective to perfect a security interest in equipment acquired by the debtor (i) prior to the name change and (ii) within four months after the name change (§ 9-507(c)) — even if the perfected or unperfected status is examined (as in this problem) on a date long after the four-month period has concluded (e.g., November 1). ZinnCo acquired Item #1 in May, within four months after the name change on March 15, so the original filing remains effective to perfect Bank's security interest in Item #1. ZinnCo acquired Item #2 in July, but without a specific date, it cannot be determined whether the purchase falls inside, or outside, the four-month period. If ZinnCo acquired Item #2 on July 10, then the original filing continues to perfect Bank's security interest in Item #2. But if ZinnCo acquired Item #2 on July 20, then Bank's filing fails to perfect its security interest in Item #2. Without more information, then, the perfected or unperfected status of Bank's security interest in Item #2 cannot be determined with certainty. Finally, ZinnCo acquired Item #3 in September, more than four months after the name change in March, so the original filing does not perfect Bank's security interest in Item #3. **Answer (C), then, is true and Answer (D) could be true.** But **Answer (C) is the better answer** because the perfected status of Item #1 is known with certainty, whereas the perfected status of Item #2 is not.

Answer (A) is incorrect because the name change has no effect on attachment, merely perfection.

Answer (B) is incorrect because Bank has a perfected security interest in at least Item #1, and perhaps Item #2.

70. **Answer (C) is the correct answer.** As a general rule (and no applicable exceptions apply in this case), a "security interest . . . continues in collateral notwithstanding sale . . . thereof unless the secured party authorized the disposition free of the security interest." *See* § 9-315(a)(1). Therefore, **Answer (A) is incorrect.** But this statute says only that the sale has not destroyed attachment; it does not address whether Bank must refile against Purchaser to remain perfected. Section 9-507(a) addresses the continued effectiveness of Bank's financing statement. Under that statute, Bank need not refile against Purchaser; instead, its financing statement filed against "BAM Corp." remains effective to perfect the security interest in the Item — even after the sale to Purchaser. (Because a financing statement filed against a seller [BAM Corp.] can remain effective against a buyer [Purchaser] under section

9-507(a), a creditor of a buyer [Purchaser] "must inquire as to the debtor's [Purchaser's] source of title and, if circumstances seem to require it, search in the name of the former owner [BAM Corp.]." § 9-507 cmt. 3. For additional discussion, including an examination of competing policy arguments on this matter, see PEB Commentary No. 3 in your statutes book, keeping in mind that the statutes discussed therein have been renumbered.)

But what if Purchaser is an entity organized under non-Delaware law and therefore is "located" in a state different from the state in which Bank filed its financing statement? Section 9-316(a)(3) addresses this situation and continues the effectiveness of Bank's filing for one year. The question asks for analysis as of November 1, a date that is within one year of the sale in March, so Bank's filing in Delaware continues to perfect its security interest in the Item, regardless of where Purchaser is "located." For this reason, **Answer (C) is correct and Answer (D) is incorrect.** Note, however, that section 9-316(b) does require Bank to file a new financing statement against Purchaser in the jurisdiction of its location (if not Delaware) within the one-year period if Bank wants to enjoy continued and uninterrupted perfection in the Item.

Answer (B) is incorrect because the location of the Item has no bearing on whether Bank's security interest in the Item remains perfected after the sale by BAM Corp. to Purchaser.

71.   Article 9 provides four methods of perfection: filing, possession (or delivery), control, and automatic. Filing works on almost all types of collateral. Possession is limited to collateral with a tangible quality. Control is unique to deposit accounts, electronic chattel paper, investment property, letter-of-credit rights, and electronic documents. Automatic perfection arises in limited situations (see § 9-309), the most common of which is when the secured party has a PMSI in a consumer good.

A certificated security (a form of investment property) is an example of collateral in which a security interest can be perfected in three different ways. The secured party may file a financing statement, obtain control of the certificate, or take delivery (possession) of the certificate (which also will constitute control if the certificate is in bearer form).

A secured party can perfect its security interest in consumer goods (excluding motor vehicles subject to certificate-of-title laws) by filing a financing statement or taking possession. If the secured party can claim a PMSI, it also can enjoy automatic perfection.

Perhaps you can come up with other examples.

72.   **Answer (D) is the correct answer. Answer (A) is incorrect** since financing statements (but not security agreements) can use supergeneric descriptions such as "all assets" or "all personal property." See § 9-504(2). (Appreciate, though, that the supergeneric description in the financing statement will not perfect a security interest in collateral that falls outside the collateral description found in the security agreement.) The remainder of the question requires an examination of the use of definitions in Article 9.

The security agreement covers "accounts, equipment, and general intangibles." "Equipment," as defined in section 9-102(a)(33), means "goods other than inventory, farm products, or consumer goods." It is a definition by exclusion, which is intended; "equipment" is the residual or default classification of goods. If it is tangible, and it is not something else, it is likely equipment. In the problem, the computers, photocopiers, and office furniture are equipment. They are not inventory because GetSmart! uses the items internally; they are neither held by GetSmart! for sale in the ordinary course of its business nor are they consumable supplies (e.g., pencils, tablets, paper clips, etc.) used in the business. And for rather obvious reasons, they are not farm products or consumer goods (the customers may be consumers, but the debtor is a business entity). The security agreement and the financing statement both cover equipment, so Omega Bank has (or will have) a perfected security interest in the office furniture, computers, and photocopiers.

Cash — presumably bills of various denominations, and pennies, nickels, dimes, and quarters — is "money" as defined in section 1-201(b)(24). Money is not an "account." The security agreement fails to mention "money," and the supergeneric collateral description in the financing statement cannot expand the pool of collateral beyond the contours of the security agreement. Therefore, Omega Bank has no security interest in the cash. (Even if Omega Bank had an enforceable security interest in the cash, the only way to perfect a security interest in money is possession (by the secured party). *See* § 9-312(a)(3).)

The checks are not "money" nor are they an "account." Instead, they are an example of an "instrument" as defined in section 9-102(a)(47). The security agreement fails to mention "instruments," and the supergeneric collateral description in the financing statement cannot expand the pool of collateral beyond the contours of the security agreement. Therefore, Omega Bank has no security interest in the checks.

Credit card receivables are, by definition, an "account." *See* § 9-102(a)(vii). Both the security agreement and the financing statement cover accounts, so Bank has (or will have) a perfected security interest in the credit card receivables.

What is the customer list? A customer list can be tangible (e.g., evidenced by one or more sheets of paper, or stored on a computer disk), and intangible (a collection of names that has value). If the list has a tangible quality, it may be equipment. But because the inherent value of the list is not found in the manner in which the information is stored, but in the information itself, the list also could be deemed a general intangible. Either way, Omega Bank is, or will be, perfected because its security agreement and financing statement cover both equipment and general intangibles.

In summary, then, Omega Bank has a perfected security interest in all of the specific assets mentioned, other than the cash and the checks. For this reason, **Answer (D) is correct and Answer (B) and Answer (C) are incorrect.**

73.   **Answer (B) is the correct answer.** The clerk indexes a financing statement by the debtor's name. *See* § 9-519(c). Therefore, whether a filing will provide the notice sought by a searcher will depend, to a great extent, on the accuracy of the debtor's name on the filing. The name of a corporation can be confirmed by objective evidence: a government-certified copy of the corporation's charter documents, which will reveal the debtor's original name and any changes to it. An individual's name, though, is more difficult to determine with accuracy. An individual's name will appear on a driver's license, a Social Security card, a tax return, a loan application, a personal check, etc., but the name may not be consistent on every source (e.g., Tom Smith, Thomas R. Smith, Thomas Robert Smith, T. Robert Smith, Tom Rob Smith, Thomas Robert Smith III, Thomas Robert Smith, Jr., etc.). *(Please note that one or more states have adopted non-uniform amendments that take the guesswork out of identifying a human debtor's "name" for filing purposes. For example, Texas provides a safe harbor when the financing statement provides "the individual's name shown on the individual's driver's license or identification certificate issued by the individual's state of residence.")* Therefore, the risk of providing a debtor's name that later is determined to be seriously misleading is

greater with an individual debtor than a corporate debtor. Recent (as of the publication of this edition) cases include the following: *Peoples Bank v. Bryan Bros. Cattle Co.*, 504 F.3d 549, 558–59 (5th Cir. 2007) (filing against "Louie Dickerson" instead of legal name of "Brooks L. Dickerson" was *not* seriously misleading); *Genoa National Bank v. Southwest Implement, Inc.*, 2007 WL 2407032, at *1–*3 (D. Neb. Aug. 20, 2007) (filing against "Mike Borden" instead of "Michael Borden" or "Michael R. Borden" was seriously misleading); *Morris v. Snap-On Credit, LLC*, 2006 WL 3590097, at *2–*3 (Bankr. D. Kan. Dec. 7, 2006) (filing against "Chris Jones" instead of full legal name of "Christopher Gary Jones" was seriously misleading); *Corona Fruits & Veggies, Inc. v. Frozsun Foods, Inc.*, 48 Cal. Rptr. 3d 868, 869–71 (Ct. App. 2006) (filing against "Armando Munoz" instead of "Armando Munoz Juarez" was seriously misleading). For this reason, Hawkeye Bank's request that Grace incorporate her business is entirely plausible, **making Answer (B) the correct answer.**

Loans to consumer debtors may indeed be an "unfair act or practice" under the FTC's credit practices regulations. *See generally* 16 C.F.R. pt. 444 (perhaps found in your statutes book). But major exceptions exist if the creditor can claim a PMSI or the collateral is not a "household good." Therefore, this reason is not likely to prompt Hawkeye Bank to insist on incorporation. **Answer (A), then, is an overbroad statement, making it less attractive as the best answer.**

As a general rule (and no exception is readily apparent here), a security interest survives the debtor's asset disposition. *See* § 9-315(a)(1). Therefore, Grace will not necessarily terminate security interests held by creditors in her business assets by transferring ownership to a corporate entity. For this reason, **Answer (C) is incorrect.**

As a general rule (and no exception applies to this transaction), financing statements are effective for five years, whether the debtor is a human or a commercial entity. *See* § 9-515(a). This cannot be the reason, then, why Hawkeye Bank wants Grace to incorporate her business. Therefore, **Answer (D) is incorrect.**

74.   **Answer (D) is the correct answer.** The check represents "proceeds" under section 9-102(a)(64)(A) ("whatever is acquired upon the sale . . . of collateral"). Under section 9-203(f), Omega Bank's enforceable security interest in BizCorp's inventory of photocopiers gives it "rights to proceeds provided by Section 9-315." Under that section, Omega Bank's security interest attaches to the check if it is an "identifiable" proceed (i.e., a proceed that can be traced to a unit of inventory). Under section 9-315(c), the security interest in the check (proceeds) is perfected because the security interest in the photocopier (the original collateral) was perfected (by a financing statement). This automatic perfection is only temporary for twenty days and terminates thereafter unless perfection continues under subsection (d). Omega Bank enjoys continued perfection under subsection (d)(2) because the check is an example of a "cash proceed" as defined in section 9-102(a)(9). Therefore, assuming that the check is traceable to a unit of inventory (the photocopier), then Omega Bank has a perfected security interest in the check, **making Answer (D) the correct answer.**

The failure to include an after-acquired property clause in the security agreement could be fatal, especially if the collateral is of a type that constantly changes in composition (e.g., inventory and accounts). (Appreciate that the after-acquired property clause need not be repeated in the financing statement. *See* §§ 9-204 cmt. 7; 9-502 cmt. 2. Also note that, when dealing with inventory and accounts, some courts have inferred the existence of an after-acquired property clause when the security agreement is silent, on the plausible assumption that no secured party in its right mind intends to limit its security interest to inventory or accounts that exist when the debtor authenticates the security agreement, but not inventory acquired or accounts created thereafter.) Here, however, BizCorp owned the photocopier for six months before selling it to the law firm in June, so BizCorp had rights in the photocopier when it executed the security agreement in February. Therefore, the omission of the after-acquired property clause from the security agreement has no importance in this question. True, BizCorp did not acquire rights in the check until June. But no proceeds-related provision of Article 9 conditions attachment or perfection of a security interest therein on the presence of an after-acquired property clause in the security agreement. For these reasons, **Answer (A) is incorrect.**

Also, no proceeds-related provision of Article 9 conditions attachment or perfection of a security interest therein on the presence of magical words — such as "proceeds" or "cash proceeds" — in the collateral description of any loan paper. Therefore, **Answer (B) is incorrect.**

As the photocopier is a unit of BizCorp's inventory, it is highly likely that the sale of the photocopier to the law firm terminated Omega Bank's security interest therein, because either Omega Bank authorized BizCorp to sell its inventory free and clear of the security interest (*see* § 9-315(a)(1)) or the law firm can invoke the protections afforded to a buyer in the ordinary course of business (*see* § 9-320(a)). But Omega Bank's loss of its security interest in the photocopier (which it has to anticipate) does not mean that Omega Bank has abandoned, or Article 9 has terminated, any possible security interest in proceeds that Omega Bank may claim. Therefore, **Answer (C) is incorrect.**

75. **Answer (A) is the correct answer.** The bookstore's insurance claim arises from damage to, or loss or destruction of, the inventory in which Trinity Finance has a perfected security interest. The insurance claim falls within the definition of "proceeds" either under section 9-102(a)(64)(D) ("claims arising out of the loss . . . or damage to . . . the collateral") or section 9-102(a)(64)(E) ("insurance payable by reason of the loss . . . or damage to . . . the collateral"). Sections 9-203(f) and 9-315(a) permit Trinity Finance to claim an interest in the insurance policy claim as an "identifiable" proceed of its perfected security interest in the inventory. Perfection of its security interest in the insurance claim is automatic for twenty days under section 9-315(c). Perfection continues thereafter because Trinity Finance can satisfy all three conditions of section 9-315(d)(1): Trinity Finance perfected its security interest in the original collateral (the inventory) by filing a financing statement; a filing in the same office will perfect a security interest in the insurance claim (either an "account" or a "general intangible"); and the bookstore's insurance claim was not acquired with cash proceeds. Therefore, **Answer (A) is the correct answer.**

Answer (B) is incorrect because, as discussed in the preceding paragraph, the perfection of Trinity Finance's security interest in the insurance claim extends beyond the automatic, but temporary, twenty-day period of section 9-315(c).

Answer (C) is incorrect because Trinity Finance has a perfected security interest in the insurance claim.

Answer (D) is incorrect because the broad exclusion of a debtor's interest in an insurance policy from the scope of Article 9 includes an exception for insurance claims that represent proceeds of collateral. *See* § 9-109(d)(8) (the "but" clause at the end).

76. **Answer (A) is the correct answer.** The $1 million check is identifiable as proceeds of the inventory. Because there is an intervening insurance claim, the check is what might be termed "second generation proceeds" or "proceeds of proceeds." Article 9 does not limit proceeds to "first generation proceeds," but also includes second, third, and other generations. *See* § 9-102 cmt. 13.c. At some point, however, the secured party's tracing duty will become difficult, if not impossible. That is not the case here, though, as the check can be easily traced back to the insurance claim, which arises from hurricane damage to the bookstore's inventory. A check is a form of "cash proceeds" as defined in section 9-102(a)(9). Therefore, Trinity Finance's perfection is not limited to the automatic, but temporary, twenty-day period of section 9-315(c), but extends beyond that period under section 9-315(d)(2). For these reasons, **Answer (A) is the correct answer.**

Answer (B) is incorrect for two reasons. First, as explained in the preceding paragraph, Trinity Finance's perfection extends beyond the twenty-day period of section 9-315(c). Second, a check is an "instrument" under section 9-102(a)(47). A security interest in an instrument can be perfected by possession (*see* § 9-313(a)), but it also can be perfected by filing (*see* § 9-312(a)).

Answer (C) is incorrect because Trinity Finance has a perfected security interest in the check. Absent indorsement and delivery, Trinity Finance may not have enforcement rights in the check under UCC Article 3. But Trinity Finance's perfected status does not turn on whether it can enforce the check.

Answer (D) is incorrect for two reasons. First, a check is not "money" as defined in section 1-201. Second, Article 9 does not exclude "money" from its scope of coverage. *See, e.g.*, § 9-312(b)(3) (discussing how a security interest in money may be perfected).

77.   **Answer (A) is the correct answer.** The bookstore's general operating bank account is a "deposit account" as defined in section 9-102(a)(29), and a deposit account (like a check) is an example of a "cash proceed" as defined in section 9-102(a)(9). Therefore, assuming that Trinity Finance can satisfy its tracing burden (which could be a challenge, with the passage of time, as the account is not a segregated "proceeds only" account), Trinity Finance has a perfected security interest in the deposit account for twenty days and beyond, as explained more fully in the preceding answer. For these reasons, **Answer (A) is the correct answer.**

Answer (B) is incorrect for two reasons. First, as already explained, Trinity Finance is perfected beyond the twenty-day period of section 9-315(c). Second, section 9-312(b)(1) does state that a security interest in a deposit account can be perfected only by control, but the opening language of section 9-312(b) defers to the proceeds-related provisions in section 9-315(c) and (d). For this reason, **Answer (C) is also incorrect.**

Answer (D) is incorrect and is a nonsense answer. Article 9 applies to security interests in deposit accounts (subject to a consumer-related exception found in section 9-109(d)(13)), regardless of how funds are deposited (e.g., cash, check, wire transfer, etc.) into the deposit account.

78.   **Answer (B) is the correct answer.** BAM Technologies can satisfy its tracing burden, so the cash and note — proceeds under section 9-102(a)(64) — are identifiable. Therefore, BAM Technologies has a security interest in the proceeds under section 9-315(a)(2), so **Answer (A) is incorrect.** That security interest is perfected for at least twenty days under section 9-315(c), but only if the security interest in the original collateral (the equipment) was perfected. MediCorp, the debtor, is a corporation and, therefore, a registered organization. Section 9-301(1) tells the secured party to file its financing statement where the debtor is located. Section 9-307(e) states that a registered organization is located in the state of its creation. MediCorp is chartered under Delaware law, so it is deemed located in Delaware. But BAM Technologies filed its financing statement in California, the state in which MediCorp operates its hospitals and clinics. BAM Technologies filed in the wrong state, leaving it unperfected in the equipment. Because its security interest in the equipment is unperfected, its security interest in the proceeds is also unperfected. Therefore, **Answer (B) is the correct answer and Answer (C) and Answer (D) are incorrect answers. Answer (C) also is incorrect** because the time of the filing (assuming the filing is recorded in the correct state) does not dictate whether the secured party can claim a perfected security interest in proceeds (although the timing may dictate priority).

79.   As of December 1, Omega Bank has a perfected security interest in the photocopier. Gershwin received the photocopier as payment for a piano (a unit of inventory), making it a "proceed" under section 9-102(a)(64). Omega Bank should be able to prove that Gershwin acquired a property interest in the photocopier by taking it from Lauren as payment for a piano (a unit of inventory), making the photocopier an "identifiable" proceed. Therefore, Omega Bank has an enforceable security interest in the photocopier under section 9-315(a)(2). Because Omega Bank had a perfected security interest in the piano, its security

interest in the photocopier is perfected for twenty days under section 9-315(c). Perfection continues thereafter because Omega Bank can satisfy the three conditions of section 9-315(d)(1): a filed financing statement covers the piano, a filing in the same office will perfect a security interest in the photocopier (equipment in the debtor's hands), and there are no intervening cash proceeds. Therefore, as of December 1, Omega Bank has a perfected security interest in the photocopier.

80.   As of December 1, Omega Bank does *not* have a perfected security interest in the photocopier. The analysis tracks the previous answer, until the twenty-day perfection period of section 9-315(c) expires. (Given the fungible nature of cash, Omega Bank may be unable to satisfy its tracing burden in the typical transaction, but the facts as stated permit Omega Bank to prove that the photocopier is an "identifiable" proceed.) Perfection of Omega Bank's security interest in the photocopier lapses on November 21 (the twenty-first day after the security interest attached to the photocopier on November 1) because Omega Bank is unable to extend perfection under section 9-315(d). It cannot satisfy subsection (d)(1) because Gershwin acquired the photocopier with cash proceeds (notice that subsection (d)(1) has three subparts, all of which must be met). Subsection (d)(2) does not apply because the photocopier is not "cash proceeds." And subsection (d)(3) offers no help because Omega Bank has failed to take any other action to perfect its interest in the photocopier (i.e., amending its original financing statement to mention the photocopier or filing a new financing statement against the photocopier). Because Omega Bank is unable to extend perfection under section 9-315, it does not have a perfected security interest in the photocopier as of December 1.

81.   **Answer (B) is the correct answer.** The act of commingling proceeds with non-proceeds does not automatically destroy a secured party's ability to "identify" some or all of the assets as its collateral. Article 9 permits the secured party to identify the proceeds "by a method of tracing, including application of equitable principles, that is permitted under law other than this article with respect to commingled property of the type involved." § 9-315(b)(2). A common "equitable principle" is the "lowest intermediate balance rule." § 9-315 cmt. 3. Under the lowest intermediate balance rule, (i) the creditor can claim an interest in commingled assets identified as proceeds, (ii) non-proceeds are considered used by the debtor before proceeds, and (iii) proceeds that are used by the debtor are not deemed replenished with subsequently commingled non-proceeds.

When the problem involves a bank account, it is helpful to run a daily balance and identify that part of the total balance that represents proceeds. The following is a summary of the bank activity:

Date	Balance	Proceeds
4/1	8,000	2,000
4/5	14,000	8,000
4/7	7,000	7,000
4/15	11,000	7,000
4/20	6,000	6,000
4/24	9,000	9,000
4/28	11,000	9,000

Because the ending number in the "proceeds" column is $9,000, **Answer (B) is the correct answer and Answers (A), (C), and (D) are incorrect answers.**

82. As of April 30, under the lowest intermediate balance rule, Lender can claim a security interest in $5,000, calculated as follows:

Date	Balance	Proceeds
4/1	8,000	2,000
4/5	14,000	8,000
4/7	7,000	7,000
4/12	11,000	11,000
4/15	15,000	11,000
4/17	7,000	7,000
4/20	2,000	2,000
4/22	4,000	2,000
4/24	7,000	5,000
4/28	9,000	5,000

83. **Answer (B) is the correct answer.** Tim received the baseballs as payment for the chess set, so the baseballs represent proceeds under section 9-102(a)(64). The baseballs are rather special, and not generic, facilitating the ability of Tim's parents to satisfy their tracing burden, making the baseballs "identifiable proceeds" in which Tim's parents can claim an enforceable security interest under section 9-315(a)(2). Therefore, **Answer (A) is incorrect.** Normally the security interest in proceeds is automatically (albeit temporarily) perfected for twenty days under section 9-315(c). But that brief period of perfection is available only if the security interest in the original collateral was perfected. Tim's parents did file a financing statement against Tim and the chess set in Ohio, where Tim (at the time) was "located" under section 9-307(b)(1). But Tim later moved to New York, a different state. This change in jurisdiction required the parents to file a new financing statement in New York within four months after the relocation if they wanted to maintain continuous and uninterrupted perfection. *See* § 9-316(a)(2). The facts do not indicate that the parents took any filing action in response to Tim's relocation, leaving them unperfected both prospectively and retroactively. *See* § 9-316(b). This means that Tim's parents cannot invoke section 9-315(c), leaving them with an unperfected security interest in the baseballs. For these reasons, **Answer (B) is the correct answer and Answer (D) is an incorrect answer.**

Answer (C) suggests that the label assigned to the chess set may be relevant to the analysis. That might be true, if Tim's parents could claim automatic perfection in the chess set. They can do so under section 9-309(1) *if* their security interest qualifies as a PMSI, *and* Tim uses the chess set as a consumer good. If both conditions are met, Tim's relocation may have an impact on the continued effectiveness of the Ohio filing, but Tim's parents could rely on the alternative method of automatic perfection, which would not be adversely affected by Tim's relocation to New York. The problem, though, is that even if Tim uses the chess set as a consumer good, the parents do not have a PMSI in the chess set. Tim used their money to take a vacation and pay off credit card; he used his own money to purchase the chess set. Therefore, the parents cannot prove (under section 9-103(a)(2)) that they hold a "purchase-money obligation" and, accordingly, do not have a PMSI that may be eligible for automatic perfection. This means that the label assigned to the chess set (e.g., consumer good, inventory, or equipment [we will safely assume the set is not a farm product]) is irrelevant. For these reasons, **Answer (C) is incorrect.**

84. **Answer (B) is the correct answer.** Section 9-102(a)(41) defines "fixtures" as "goods that have become so related to particular real property that an interest in them arises under real property." Notice that a fixture must be a "good," a term defined in section 9-102(a)(44). Revenues are not "goods," but are something else (e.g., accounts). Therefore, **Answer (D) is incorrect.** The definition of "goods" also excludes "oil, gas, or other minerals before extraction," so coal in the ground is not a fixture and **Answer (A) is incorrect.** A grand piano may not be easily removable from a room in which it is located, but it remains movable within that room, so **Answer (C) is incorrect.** A large video screen, almost certainly bolted or otherwise affixed to the ceiling, could be a fixture, **making Answer (B) the correct answer.**

Appreciate that Article 9 excludes from its coverage not only real estate collateral (which would include pre-extracted minerals), but also "a lease or rents" arising from real estate. *See* § 9-109(d)(11). Therefore, a secured party that takes as collateral an interest in a revenue stream (e.g., accounts) of a debtor in the real estate business (e.g., a hotel, a golf course, an apartment complex, etc.) should consult local real estate law and consider recording an "assignment of rents" document in the real estate records and not rely solely on its security agreement and financing statement.

85. **Answer (A) is the correct answer.** The contents of an effective fixture filing are summarized in section 9-502(b). A fixture filing must include the same information as a regular financing statement. It also must (i) state that it covers fixtures, (ii) state that it is to be filed in the real estate records, (iii) provide a description of the real estate, and (iv) provide the name of the record owner of the real estate if the debtor does not have a recorded interest. Only Answer (A) mentions information that the statute requires, so **Answer (A) is the correct answer.** Section 9-502(b) does not require the record owner of the real estate to authorize the fixture filing, even if the debtor does not have an interest of record in the real estate, so **Answer (B) is incorrect.** Nor does section 9-502(b) require the filing to be authenticated or notarized, so **Answers (C) and (D) are incorrect answers.**

86. **Answer (D) is the correct answer.** Answers (C) and (D) both suggest that Quality Contractors should file a fixture filing, with the only difference being the location of the filing. Standard financing statements are filed where the debtor is located (*see* § 9-301(1)), and Molly (a human) is deemed located at her primary residence (*see* § 9-307(b)(1)). Therefore, Minnesota may appear to be the correct state in which to file the fixture filing. However, a fixture filing is not recorded where the debtor is located, but where the relevant real estate is located. *See* § 9-501(a)(1). The fixtures will be affixed to real estate located in Phoenix, so Quality Contractors should file its fixture filing in the relevant Arizona county. For these reasons, **Answer (D) is the correct answer and Answer (C) is an incorrect answer.**

A secured party whose collateral is, or may become, a fixture should always file a fixture filing. The primary reason for doing so is that the filing increases the likelihood under section 9-334 that the secured party can win a priority dispute with a real estate encumbrancer (e.g., a mortgagee) that also claims the fixtures as its collateral. **Answer (A) and Answer (B) are incorrect** because they erroneously suggest that there is no reason to file a fixture filing. Quality Contractors does have a PMSI in the fixtures, which are consumer goods as used by Molly, so its security interest in the fixtures is automatically perfected. *See* § 9-309(1). Even so, for the reason mentioned above, Quality Contractors should file a fixture filing. And **Answer (B) is incorrect for the additional reason** that Article 9 includes within, rather than excludes from, its scope of coverage the debtor's use of residential fixtures as collateral. *See* § 9-109(d)(11).

87. **Answer (C) is the correct answer.** The priority rules concerning fixture disputes are found in section 9-334. The default rule is found in subsection (c), which awards priority to Bay Area Bank (the real estate encumbrancer) unless BAMCO can claim priority under another subsection. BAMCO has engaged in seller financing, so it can claim a purchase-money security interest in the tanks under section 9-103(a) and (b)(1). And Bay Area Bank's interest in the real estate arose in January, before the tanks became fixtures in August. Therefore, BAMCO's security interest in the tanks enjoys priority if it files a fixture filing no later than the twentieth day "after the goods become fixtures." § 9-334(d). That date is August 5, not July 8 (the purchase date). So BAMCO's fixture filing is timely if it is filed on or before August 25. A fixture filing on August 23, then, is timely, and BAMCO can claim priority. Therefore, **Answer (C) is the correct answer.** Absent a fixture filing, BAMCO cannot claim priority over Bay Area Bank under any other subsection of 9-334 (subsection (e)(1) requires a fixture filing, subsection (e)(2) is inapplicable because the tanks are not readily removable, and no other subsection applies). BAMCO can rely on a standard financing statement to perfect its security interest, but that filing is of little comfort in a priority dispute with a real estate claimant. Therefore, **Answer (B) is incorrect.**

The tanks are being offered as collateral by GC, a corporation. Therefore, the tanks are not consumer goods (but instead are equipment). This means that BAMCO's seller-financed PMSI is not eligible for automatic perfection under section 9-309(1) (or any other section), so **Answer (D) is incorrect.**

Even though the tanks are fixtures, BAMCO can perfect its security interest by filing a standard financing statement in the central filing office of the state where the debtor (GC) is located. *See* §§ 9-501(a)(2), 9-301(1). GC, a corporation, is a "registered organization" under section 9-102(a)(70). A registered organization is deemed located in the state of its creation (*see* § 9-307(e)), so BAMCO should file its standard financing statement in Delaware, the state in which BAMCO is incorporated. **Answer (A) is incorrect** because Delaware (the state of incorporation), rather than California (the location of business operations), is the correct state in which to file a standard financing statement.

88. **Answer (C) is the correct answer.** Section 9-604 provides the fixture creditor with a choice: it can exercise its rights and remedies afforded by Part 6 of Article 9, or it can elect to pursue its rights and remedies under the relevant real estate law. *See* § 9-604(b). **Answer (A) is incorrect** because it erroneously suggests that BAMCO is governed exclusively by real estate law. If BAMCO decides to pursue its rights and remedies under Article 9, it can remove the fixtures — but only if its security interest enjoys priority. *See* § 9-604(c). Therefore, **Answer (C) is the correct answer.** Subsection (c) does not condition removal on

the debtor's consent (although BAMCO cannot breach the peace), so **Answer (B) is incorrect.** Nor does subsection (c) prohibit removal if the debtor has paid off a certain percentage of the debt, so **Answer (D) is incorrect.**

89. **Answer (B) is the correct answer.** Section 9-604(d) states that BAMCO "need not reimburse the encumbrancer [Bay Area Bank] or owner [GC] for any diminution in value of the real property caused by the absence of the goods removed [the tanks] or by any necessity of replacing them." Therefore, neither Bay Area Bank nor GC is entitled to $36,000 (or $42,000), so **Answer (A) and Answer (C) are incorrect answers.** BAMCO is liable for damage that it causes during removal — but to whom? Section 9-604(d) states that BAMCO "shall promptly reimburse any encumbrancer or owner of the real property, other than the debtor, for the cost of repair of any physical injury caused by the removal." This means that BAMCO must pay $6,000 to Bay Area Bank rather than to GC, **making Answer (B) the correct answer and Answer (D) an incorrect answer.**

90. **Answer (A) is the correct answer.** This problem seems to involve fixtures, but it does not. The units have yet to be installed, so they have not become fixtures. Until they become fixtures, Gilmore Finance has no interest in them (at least through its mortgage). The units retain their character as personal property covered solely by Article 9. This is a one-party dispute, easy to resolve in favor of FrigiTech under section 9-201(a), **making Answer (A) the correct answer.** Gilmore Finance cannot win a priority dispute unless it has an enforceable interest in the collateral, so **Answers (B), (C), and (D) are incorrect.** As we will see in the next question and answer, however, the analysis changes if the units become fixtures before M&Z files its bankruptcy petition.

91. Gilmore Finance enjoys priority in the units, which became fixtures upon their installation. Section 9-334(h) awards priority to Gilmore Finance because its interest arises in the units under a construction mortgage that was recorded in the real property records before the units became fixtures (and the units became fixtures before construction had been completed). FrigiTech cannot invoke the exception found in section 9-334(e)(1) because it never filed a fixture filing. Nor can FrigiTech invoke the exception found in section 9-334(e)(2) because the units are not readily removable. No other exception in section 9-334(e) or section 9-334(f) is available. Therefore, Gilmore Finance, as a construction mortgagee, enjoys priority in the units.

Construction mortgages have priority over purchase-money interests in fixtures on the theory that vendors such as FrigiTech will be paid from a draw or advance under the construction loan (and FrigiTech should know that and either require a check from the construction lender or, if it is willing to extend purchase-money credit to the property owner, negotiate a subordination agreement with the construction lender).

92. No, the bankruptcy trustee will not be successful in its attempt to convert FrigiTech's secured claim into an unsecured claim by avoiding FrigiTech's security interest under the strong-arm clause of the Bankruptcy Code. The strong-arm clause (11 U.S.C. § 544(a)(1)) effectively permits the trustee to avoid any security interest that is unperfected, or otherwise subordinate to the interest of a hypothetical lien creditor arising, on the petition date (perhaps an oversimplication, but one that suffices for this problem). FrigiTech filed a standard financing statement, which perfected its security interest in the units under section 9-501(a)(2). Therefore, FrigiTech's interest is senior to the trustee's hypothetical lien (which

arises "by legal or equitable proceedings") under section 9-334(e)(3), which arose (hypothetically) after FrigiTech perfected its security interest by a central filing (a "method permitted by this article," particularly section 9-501(a)(2)). In summary, then, FrigiTech's perfected security interest in the units cannot be avoided by the bankruptcy trustee under the strong-arm clause (notwithstanding the absence of a fixture filing). *See* § 9-334 cmt. 9.

93.   **Answer (A) is the correct answer.** The dispute between two secured but unperfected
creditors is resolved by the rule found in section 9-322(a)(3): priority is awarded to the
creditor whose security interest attached first. Although the facts do not provide specific
dates, the timeline does indicate that the security interest held by Meredith's parents (Tim
and Lisa) became enforceable, or attached, earlier than the security interest held by
Meredith's sister (Grace). Therefore, the parents enjoy priority and have the senior claim to
the proceeds in an amount not exceeding their debt. This means that Ethan should take the
proceeds of $20,000 and pay $15,000 to his parents (paying off their claim) and the balance of
$5,000 to Grace (leaving her with an unsecured claim for the remaining unpaid $5,000
balance of her $10,000 loan). Therefore, **Answer (A) is the correct answer.**

Answer (B) is incorrect because Article 9 gives priority to the first security interest to
attach, rather than bestowing an equal rank on all unperfected security interests.

Answer (C) is incorrect because Article 9 does not award priority based on a *pro rata*
percentage of unpaid debt secured by the unperfected claims.

Answer (D) is incorrect. Article 9 does exclude from its scope real estate *collateral* (*see* § 9-
109(d)(11)), but it does not exclude from its scope the use of personal property (e.g., a piano)
to secure real estate *debt*.

94.   **Answer (A) is the correct answer.** The analysis remains the same, although the dispute is
resolved under a different rule. Because both security interests are perfected, section 9-
322(a)(1) awards priority to the secured party that is the first to file a financing statement, or
the first to perfect its security interest (whichever is earlier). Tim and Lisa were the first to
file a financing statement (April 2010 v. no filing date), and they were the first to perfect their
security interest (filing in April 2010 v. possession in September 2010). So Tim and Lisa have
the senior claim, and, as before, Ethan should award $15,000 to his parents and the $5,000
balance to Grace. For these reasons, **Answer (A) is the correct answer.**

Possession of some types of collateral (e.g., stock certificates) may bestow on the possessor
a superior claim over a security interest perfected by an earlier filing. But possessing a
piano will not trigger any such result, so **Answer (B) is incorrect.**

Priority rules that turn on knowledge or notice raise difficult proof issues and may reward
ignorance, which explains (at least in part) why the drafters of Article 9 declined to adopt
such rules. Whether Grace knew of the prior loan or the earlier security interest is
irrelevant in this priority dispute (and appreciate that Grace could easily have learned of the
prior claim by ordering a UCC search against Meredith that should have disclosed the filing
by Tim and Lisa). So **Answer (C) is incorrect.**

Answer (D) is an incorrect answer. Security interests that arise after a previous creditor
has filed its financing statement can be perfected by possession (or filing or some other
method permitted by Article 9). Those later security interests may not enjoy priority, but

they are protected in at least two ways. First, a junior claim may move up the priority ladder as the earlier claim is paid in full. Second, a junior claim may be entitled to receive proceeds that remain after the earlier claim is paid in full.

95.   As of the petition date (October 1, 2015), the security interest held by Grace enjoys priority over the competing security interest held by her parents. Financing statements are effective for five years (*see* § 9-515(a)). Tim and Lisa filed their original financing statement in April 2006, so its effectiveness expired in April 2015 unless they *timely* filed a continuation statement. A continuation statement must be filed within the six-month period preceding the expiration of the five-year period of effectiveness (*see* § 9-515(d)). Tim and Lisa filed their continuation statement in June 2015, *after* the five-year period had recently expired. Therefore, notwithstanding the fact that the continuation statement has been filed and gives notice, the untimely filing is ineffective (*see* § 9-510(c)). Therefore, Tim and Lisa are unperfected both prospectively and, as against Grace as a "purchaser of the collateral for value," retroactively (*see* § 9-515(c) and definitions of "purchaser" and "purchase" in § 1-201). Grace remains perfected by her original filing in December 2010 because its five-year period of effectiveness has not expired by the bankruptcy petition date. Grace wins the dispute with her parents as of the petition date because a perfected security interest is senior to an unperfected security interest (*see* § 9-322(a)(2)).

96.   **Answer (A) is the correct answer.** MegaHealth is a Delaware corporation and, therefore, a registered organization under section 9-102(a)(70). Section 9-301(1) tells a secured party to file its financing statement where the debtor is located, and section 9-307(e) tells the secured party that a registered organization is located in the state of its creation. Therefore, MegaHealth's creditors must file their financing statements in Delaware (state of incorporation), rather than Washington (state of chief executive office). First Bank filed in the correct state, and Second Bank did not. MegaHealth acquired the Item in February, before it authenticated the security agreement in favor of First Bank, so the omission of an after-acquired property clause from the security agreement is not fatal in this question. First Bank has a perfected security interest in the Item, and Second Bank does not. This means that First Bank wins the dispute under section 9-322(a)(2), which favors perfected claims over unperfected claims. Therefore, **Answer (A) is the correct answer.**

       Answer (B) is incorrect because Second Bank does indeed have a security interest in the Item. Second Bank filed its financing statement in the wrong state, leaving it unperfected. But the security interest remains enforceable.

       Answer (C) is incorrect because it erroneously states that First Bank's interest is unperfected and Second Bank's interest is perfected. The status of each respective claim is just the opposite.

       Answer (D) is incorrect. If both security interests are unperfected (which is not the case), then Article 9 favors the first claim to attach, rather than declare a "tie" between the unperfected claims.

97.   **Answer (C) is the correct answer.** MegaHealth authenticated First Bank's security agreement in April. MegaHealth acquired the Item in July. First Bank's security agreement failed to include an after-acquired property clause, so its collateral does not include this Item. First Bank has no security interest in it. For reasons explained in the previous answer, Second Bank filed in the wrong state, leaving it with an enforceable, but unperfected,

security interest in MegaHealth's equipment (including this Item). Therefore, what appears to be a two-creditor dispute is actually a one-creditor dispute. Second Bank is the only creditor that can claim an enforceable security interest in the Item, **making Answer (C) the correct answer.**

Answer (A) is incorrect because filing a financing statement first, and in the correct state, will not perfect a security interest that never attaches.

Answer (B) is incorrect because the omission of an after-acquired property clause from the collateral description prevented First Bank's security interest from attaching to this Item.

Answer (D) is incorrect because First Bank has no security interest in the Item, and Second Bank has an unperfected security interest in the Item.

98.   Even if the second security agreement again fails to include an after-acquired property clause, the security agreement will be effective to create an enforceable security interest in equipment acquired by MegaHealth prior to its authentication of the agreement. Therefore, MegaHealth's authentication of a security agreement in November will create an enforceable security interest in a piece of equipment that it acquired earlier in July. The omission of the after-acquired property clause from the financing statement is irrelevant (*see* §§ 9-204 cmt. 7; 9-502 cmt. 2), so First Bank's filing in Delaware in April perfects its security interest in the Item when MegaHealth acquires the Item in July. Now First Bank wins the dispute because its perfected security interest defeats Second Bank's unperfected security interest under section 9-322(a)(2).

Hopefully this problem illustrates that a subsequent creditor cannot draw absolute comfort from the omission of an after-acquired property clause from a security agreement previously authenticated by the debtor in favor of another creditor who also filed first. The omission is readily cured by a second (or third or fourth) security agreement that breathes new life into the earlier filing.

99.   **Answer (D) is the correct answer.** The general priority rule used to resolve disputes between two secured creditors with perfected security interests is the "first to file or perfect, whichever is earlier" rule under section 9-322(a)(1). A creditor's knowledge is irrelevant (it is too difficult and costly to prove and can reward ignorance), so **Answer (C) is incorrect.** And both creditors have a perfected security interest, so the "first to attach" rule in section 9-322(a)(3) does not apply, **making Answer (A) an incorrect answer.** Alpha Bank perfected its security interest on May 31, when Debtor authenticated the security agreement and Alpha Bank gave value (Debtor had previously acquired rights in the equipment on May 29, and Alpha Bank had previously filed its financing statement on May 23). Omega Bank perfected its security interest on May 29, when Debtor acquired rights in the equipment (Omega Bank had previously given value on May 20 and filed its financing statement on May 27, and Debtor had previously authenticated the security agreement on May 20). Although Omega Bank's perfection date of May 29 is earlier than Alpha Bank's perfection date of May 31, Alpha Bank's security interest enjoys priority because its filing date of May 23 is earlier than Omega Bank's filing date of May 27. Therefore, **Answer (D) is the correct answer and Answer (B) is an incorrect answer.** The result is justified because Alpha Bank was the first party to announce to the world (via its financing statement) that it might be claiming an interest in Debtor's equipment. Omega Bank could have won the filing race, had it filed its financing statement no later than when it funded the $1 million loan on May 20.

100. **Answer (C) is the correct answer.** The four answers require you to determine how many of the secured parties can claim an interest in the check. Bonnie paid for the furniture with a check, so the collateral started out as inventory and created cash proceeds in the form of an instrument. (The furniture had been part of Odyssey's inventory for several months, negating any possibility that the furniture itself represents proceeds of an account, a deposit account, or otherwise.) The collateral in this question is never an account or a deposit account, so neither First Finance nor AmeriBank has any claim to the check as a proceed of its original collateral. This is a one-party dispute that Midway Bank wins because the check represents proceeds of inventory in which it can claim a perfected security interest. *See* §§ 9-315(a)(2) (attachment), 9-315(c) (temporary perfection), 9-315(d)(2) (continued perfection), 9-102(a)(9) (definition of "cash proceeds"). Therefore, **Answer (C) is the correct answer and Answers (A), (B), and (D) are incorrect answers.**

101. **Answer (A) is the correct answer.** Now the collateral path looks like this: inventory, then an instrument, then a deposit account. In the absence of any account, First Finance has no claim yet, making this a two-party dispute between Midway Bank (inventory and its proceeds) and AmeriBank (deposit account). Therefore, **Answer (B) and Answer (D) are incorrect.** The deposit account is a "proceeds only" account, so Midway Bank has an enforceable security interest in the $3,500 credit entry under section 9-315(a)(2) that is automatically perfected for twenty days under section 9-315(c). The perfection continues thereafter under section 9-315(d)(2) because a check and a deposit account are examples of "cash proceeds" as defined in section 9-102(a)(9). So Midway Bank has a perfected security interest in the $3,500 credit entry. AmeriBank also has a security interest in the $3,500 credit entry (and the entire deposit account). Its enforceable security interest is perfected by "control" under section 9-104(a)(1), as AmeriBank is the financial institution that maintains the deposit account (and AmeriBank's failure to file a financing statement is a red herring, since section 9-312(b)(1) states that "a security interest in a deposit account [as original collateral] may be perfected only by control"). If the general priority rule used to resolve disputes between two perfected security interests (section 9-322(a)(1)) applied, Midway Bank would have priority because its filing date in March is earlier than AmeriBank's perfection date in September. But the opening language of section 9-322(a) warns that other priority rules in section 9-322 may apply, and subsection (f)(1) states that subsection (a) is subject to priority rules found elsewhere in "this part" of Article 9 (e.g., Part 3, or any rule codified as section 9-3xx). One of those other rules is section 9-327. Under section 9-327(1), AmeriBank's security interest in the $3,500 credit entry enjoys priority because, with respect to conflicting security interests in a deposit account, a security interest perfected by control enjoys priority over a competing security interest not perfected by control (e.g., filing). For these reasons, **Answer (A) is the correct answer.**

Answer (C) is an incorrect answer. Midway Bank is perfected for twenty days following the deposit (*see* § 9-315(c)) and thereafter (*see* § 9-315(d)(2)). Even so, it will not enjoy priority over AmeriBank's competing security interest that is perfected by control, even during the twenty-day period following the deposit.

102. **Answer (C) is the correct answer.** The credit card receivable is an "account" under section 9-102(a)(2)(vii). Therefore, First Finance has a perfected security interest in the credit card receivable because its collateral includes accounts, its loan documentation includes an after-acquired property clause, and First Finance has filed a financing statement. Midway Bank has a perfected security interest in the credit card receivable on a proceeds theory under

section 9-315(c) and (d)(1). The problem does not yet involve a deposit account, so AmeriBank has no interest in the receivable. This is a two-party dispute, so **Answers (B) and (D) are incorrect.** The general priority rule of section 9-322(a)(1) (and, with respect to any proceeds, (b)(1)) resolves this two-party dispute. Under those rules, the security interest of First Finance enjoys priority because First Finance filed its financing statement on March 29, before Midway Bank filed its financing statement on June 13. For these reasons, **Answer (C) is the correct answer and Answer (A) is an incorrect answer.**

This question illustrates that a party such as Midway Bank can be the first party to perfect a security interest in inventory by filing, and yet lose a priority dispute to an earlier filer who claims a security interest in a different type of collateral (e.g., accounts) that may be deemed a proceed of the inventory. Therefore, a secured party must be concerned about previous filings, whether or not those filings specifically mention the type of collateral in which the subsequent filer is claiming as its original collateral.

Furthermore, appreciate that First Finance may enjoy priority in this two-party dispute today, but it will lose priority in a three-party dispute if and when Odyssey receives payment of the receivable, and that payment finds its way into the "proceeds only" deposit account maintained by AmeriBank. At that time, AmeriBank's security interest (perfected by control) enjoys priority over the "proceeds" claims of First Finance (and Midway Bank) under section 9-327(1).

103. Midway Bank is the only creditor with an enforceable interest in the contract, so it will win this one-party dispute. The title reservation clause creates a security interest in favor of Midway Bank. *See* § 1-201(b)(35) (penultimate sentence of definition of "security interest"). This clause, together with the provisions that address Bonnie's monetary obligations, combine to create "chattel paper" under section 9-102(a)(11). The collateral has gone from furniture (inventory) to a proceed in the form of a contract (chattel paper). The transaction has failed to create an account or a deposit account, so First Finance and AmeriBank never have an enforceable security interest in the contract. Midway Bank does so, though, on a proceeds theory. And its interest in the chattel paper is perfected not just for twenty days under section 9-315(c) but also thereafter under section 9-315(d)(1).

As before, though, Midway Bank will lose a priority dispute with AmeriBank if Bonnie honors her monetary obligations with payments that find their way into the "proceeds only" deposit account.

And, as you will learn, Midway Bank may lose a priority dispute with a party that has purchased, and taken possession of, the contract. *See generally* § 9-330(a), (b).

104. **Answer (B) is the correct answer.** The accounts and chattel paper contracts resulted from inventory sales, so FNB can claim an enforceable security interest in them as proceeds under sections 9-203(f) and 9-315(a)(2). The security interest is perfected for twenty days under section 9-315(c) and thereafter under section 9-315(d)(1). ZinnCo's sale of accounts and chattel paper falls within the scope of Article 9 (*see* § 109(a)(3)), making ZinnCo a debtor and Markell Finance a secured party (*see* § 9-102(a)(28)(B) (defining "debtor"), 9-102(a)(72)(D) (defining "secured party")). Markell Finance has a security interest in the accounts and chattel paper that it has purchased. *See* § 1-201(b)(35) (defining "security interest"). FNB's perfected security interest in the accounts enjoys priority over Markell Finance's unperfected security interest under section 9-322(a)(2). (Markell Finance, which never filed a financing statement, also loses even if its security interest in the accounts is

automatically perfected under section 9-309(2) because FNB's filing date of February 15 is earlier than Markell Finance's perfection date in June.) But under section 9-330(a), Markell Finance, a purchaser of the chattel paper contracts, has priority over FNB's perfected security interest claimed merely as proceeds of inventory. Markell Finance acquired the contracts in the ordinary course of its business, took possession of the contracts, and gave "new value" under section 9-102(a)(57) in the form of $14,000. Furthermore, the facts do not indicate that the contracts included any type of legend indicating they had been assigned to FNB or any other party, and its knowledge of FNB's filed financing statement should not preclude Markell Finance from satisfying the requirement of good faith as defined in section 1-201(b)(20) (*see* § 9-330 cmts. 5 and 6). In summary, then, FNB enjoys priority in the accounts, and Markell Finance has priority in the contracts. Therefore, **Answer (B) is the correct answer. Answers (A), (C), and (D) are incorrect** because they misstate one or both priority dispute results.

105. **Answer (C) is the correct answer.** Trinity Finance's security interest in the piano became perfected on October 1, when MegaChurch acquired the piano (the security agreement was in place on September 1, Trinity Finance had given value on September 1, and Trinity Finance had filed its financing statement on September 10). Salem Bank's security interest in the deposit account was perfected by control under section 9-104(a)(1) on May 1. It can claim an enforceable security interest in the piano under section 9-315(a)(2) as an "identifiable proceed" of the funds in the deposit account. Therefore, **Answer (A) is incorrect.** Salem Bank's security interest in the piano is perfected for at least twenty days from the date of attachment under section 9-315(c), which runs through the dispute resolution date of October 10. Therefore, **Answer (B) is incorrect.** So as of October 10, both Trinity Finance and Salem Bank have a perfected security interest in the piano. Under the general "first to file or perfect" rule of section 9-322(a)(1), Salem Bank has priority because its perfection date of May 1 is earlier than Trinity Finance's filing date of September 10 and perfection date of October 1. But by its own opening language, section 9-322 is subject to other priority rules. The rule that applies to this dispute is found in section 9-322(d). Under that section, a creditor's security interest in proceeds of a deposit account does not enjoy priority if another creditor filed first against those proceeds. This means that Salem Bank's security interest in the piano (claimed as a proceed of MegaChurch's deposit account) is junior to the competing security interest claimed by Trinity Finance, which filed first against MegaChurch's equipment. Therefore, **Answer (C) is the correct answer and Answer (D) is an incorrect answer.**

To avoid this result, a party (such as Salem Bank) that takes a security interest in a deposit account to which the debtor continues to enjoy withdrawal rights should (i) promptly file a financing statement against any assets that the debtor might acquire with funds drawn from the deposit account and (ii) review the filing records to assure itself that no other creditor has filed a financing statement against the debtor. For additional reading, see section 9-322 cmts. 7, 8, and 9.

106. **Answer (D) is the correct answer.** Salem Bank's filing on October 18 extends its automatic perfection beyond the twenty-day period of section 9-315(c) to the dispute resolution date of November 1. *See* § 9-315(d)(3). But Trinity Finance continues to enjoy priority under section 9-322(d) for reasons explained in the previous answer. Therefore, **Answer (D) is correct and**

Answer (C) is incorrect.

Trinity Finance has an enforceable security interest in the current and after-acquired equipment. Its financing statement describes the collateral in a manner that omits any reference to after-acquired equipment. This is a red herring, though, as the after-acquired property clause need not be mentioned in the financing statement. *See* §§ 9-204 cmt. 7; 9-502 cmt. 2. Therefore, **Answer (A) is incorrect.**

A secured party may violate what one of your authors refers to as "the clearly stupid rule" if it permits the debtor to withdraw funds from a deposit account that serves as collateral. Nevertheless, Article 9 makes clear that a secured party can have "control" over the deposit account, even if the debtor continues to enjoy access to the funds therein. *See* § 9-104(b). Therefore, **Answer (B) is incorrect.**

107. **Answer (A) is the correct answer.** If the judge relies on the general priority rule of section 9-322(a)(1), then she should rule in favor of Polk Finance because its filing date (2009) is earlier than Albany Bank's filing date (2010). But if she does so, she would be wrong. Section 9-322(a) is subject to section 9-322(f), which states that priority rules found elsewhere in sections 9-301 through 9-342 (part 3 of Article 9, or "this part") may control. One of those rules is section 9-325(a), which states: "[A] security interest created by a debtor [AlphaCorp] is subordinate to a security interest in the same collateral created by another person [OmegaTech] if: (1) the debtor [AlphaCorp] acquired the collateral subject to the security interest created by the other person [OmegaTech]; (2) the security interest created by the other person [OmegaTech] was perfected when the debtor [AlphaCorp] acquired the collateral; and (3) there is no period thereafter when the security interest is unperfected." Clause (1) is satisfied because Albany Bank's security interest survives the unauthorized sale under sections 9-201 and 9-315(a), and AlphaCorp's acquisition does not terminate the security interest under section 9-320(a) (AlphaCorp is not a buyer in the ordinary course of business because the Item in OmegaTech's hands is equipment, not inventory) or section 9-320(b) (neither AlphaCorp nor OmegaTech hold the Item as a consumer good, and Albany Bank has filed a financing statement). Therefore, **Answer (D) is incorrect.** Clause (2) is met because Albany Bank's financing statement remained effective at the time of sale and, under section 9-507(a), thereafter. Therefore, **Answer (C) is incorrect.** And section 9-325(b) applies to subordinate the security interest of Polk Finance to the security interest of Albany Bank because otherwise Polk Finance would enjoy priority under section 9-322(a). For these reasons, **Answer (A) is the correct answer and Answer (B) is an incorrect answer.**

The result should not be surprising. It is an instance of *"nemo dat"*: a person can give only what it has. If AlphaCorp acquires the Item subject to the security interest held by Albany Bank, then AlphaCorp's creditors (e.g., Polk Finance) also take the Item subject to the security interest held by Albany Bank. Perhaps rephrased, a secured party can only take a security interest in the limited, and possibly encumbered, rights held by its debtor.

108. Polk Finance enjoys priority under the revised facts. Under the original facts, both OmegaTech (the selling debtor) and AlphaCorp (the buying debtor) were located in Delaware, the state in which their respective creditors filed financing statements. Under the revised facts, AlphaCorp is a Texas corporation and, therefore, deemed located in that state for filing purposes. *See* §§ 9-301(1), 9-307(e). Albany Bank must be concerned, then, with what effect this difference in jurisdiction might have on the continued effectiveness of its

Delaware filing against OmegaTech. The answer is found in section 9-316(a)(3), which continues the effectiveness of the Delaware filing for one year from the transfer date. OmegaTech sold the Item to AlphaCorp on August 10, 2011, more than a year before the dispute resolution date of September 1, 2012. The facts do not suggest that Albany Bank filed a new financing statement in Texas, so its security interest in the Item has become unperfected prospectively and, as against Polk Finance as "a purchaser of the collateral for value," retroactively. *See* § 9-316(b). Albany Bank can no longer navigate section 9-325(a)(3), so the protections afforded by section 9-325 (as under the original facts) are no longer available. No other exception to the general rule applies, so Polk Finance and its perfected security interest enjoy priority under section 9-322(a)(2) over Albany Bank and its unperfected security interest.

109. **Answer (C) is the correct answer.** A security interest in investment property can be perfected by filing. § 9-312(a). The general rule on filing location is found in section 9-301(1), which tells the secured party to file its financing statement where the debtor is located. But the opening language of section 9-301(1) defers to rules found in sections 9-303 through 9-306, if applicable. Section 9-305 applies in this question because the collateral is investment property. Subsection (c)(1) states the same filing rule found in section 9-301(1): file where the debtor is located. In this problem, BAMCO is the debtor. It is a corporate entity and, therefore, a registered organization. A registered organization is located in its state of creation. § 9-307(e). BAMCO is incorporated under Delaware law, so it is deemed located in Delaware. Therefore, a secured party that seeks to perfect its security interest in BAMCO's investment property by filing must file its financing statement in Delaware. **Answer (A) is incorrect**, then, because it erroneously suggests that a filing in Texas (the state in which Zee-Con, the issuer of the investment property, is located) is effective. Answer (B) correctly identifies Delaware as the place to file. But if First Bank does not file in Delaware until August 9, it will lose the priority dispute to an earlier filer under the general "first to file or perfect" rule of section 9-322(a)(1). Second Bank did file its financing statement earlier, on August 8. So **Answer (B) is an incorrect answer.**

Answer (C) implicitly, but correctly, suggests that First Bank can perfect its security interest in the Zee-Con stock certificate by taking delivery of it. *See* § 9-313(a). If the stock certificate was issued in bearer form (issued to "bearer" or in blank), then First Bank would have "control" of the certificate under section 8-106(a) by taking delivery of it. Perfection by control trumps perfection by filing. *See* § 9-328(1). But the facts state that the certificate is in registered form. Taking delivery of a certificate in registered form, without more, does not give First Bank control. *See* § 8-106(b) (requiring delivery plus either indorsement or registration). So it is possible, without knowing more facts, that First Bank does not have control of the Zee-Con stock certificate even though it has taken delivery. And without control, it cannot invoke the priority rule of section 9-328(1). Even so, though, First Bank enjoys priority under section 9-328(5). That section states: "A security interest in a certificated security in registered form which is perfected by taking delivery . . . and not by control . . . has priority over a conflicting security interest perfected by a method other than control." Second Bank perfected by filing, not by control. Therefore, the rule applies and First Bank enjoys priority, **making Answer (C) the correct answer.**

Many security agreements prohibit the debtor from granting additional security interests in the collateral. The debtor may violate that provision, triggering a default that permits the secured party to exercise its rights and remedies against the debtor and the collateral. Nevertheless, contract defaults do not affect the priority rules of Article 9. Therefore, **Answer (D) is an incorrect answer.**

110. **Answer (B) is the correct answer.** Lender's search against the debtor's current legal name of "Houston Healthcare Corp." has failed to reveal Bank's previous filing against "HealthNet Corp." Therefore, under section 9-506(c), the debtor's name change has caused Bank's financing statement to become seriously misleading. Nevertheless, the filing against "HealthNet Corp." remains effective to perfect a security interest in equipment acquired by the debtor (i) prior to the name change and (ii) within four months after the name change (§ 9-507(c)) — even if the perfected or unperfected status is examined (as in this problem) on a date long after the four-month period has concluded. The debtor acquired Item #1 on May 10, within four months after the name change on March 15, so the original filing remains effective to perfect Bank's security interest in Item #1. The debtor acquired Item #2 on July 20 and Item #3 on September 18. These two dates fall outside the four-month period that concluded on or about July 15. Therefore, Bank's filing does not perfect its security interest in those two items. Bank remains perfected in Item #1 by its filing, so it has priority in Item #1 under the "first to file or perfect" rule of section 9-322(a)(1) because it filed in January, and Lender filed in August. But Lender has priority in Items #2 and #3 under the "perfected beats unperfected" rule of section 9-322(a)(2), because Lender's filing perfected its security interest in all of the equipment, but Bank's security interest in Items #2 and #3 is unperfected. The debtor's name change has rendered the filing seriously misleading and those two items were acquired by the debtor more than four months after the name change. These priority results are correctly stated in Answer (B), **making Answer (B) the correct answer and Answers (A), (C), and (D) incorrect answers.**

111. The court should award priority to Matthew. The court must address whether Esther's relocation from Texas to Arizona may have had an adverse impact on the continued effectiveness of Matthew's filing in Texas. Section 9-316(a)(2) addresses Matthew's concern, stating that the Texas filing remains effective for four months following Esther's relocation. Esther moved to Phoenix sometime in February 2011. The dispute date is May 20, 2011, a date that falls within the four-month period. Therefore, as of the dispute date, Matthew's filing in Texas remains effective to perfect his security interest in the chess sets. Because he filed in 2010, before Shelby filed in 2011, the court should award priority to Matthew under the general "first to file or perfect" rule of section 9-322(a)(1).

112. The court should award priority to Shelby. The dispute date of September 1, 2011, falls outside the four-month period that commenced when Esther moved from Texas to Arizona in February 2011. As a result, the court should conclude, under section 9-316(b), that Matthew's security interest has become unperfected prospectively and, as against Shelby as "a purchaser of the collateral for value," retroactively. Shelby remains perfected. The court should award priority to Shelby under the "perfected beats unperfected" rule of section 9-322(a)(2), a result that is not affected by Shelby's knowledge of Matthew's prior loan and his Texas filing.

113.   **Answer (C) is the correct answer.** Because the second piano is used by Ellie's family for personal use more than 50% of the time, the piano is a consumer good under section 9-102(a)(23). Ellie's parents can attempt to claim an enforceable security interest in the second piano through the after-acquired property clause in their security agreement. But section 9-204(b)(1) negates the reach of an after-acquired property clause to a consumer good unless the debtor acquires the consumer good within ten days after the secured party has given any value. (Presumably the limitation has the intended purpose, at least in part, of discouraging overreaching, or possible predatory practices, by a secured party who seeks to claim a property interest in a consumer's goods against which the secured party advanced no funds and which have little value to anyone other than the consumer (think "hostage value" rather than "commercial value")). Under the facts, Ellie's parents funded the $4,000 loan last July, but Ellie did not buy the second piano until this year, creating more than a ten-day gap between the purchase date of the piano and the funding date of the loan (and the facts do not suggest that Ellie's parents have given any other value). This means that Ellie's parents cannot rely on the after-acquired property clause, without which they cannot claim an enforceable security interest in the second piano. The facts state that Dealer "retained an enforceable security interest in the piano," so it wins this one-party dispute, **making Answer (C) the correct answer, and Answers (A), (B), and (D) incorrect answers.**

Because Dealer is claiming a PMSI in a piano that is a consumer good, its failure to file a financing statement is not fatal. Instead, Dealer can claim automatic perfection of its security interest under section 9-309(1). But Dealer's perfection, or lack thereof, becomes meaningless if Ellie's parents cannot claim an enforceable security interest in the piano. For the same reason, any discussion of the superpriority rule of section 9-324(a) is unnecessary.

114.   If the percentage breakdown between personal use and business use changes from 55:45 to 50:50, then Ellie's parents enjoy priority. To be a consumer good under section 9-102(a)(23), the piano must be used "primarily" for personal use. If the percentages of personal use and business use are each an identical 50%, then neither use is a "primary" use. This means that the piano is equipment (defined in section 9-102(a)(33) as a good that is not something else). Because the piano is equipment (rather than a consumer good), Ellie's parents need not worry about section 9-204(b) and now can rely on the after-acquired property clause (and their financing statement) to claim an enforceable (and perfected) security interest in the second piano. But switching the label on the second piano from "consumer good" to "equipment" also means that Dealer cannot rely on automatic perfection of its PMSI under section 9-309(1). And because Dealer no longer has possession of the piano and has not filed a financing statement, its PMSI is unperfected. Therefore, Ellie's parents have priority under section 9-322(a)(2), which favors perfected security interests over unperfected security interests.

115.   **Answer (A) is the correct answer.** Because Ellie's primary use is a business use, the piano

is equipment. Therefore, Dealer must perfect its nonpossessory security interest by timely filing a financing statement if it hopes to claim superpriority under section 9-324(a). Dealer has filed a financing statement, but the filing names "ES Music Studio" as the debtor. The law does not treat an individual and his or her sole proprietorship as separate legal entities. Ellie is the debtor, and Dealer should have used her individual name on the filing, as trade names and dba's are insufficient. *See* §§ 9-502(a)(1), 9-503(a)(4)(A), 9-503(c). Dealer's failure to correctly identify the debtor means that its filing is ineffective to perfect its security interest in the piano, leaving Dealer unable to claim superpriority under section 9-324(a). Therefore, Ellie's parents, who hold a perfected security interest, enjoy priority over Dealer, which has an unperfected security interest. *See* § 9-322(a)(2). For these reasons, **Answer (A) is the correct answer.**

Answer (B) and Answer (C) are incorrect because they erroneously suggest that the timing of Dealer's filing may dictate priority. That may indeed be true, if the filing is otherwise effective. But Dealer failed to correctly identify the debtor on its filing, so the timing of its filing is irrelevant.

Answer (D) is incorrect because Ellie's parents, rather than Dealer, enjoy priority.

116. **Answer (D) is the correct answer.** BizCorp can claim the superpriority afforded to equipment sellers by section 9-324 if, and only if, its security interest is perfected no later than twenty days after ZinnCo took possession of the photocopiers. ZinnCo took possession of the photocopiers in March, but BizCorp did not file its financing statement until July 17. It appears, then, that BizCorp's filing is not timely. But as illustrated by the last paragraph of Official Comment 3 to section 9-324, the twenty-day period did not commence in this transaction until the photocopier became "collateral." That occurred in July, when the parties terminated the lease and entered into a secured transaction. Therefore, the filing is timely (**making Answer (C) an incorrect answer**), and BizCorp enjoys superpriority under section 9-324(a). For these reasons, **Answer (D) is the correct answer.**

Answer (A) is incorrect because BizCorp enjoys superpriority under the non-temporal rule of section 9-324(a) (perhaps rephrased, "the second in time can be the first in line").

Answer (B) is incorrect because BizCorp does have a PMSI in the photocopiers. ZinnCo did acquire a property interest in the photocopiers as a lessee. But it acquired additional property rights (e.g., ownership rights, and possessory rights that now extend beyond the original lease term) when it agreed to purchase the equipment on credit from BizCorp, who is willing to extend seller financing. Therefore, notwithstanding that it follows a lease transaction, the secured transaction creates a PMSI in favor of BizCorp.

117. **Answer (A) is the correct answer.** Dealer has a PMSI in the machine. Dealer perfected its PMSI by filing a financing statement on August 2, which is within twenty days of the possession date (July 15). True, it is not within twenty days of the attachment date (July 2), but section 9-324(a) uses the possession date, rather than the attachment date (perhaps because the former is easier to determine and subject to less debate and potentially misleading manipulation). Therefore, Dealer's filing is timely, and it enjoyed superpriority in the machine under section 9-324(a) (**making Answer (C) an incorrect answer**). That section also extends the superpriority to identifiable proceeds (**making Answer (D) an incorrect answer**). Therefore, assuming that the $150,000 remains identifiable as proceeds from the sale of the machine, Dealer has the senior claim, **making Answer (A) the correct answer.**

Answer (B) is an incorrect answer because section 9-322(a), by its own terms, defers to other priority rules, including the superpriority rule in section 9-324(a).

118. **Answer (B) is the correct answer.** Under section 9-324(a), a PMSI in non-inventory enjoys priority over a conflicting security interest if the PMSI is perfected "when the debtor receives possession of the collateral or within twenty days thereafter." Debtor obtained possession of the equipment on June 5, but Dealer did not file its financing statement until June 29. Dealer's failure to timely file its financing statement prevents it from invoking section 9-324(b), leaving Lender with priority under section 9-322(a) as the earlier filer. Therefore, **Answer (B) is the correct answer and Answer (A) is incorrect.**

Dealer provided seller financing for the equipment, which secures payment of its purchase price. Dealer, then, had a PMSI in the equipment under section 9-103. Answers (C) and (D) suggest, though, that Dealer's failure to timely file its financing statement may have destroyed its PMSI, leaving Dealer with a generic security interest. That is not so. PMSI status is dictated by section 9-103, not when (or if) the PMSI is timely (or ever) perfected. Dealer's security interest continues to remain a PMSI, notwithstanding its untimely filing and lack of superpriority. Therefore, **Answer (C) and Answer (D) are incorrect answers.**

Answer (D) also is incorrect because a filing, even a filing that is not timely under section 9-324(a), is effective to perfect a security interest.

119. **Answer (B) is the correct answer.** (As a matter of review, recall that consignments — as that term is defined in section 9-102(a)(20) — fall within the scope of Article 9. *See* § 9-109(a)(4).) In this consignment transaction, ToyCo is the consignor, and the Zoo is the consignee. *See* § 9-102(a)(19) (defining "consignee"), 9-102(a)(21) (defining "consignor"). ToyCo's property interest in the consigned goods is a "security interest" under section 1-201(b)(35). That security interest also is a PMSI under section 9-103(d). Therefore, if ToyCo wants to enjoy superpriority over a competing claim held by Lender, an earlier filer, ToyCo must comply with the requirements of section 9-324(b) and (c). Section 9-324(b)(1) affords superpriority to the purchase-money creditor only if the PMSI is perfected when the debtor receives possession of the inventory. ToyCo, then, must file its financing statement before delivering the toy animals to the Zoo, **making Answer (B) the correct answer.**

Article 9 contemplates that consigned goods do become part of the consignee's inventory and may be subject to security interests. Therefore, **Answer (A) is incorrect.**

Unlike section 9-324(a), which affords superpriority to non-inventory creditors, section 9-324(b) and (c) afford no post-delivery grace period for inventory creditors. Therefore, **Answer (C) is incorrect.**

Even though Article 9 bestows purchase-money status on the toy animals, that status alone is insufficient for perfection or priority. The inventory creditor must file a financing statement to perfect its security interest, and it must do so before delivering the goods to the debtor if it hopes to enjoy priority over an earlier filer. **Therefore, Answer (D) is incorrect.**

120. **Answer (B) is the correct answer.** As noted in the previous answer, if ToyCo wants to enjoy superpriority over a competing claim held by Lender, an earlier filer, ToyCo must comply with the requirements of section 9-324(b) and (c). Section 9-324(b)(2) obligates the purchase-money creditor to send notice of its PMSI to a previous filer, **making Answer (D) an**

incorrect answer. Additionally, section 9-324(b)(3) offers superpriority only if the previous filer receives the notice before the debtor receives possession of the consigned goods. Therefore, ToyCo will enjoy priority over Lender only if Lender receives ToyCo's notice before the Zoo receives the toy animals, **making Answer (B) the correct answer.**

Answer (A) is true, but it fails to recognize that *receipt* must be timely, **making Answer (A) an incorrect answer.**

Answer (C) is incorrect because the notice must be received before the goods are delivered; there is no post-delivery grace period.

121.   **Answer (C) is the correct answer.** ToyCo will never enjoy priority in proceeds generated by sales of the toy animals unless it first enjoys superpriority in the toy animals themselves. As the previous two answers state, ToyCo cannot enjoy superpriority in the toy animals unless it satisfies time-sensitive filing and notice obligations. Because it is possible that ToyCo may not satisfy both of these duties, it is impossible to conclude that ToyCo will always win a priority dispute in proceeds of any form, **making Answer (A) and Answer (B) incorrect answers.** If ToyCo did satisfy its filing and notice duties and enjoyed superpriority in the toy animals, then section 9-324(b) extends the superpriority to "identifiable cash proceeds [that] are received [by the debtor] on or before the delivery of the inventory to a buyer." A check is an example of a "cash proceed" under section 9-102(a)(9) (as is an electronic receivable created by swiping a debit card), so it is possible, although not a certainty, that ToyCo might enjoy priority in proceeds consisting of a check. Rephrased, Lender will not win a priority dispute in cash proceeds consisting of a check if ToyCo enjoyed superpriority in the toy animals. Therefore, **Answer (D) is incorrect.** Proceeds that consist of credit card receivables are "accounts" under section 9-102(a)(2)(vii) (and "noncash proceeds" under section 9-102(a)(58)), and section 9-324(b) never extends superpriority to accounts. Whether or not ToyCo enjoys superpriority in the toy animals, its superpriority will not extend to proceeds generated by the sales of toy animals to patrons who pay by using a credit card. Lender (whose collateral includes accounts) will always win that priority dispute, **making Answer (C) the correct answer.**

122.   **Answer (B) is the correct answer.** Both Dealer and Martin can claim a purchase-money security interest in the freezers under section 9-103(a) and (b)(1). Dealer has a PMSI for the 25% down payment (seller financing), and Martin has a PMSI for the remaining 75% of the purchase price (third-party financing). In the hands of BAM, Inc., the freezers are equipment. And both Dealer (July 2) and Martin (June 30) perfected their security interests in the freezers by filing financing statements no later than twenty days after the restaurant took possession of the freezers (June 20). As between Dealer and Martin, Dealer's security interest enjoys priority under section 9-324(g)(1), which favors the seller over a third-party financer. *See* § 9-324 cmt. 13. So Dealer's unpaid debt is repaid first ($20,000), with the remaining $40,000 paid to Martin (to be applied against her $80,000 debt). This result is found in **Answer (B), making it the correct answer and Answers (A), (C), and (D) incorrect answers.**

123.   As in the previous question, this fact pattern involves competing purchase-money security interests. Fidelity Bank, regardless of whether it files on June 27 or July 1, joins Dealer (July 2) as a party entitled to superpriority under section 9-324(a). Neither purchase-money creditor is the seller, however, so section 9-324(g)(1) does not apply. Instead, subsection (g)(2) applies and directs the reader to the general priority rule of section 9-322(a). Under

section 9-322(a)(1), Fidelity Bank enjoys priority if its filing date is June 27 (earlier than Martin's filing date of June 30), but Martin enjoys priority if Fidelity Bank does not file until July 1 (later than Martin's filing date of June 30). Under the first scenario, the liquidator should distribute the first $20,000 to Fidelity Finance and the remaining $40,000 to Martin. But under the second scenario, the liquidator should distribute the entire $60,000 to Martin.

124.   **Answer (A) is the correct answer.** BigBank has an enforceable security interest in the furnishings through its after-acquired property clause. That interest is perfected by BigBank's filing. Because BigBank filed its financing statement two years ago, long before FurniCo filed this year, FurniCo will not enjoy priority in any of the furnishings or proceeds therefrom unless FurniCo's security interest is a purchase-money security interest. Prior to the enactment of revised Article 9, some courts held that the inclusion of after-acquired property clauses and future advance clauses destroyed, or transformed, a PMSI into a non-PMSI because cross-collateralization upset the traditional one-to-one relationship between a unit of collateral and its unpaid purchase price. Some courts disagreed, concluding that a security interest could be both a PMSI and a non-PMSI. As revised, Article 9 adopts this latter approach, often referred to as the "dual status rule." *See* § 9-103(f) and cmt. 7.

Under the dual status rule, all of the furnishings secure FurniCo's unpaid debt of $120,000. Because the contract requires application of payments to oldest debts first (enforceable under section 9-103(e)(1)), the $120,000 represents $60,000 unpaid on the sofa-sleeper beds and $60,000 unpaid on the lamps. (The aggregate purchase price of all three items is $200,000. At the time of default, ZinnMark owes $120,000 to FurniCo, indicating that ZinnMark has repaid $80,000. Under the contract terms, that $80,000 repaid the entire purchase price of the framed pictures [$40,000] and part of the purchase price of the beds [$40,000].) To the extent that an item secures repayment of its own purchase price, the security interest is a PMSI. But because the purchase price of the pictures has been paid in full, the security interest in the pictures is not a PMSI. So FurniCo cannot claim any superpriority in the pictures under section 9-324(a). Instead, FurniCo receives $0 and BigBank is entitled to the entire $25,000 under section 9-322(a)(1) because BigBank filed its financing statement before FurniCo did. This result is found in **Answer (A), making it the correct answer and Answers (B), (C), and (D) incorrect answers.**

125.   **Answer (C) is the correct answer.** Under the dual status rule, the beds secure FurniCo's unpaid debt of $120,000. As noted in the previous answer, the $120,000 represents $60,000 unpaid on the beds and $60,000 unpaid on the lamps. To the extent that an item secures repayment of its own purchase price, the security interest is a PMSI. So FurniCo can claim a PMSI in the beds for $60,000. And FurniCo's PMSI enjoys priority over BigBank's security interest under section 9-324(a). FurniCo cannot claim a PMSI in the extra $10,000. BigBank receives that $10,000 under section 9-322(a)(1) because it filed its financing statement before FurniCo did. Therefore, the liquidator should pay $60,000 to FurniCo and $10,000 to BigBank. This result is found in **Answer (C), making it the correct answer and Answers (A), (B), and (D) incorrect answers.**

126.   **Answer (D) is the correct answer.** Under the dual status rule, the lamps secure FurniCo's unpaid debt of $120,000. As noted in the previous answer, the $120,000 represents $60,000 unpaid on the beds and $60,000 unpaid on the lamps. To the extent that an item secures repayment of its own purchase price, the security interest is a PMSI. So FurniCo can claim a PMSI in the lamps for $60,000. And Dealer's PMSI enjoys priority over BigBank's security

interest under section 9-324(a). The liquidator should pay the entire $40,000 to FurniCo, **making Answer (D) the correct answer and Answers (A), (B), and (C) incorrect answers.**

127. **Answer (D) is the correct answer.** This question involves a priority dispute in an "accession." Section 9-102(a)(1) defines an "accession" as "goods that are physically united with other goods in such a manner that the identity of the original goods is not lost." The sound board, the keyboard, and the piano each retained their identity after the sound board and the keyboard were installed in the piano. Therefore, from MusiCorp's perspective, the piano is an "accession"; from Kline Music's perspective, the sound board and keyboard are "accessions." *See* § 9-335 cmt. 3. But the collateral does not involve a certificate of title, so priority in the liquidation proceeds is dictated by rules found outside section 9-335. *See* § 9-335(c).

Determining which priority rule resolves the dispute between Kline Music and MusiCorp requires knowing whether their security interests are perfected and qualify for purchase-money status. Both creditors hold a purchase-money security interest under section 9-103; Kline Music offered seller financing for the piano, and MusiCorp offered seller financing for the replacement parts. (The creditors are not claiming a PMSI in common collateral, so section 9-324(g) is inapplicable.) Both creditors perfected their interests by filing, and MusiCorp's filing on August 17 was within twenty days of the delivery date of the replacement parts (August 4), so MusiCorp can claim the superpriority afforded by section 9-324(a). Therefore, it has priority in the proceeds associated with its purchase-money collateral (sound board and keyboard). *See* § 9-335 cmt. 6. For that reason, the liquidator should pay $6,000 to MusiCorp and the balance of $7,500 to Kline Music, **making Answer (D) the correct answer and Answers (A), (B), and (C) incorrect answers.**

128. **Answer (C) is the correct answer.** This fact pattern is based upon Example 1 in cmt. 4 to section 9-336. It involves commingling of goods, which is governed by section 9-336. Section 9-336 specifically permits the continuation of a security interest in a product or mass (bottles of pasta sauce) that is made up of commingled goods (spices, tomatoes, etc.). Both Smith and Jones have security interests in pre-commingled collateral. Attachment continues, following the commingling, but now the security interest attaches to the product (the pasta sauce), as stated in section 9-336(b). Because both creditors were perfected before the ingredients were commingled, perfection continues after the commingling, but now the perfection extends to the product (the pasta sauce), as stated in section 9-336(d). As both Smith and Jones had perfected security interests in pre-commingled goods, their priority in the pasta sauce is dictated by section 9-336(f)(2), which states: "the security interests rank equally in proportion to the value of the collateral at the time it became commingled goods." That means that Smith and Jones have claims to the $1,500 in the ratio of their original contributions to the final product: $1000:$2000 (or 1:2). This formula yields a distribution of $500 to Farmer Smith and $1,000 to Farmer Jones, **making Answer (C) the correct answer.**

Answer (D) is incorrect because the formula in section 9-336(f)(2) relies on the ratios of collateral values (1:2), not unpaid debts (2:3).

Answer (A) and Answer (B) are incorrect because filing dates are irrelevant when both creditors file before the collateral is commingled.

129. If the liquidator sells the pasta sauce for $2,100, then he should distribute $800 to Farmer Smith and $1,200 to Farmer Jones, leaving a $100 surplus for Pasta Company. The formula of section 9-336(f)(2) continues to apply, but neither creditor is entitled to receive proceeds greater than its unpaid debt. The formula yields a payout of $700 to Farmer Smith and $1,400 to Farmer Jones. But Farmer Jones has unpaid debt of only $1,200, so he receives that amount, and no more. The excess $200 is applied to Farmer Smith's remaining debt of $100. The liquidator should return the remaining $100 surplus to Pasta Company under section 9-615(d).

130. If Farmer Smith files his financing statement after his spices are added to other ingredients and become commingled goods, then the liquidator should distribute $1,200 to Farmer Jones (the full amount of his unpaid debt) and the $300 balance to Farmer Smith (to be applied against his unpaid debt of $800). The "collateral value" formula of section 9-336(f)(2) applies only to resolve disputes between creditors who are perfected before collateral is commingled. Here, Farmer Smith filed after his spices became commingled. Now section 9-332(f)(1) applies, and it favors the creditor who is perfected before commingling occurs. Farmer Jones did perfect his security interest in the tomatoes before processing began, so he enjoys priority. Therefore, the liquidator should distribute all of the $1,500 to Farmer Jones, capped at his unpaid debt of $1,200, with the $300 balance to be remitted to Farmer Smith.

131. The liquidator should pay Bank's claim first, with any proceeds remaining distributed to Farmer Smith and Farmer Jones in the 1:2 ratio they enjoy under section 9-336(f)(2). *See* § 9-336 cmt. 7. Section 9-336 continues to address the priority of claims held by Farmer Smith and Farmer Jones, but because Bank's claim is in the finished product (the pasta sauce) rather than in any specific ingredients (spices, tomatoes), other priority rules address Bank's claim. *See* § 9-336(e). The facts indicate that Bank filed earlier than Smith and Jones, so its claim enjoys priority under section 9-322(a)(1).

132. **Answer (D) is the correct answer.** The absence of the after-acquired property clause from TNB's financing statement is a red herring. That clause must appear in the security agreement, but it need not appear in the financing statement. *See* §§ 9-204 cmt. 7; 9-502 cmt. 2. Therefore, **Answer (A) is incorrect.**

Both TNB and ZinnMark have perfected security interests in the furniture sold by ZinnMark to Friendly Furniture. TNB filed its financing statement on February 10, and ZinnMark filed its financing statement on July 18. Therefore, under the general priority rule of section 9-322(a)(1), TNB will enjoy priority because it filed first. By its own language, however, the general priority rule is subject to other applicable priority rules found in section 9-322 and elsewhere in Part 3 (e.g., the 9-300 series), one of which is section 9-324, which affords superpriority to purchase-money creditors. ZinnMark provided seller financing and retained a security interest in the furniture to secure the unpaid purchase price, so ZinnMark has a PMSI. Friendly Furniture operates a furniture store, so the sofas and bookcases are inventory. Section 9-324(b) and (c) address the superpriority available to secured parties with a PMSI in inventory. Parsing the statute reveals that ZinnMark must satisfy four requirements in order to achieve superpriority. First, ZinnMark's security interest must be perfected when Friendly Furniture receives the sofas and bookcases. *See* § 9-324(b)(1). ZinnMark perfected its security interest by filing a financing statement on July 18. Friendly Furniture received the sofas on July 15 and the bookcases on July 22.

Therefore, ZinnMark cannot claim superpriority in the sofas (**making Answer (C) an incorrect answer**) but might be able to claim superpriority in the bookcases. Second, ZinnMark must send notice of its PMSI to TNB (a previous filer entitled to such notice under section 9-324(c)) before Friendly Furniture receives the bookcases. *See* § 9-324(b)(2). ZinnMark sent notice on July 7, before Friendly Furniture received the bookcases on July 22. Third, TNB must receive ZinnMark's notice before Friendly Furniture received the bookcases. *See* § 9-324(b)(3). TNB received the notice on July 14, before Friendly Furniture received the bookcases on July 22. Fourth, ZinnMark's must state that it "has or expects to acquire a purchase-money security interest in inventory of [Friendly Furniture] and describe the inventory." *See* § 9-324(b)(4). The facts state that the notice satisfied these requirements. ZinnMark can satisfy all four of the statutory requirements, so it enjoys superpriority in the bookcases. It does not have superpriority in the sofas (failing the opening requirement), so TNB claims priority in them under the general "first to file or perfect" rule of section 9-322(a). These results are correctly stated in Answer (D), **making Answer (D) the correct answer and Answer (B) an incorrect answer.**

133.   **Answer (C) is the correct answer.** First, section 9-324(b) extends superpriority to proceeds of inventory sales only if the purchase-money creditor had superpriority in the inventory itself. The previous answer revealed that ZinnMark did not have superpriority in the sofas, so it will not have superpriority (or priority) in any proceeds from the sales of sofas. Therefore, ZinnMark cannot claim priority in Grace's check or Meredith's credit card receivable. **Answer (A), then, is an incorrect answer.** ZinnMark did have superpriority in the bookcases. Therefore, section 9-324(b) extends the superpriority to "identifiable cash proceeds [that] are received [by Friendly Furniture] on or before the delivery of the inventory to a buyer." Cash is an obvious example of a "cash proceed" under section 9-102(a)(9), so ZinnMark has priority in Ethan's cash, **making Answer (D) an incorrect answer.** The retail installment contract with a title-retention clause is probably chattel paper (a writing that evidences Bruce's monetary obligation and, under section 1-201(b)(35), creates a security interest in the bookcases via the title-retention clause). Section 9-324(b) does extend superpriority to chattel paper, but only if the creditor claiming superpriority can navigate section 9-330. ZinnMark cannot do so because Friendly Furniture, rather than ZinnMark, possesses the contract. Therefore, ZinnMark does not have priority in Bruce's contract, **making Answer (B) an incorrect answer.**

In summary, then, ZinnMark has priority in Ethan's cash. TNB has priority in Grace's check, Meredith's credit card receivable, and Bruce's contract, **making Answer (C) the correct answer.**

134. **Answer (D) is the correct answer.** The baseline rule in any priority dispute between the secured party and a buyer of collateral is this: the secured party wins. Section 9-201(a) says as much, with the caveat, "Except as otherwise provided in [the Uniform Commercial Code]." One major exception is found in section 9-315(a)(1): "a security interest . . . continues in collateral notwithstanding sale . . . thereof unless the secured party authorized the disposition free of the security interest." MegaBank has triggered the "unless" clause of the quoted language because its security agreement permits ZinnMark to sell the collateral in the ordinary course of its business. ZinnMark sells office equipment, so a "routine cash sale of three photocopiers" is, presumably, a transaction in the ordinary course of ZinnMark's business. Permitting such sales is expected, as a secured party wants its debtor to sell its inventory to generate profits that enable the debtor to repay the secured debt. The secured party may have an interest in blocking non-inventory dispositions, but presumably not routine inventory dispositions. In effect, then, ZinnMark's sale of the photocopiers to the law firm has terminated MegaBank's security interest in the photocopiers, **making Answer (D) the correct answer.**

Answer (A) is incorrect not because MegaBank will not lose, but because MegaBank will lose for reasons discussed above. Whether it has a duty to file against the law firm is irrelevant under the facts of this transaction.

Answers (B) and (C) are incorrect because MegaBank's security interest is terminated at the point of sale, regardless of what knowledge (if any) that the law firm had about MegaBank's security interest or filing. That knowledge might merit some discussion if the law firm asserted priority under section 9-320(a) based on its alleged status as a buyer in the ordinary course of business, but that is not the case in this transaction.

135. Under the revised facts, MegaBank will probably lose, but for different reasons than before. Because the sale was not permitted by the security agreement, MegaBank's security interest survives the disposition this time under section 9-315(a)(1). The law firm, however, will invoke the protection afforded by section 9-320(a), which states: "a buyer in the ordinary course of business . . . takes free of a security interest created by the buyer's seller, even if the security interest is perfected and the buyer knows of its existence." The security interest was indeed created by the law firm's seller — ZinnMark — so the law firm can win the priority dispute if it is a "buyer in the ordinary course of business," a term defined in section 1-201(b)(9). The definition requires the law firm to (1) buy (yes, as contrasted with taking by gift, for example) (2) goods (the photocopiers), (3) without knowledge that the sale violates MegaBank's rights (probably, but fact-sensitive), and (4) in the ordinary course of the seller's business (ZinnMark is in the business of selling photocopiers). The definition also states: "A person buys goods in the ordinary course if the sale to the person comports with the usual or customary practices in the kind of business in which the seller is engaged or with the seller's own usual or customary practices." Therefore, the fact that the law firm executed a

note — the standard form used by ZinnMark, and a form that comports with industry-wide standards — will not preclude the law firm from being a buyer in the ordinary course. And if the law firm does meet the definition, it will win the priority dispute.

136.   **Answer (D) is the correct answer.** A cashier's check is an example of "cash proceeds" under section 9-102(a)(9), as is a deposit account. Therefore, assuming MegaBank can satisfy its tracing burden, it has a perfected security interest in the $30,000 for twenty days under section 9-315(c), and thereafter under section 9-315(d)(2). Therefore, **Answer (D) is the correct answer and Answer (C) is an incorrect answer.**

Answer (A) is incorrect because MegaBank can claim a security interest in proceeds that are identifiable, whether or not the collateral description mentions "proceeds" or any derivation thereof. *See* §§ 9-203(f), 9-315(a)(2).

Answer (B) is incorrect because MegaBank can release (or otherwise lose) its security interest in the photocopiers, without abandoning its claim to identifiable proceeds. *See* § 9-315 cmt. 2 (second paragraph).

137.   **Answer (C) is the correct answer.** Friendly Furniture's security interest survives the sale under section 9-315(a)(1) because the sale was unauthorized. Nevertheless, the buyer can win the lawsuit if the buyer can navigate the protection afforded by section 9-320(b) (often referred to as the "garage sale" provision). To do so, the dining room suite must be a consumer good in the hands of both the seller and the buyer, the buyer must purchase the goods without knowledge of the security interest, and the sale must precede any filing by the creditor. Answer (C) offers an answer that meets all conditions, so **Answer (C) is the correct answer.**

Friendly Furniture engaged in seller financing with Sandra and can claim a PMSI in the furniture under section 9-103(a) and (b)(1). In Sandra's hands, the furniture was a consumer good. Because Friendly Furniture has a PMSI in consumer goods, its security interest is automatically perfected under section 9-309(1). Therefore, **Answer (A) is incorrect.**

Just because the sale generated identifiable cash proceeds — in which Friendly Furniture has a continuing perfected security interest — does not necessarily mean that Friendly Furniture loses any priority dispute in the original collateral itself. Therefore, **Answer (B) is incorrect.**

Friendly Furniture may win the lawsuit. But it also may lose the lawsuit, as suggested by facts found in Answer (C). Without more information, the absolute truth of Answer (D) remains unknown, **making Answer (D) an incorrect answer.**

138.   Friendly Furniture wins the conversion lawsuit under the revised facts. Its security interest is effective against all buyers under section 9-201(a), unless an exception applies. Because Sandra's sale was not authorized, Friendly Furniture's security interest survives the sale under section 9-315(a)(1). The buyer cannot claim the protection afforded by section 9-320(a) to buyers in the ordinary course of business because Sandra, the seller, is not in the business of selling dining room suites. Nor can Sandra's buyer — even one who uses the furniture as a consumer good and who purchases the furniture with no knowledge of Friendly Furniture's security interest — claim the protection afforded by section 9-320(b). Why? Because Friendly Furniture filed a financing statement against Sandra and the dining room suite under the revised facts, blocking the buyer from successfully navigating through

section 9-320(b)(4). (One could criticize this statutory hurdle, given that most buyers of consumer goods rarely, if ever, request a UCC search report before buying the goods.) Finally, Friendly Furniture's security interest is perfected at the time of sale (automatically, and by filing), and also when the buyer takes possession, so the buyer cannot invoke section 9-317(b). No other exception to the general rule applies to these facts, so Friendly Furniture will win its conversion lawsuit.

139. **Answer (C) is the correct answer.** Omega Bank's security agreement prohibits AMC from selling its inventory on credit. Therefore, Omega Bank may argue that its security interest survived AMC's sale of the harp to Ima, invoking section 9-315(a)(1). That section, however, opens with the phrase "Except as otherwise provided in this article." And Ima will rely on section 9-320(a), which states: "a buyer in the ordinary course of business . . . takes free of a security interest created by the buyer's seller, even if the security interest is perfected and the buyer knows of its existence." The security interest was indeed created by Ima's seller (AMC), and Ima had no knowledge of the business relationship between AMC and Omega Bank. Therefore, Ima will win the priority dispute if she is a "buyer in the ordinary course of business," a term defined in section 1-201(b)(9). The only concern is that she executed a promissory note as her form of payment, which was not authorized by Omega Bank's security agreement. Nevertheless, the facts indicate that promissory notes are an "industry practice" for expensive items, permitting Ima to meet this language from the definition: "A person buys goods in the ordinary course if the sale to the person comports with the usual or customary practices in the kind of business in which the seller is engaged or with the seller's own usual or customary practices." Ima can successfully invoke the protections of section 9-320(a), **making Answer (C) the correct answer.**

Even though Omega Bank did not consent to AMC's credit sale of the harp to Ima, Omega Bank does not necessarily win the priority dispute under section 9-315(a)(1). That section is subject to other rules, one of which is section 9-320(a). And in this question, that section favors Ima, **making Answer (A) an incorrect answer.**

The fact that Ima is using the harp as equipment, rather than a consumer good, prevents her from claiming priority under section 9-320(b) (which will not apply for other reasons, as well). But her use is irrelevant under section 9-320(a), the conditions of which she satisfies. Therefore, **Answer (B) is an incorrect answer.**

If Omega Bank's security interest in the harp survives the sale by AMC to Ima, it also remains perfected by Omega Bank's original filing. *See* § 9-507(a). Ima and AMC are both located in Texas, so Omega Bank need not worry about any change in jurisdiction that might trigger an additional filing under section 9-316(a). Therefore, Ima cannot claim priority under section 9-317(b) or otherwise, on the theory that Omega Bank's security interest is not perfected after the sale. Ima does enjoy priority (under section 9-320(a)), but for reasons different than stated in Answer (D), **making Answer (D) an incorrect answer.**

140. **Answer (C) is the correct answer.** AMC is in the business of selling musical instruments and related items. Therefore, AMC used the computer equipment as "equipment," rather than "inventory." Omega Bank's security interest extends to equipment, and its security agreement prohibits AMC from selling its equipment. Omega Bank, then, can recover the equipment from Hewey under sections 9-201(a) and 9-315(a), unless some other provision favors Hewey. He cannot invoke the protection afforded to buyers under section 9-320(a). Hewey is not a "buyer in ordinary course of business" as defined in section 1-201(b)(9)

because AMC does not sell computer equipment in the ordinary course of its business. Therefore, **Answer (B) is incorrect.** Also, Hewey cannot invoke the protection afforded to buyers under section 9-320(b) because the computer equipment is not a consumer good in the hands of AMC (and Omega Bank had filed a financing statement against the equipment). Therefore, **Answer (A) is incorrect.** No provision that might favor Hewey turns on whether he is or is not an employee of the debtor, **making Answer (D) an incorrect answer.** (If Hewey was an in-house lawyer who negotiated the transaction with Omega Bank, then perhaps he would fail a "good faith" or "no knowledge" requirement, but those facts are not present in this question.) Hewey cannot successfully invoke any buyer-protection statute, so Omega Bank wins the priority dispute in reliance on sections 9-201(a) and 9-315(a), **making Answer (C) the correct answer.**

141. **Answer (D) is the correct answer.** The term "buyer in ordinary course of business" is defined in section 1-201(b)(9). The phrase "ordinary course of business" refers to the seller's course of business, not the buyer's course of business. Dealer is in the business of selling sports memorabilia, so Mickey may meet the definition, regardless of what business he is in, and no matter how he intends to use the baseballs. Therefore, **Answer (B) is incorrect.** To qualify as a buyer in the ordinary course of Dealer's business, Mickey must purchase the baseballs "without knowledge that the sale violates the rights of [Redbird Bank] in the goods." Mickey's mere knowledge of an existing security interest and awareness of an accompanying filing is acceptable. *See* § 9-320(a) (last clause) and cmt. 3. Therefore, **Answer (C) is incorrect.** Because the terms of sale violated Omega Bank's security agreement, Omega Bank's security interest may survive the disposition under section 9-315(a). But that contract breach does not, by itself, preclude Mickey from qualifying as a buyer in the ordinary course of Dealer's business. Therefore, **Answer (A) is incorrect.** Payment terms can pose a problem, though, as the definition states: "A person buys goods in the ordinary course if the sale to the person comports with the usual or customary practices in the kind of business in which the seller is engaged or with the seller's own usual or customary practices." Here, Mickey paid by executing a negotiable, unsecured promissory note. Unless that payment device is customary for either Dealer or the sports memorabilia industry, Mickey will not be a buyer in the ordinary course of business. Answer (D) raises that possibility, **making Answer (D) the correct answer.**

142. ZinnBank will win the priority dispute. ZinnBank can claim priority under sections 9-201(a) and 9-315(a) because a sale of camera equipment in exchange for a photocopier is not a customary transaction. Therefore, ZinnBank's security interest survived the disposition. For the same reason, the exchange of camera equipment for a photocopier prevents Gwen from acquiring the camera equipment free of ZinnBank's security interest under the protection afforded by section 9-320(a) to a buyer in the ordinary course of business. Gwen finds no help in section 9-320(b) because ZinnBank had filed a financing statement and Markells was holding the camera equipment as inventory (rather than consumer goods). And ZinnBank's security interest remained perfected following the sale to Gwen under section 9-507(a), so Gwen finds no help in section 9-317(b). Therefore, ZinnBank wins any priority dispute with Gwen and, accordingly, Ethan (her non-buyer transferee).

143. **Answer (D) is the correct answer.** ZinnBank's collateral includes current and future equipment, so its security interest extends to the photocopier (equipment in the hands of a camera equipment store). Its interest in the photocopier is perfected by its Texas filing. The

security interest survives the sale to BizSmart under section 9-315(a) because ZinnBank has consented to dispositions in the ordinary course of business. Rephrased, Markells can sell its inventory, but not anything else (including equipment).

Ashley, paying cash for the photocopier and buying it from BizSmart, which had held it as a unit of inventory, appears to be a buyer in the ordinary course of business. Nevertheless, Ashley cannot claim the protection afforded by section 9-320(a) because Markells, rather than BizSmart, created the security interest in favor of ZinnBank (observe the statutory language, "a security interest created by the buyer's seller"). Therefore, **Answer (C) is an incorrect answer.** Ashley cannot win under section 9-320(b) even if she uses the photocopier primarily as a consumer good, because that provision applies only if the seller (BizSmart) also used the photocopier as a consumer good, which is not the case. Therefore, **Answer (B) is an incorrect answer.** Absent additional facts involving a change in jurisdiction and application of section 9-316(a), ZinnBank's security interest remains perfected in the photocopier under section 9-507. No other section affords buyer protection to Ashley, so she loses to ZinnBank under sections 9-201 and 9-315, **making Answer (D) the correct answer.**

Answer (A) is incorrect because ZinnBank's ability to claim a perfected security interest in identifiable cash proceeds does not automatically preclude ZinnBank from continuing to enjoy priority in the collateral that generated the proceeds.

144.   **Answer (A) is the correct answer.** Section 9-317(a) states the general rule that resolves priority disputes between secured parties and "lien creditors" (as that term is defined in section 9-102(a)(52)). That section states: "A security interest . . . is subordinate [i.e., junior, inferior, etc.] to the rights of . . . (2) a person that becomes a lien creditor before . . . (A) the security interest is perfected." Observe that the lien creditor's interest must arise "before" the secured party is perfected. MegaBank will be perfected in collateral when it files its financing statement, if ZinnCorp then has rights in the collateral (assuming previous value, and a security agreement is in place). MegaBank will be perfected in subsequent collateral when ZinnCorp acquires rights in it (assuming previous value, a security agreement is in place, and a previous filing). MegaBank's security agreement includes an after-acquired property clause, and it filed its financing statement long before BAMCO became a lien creditor. BAMCO's lien cannot encumber ZinnCorp's assets until ZinnCorp acquires rights in those assets. But at that very moment, MegaBank's security interest will become perfected in those same assets (by the earlier filing). In that case, there is a "tie" between the moment of MegaBank's perfection and BAMCO's lien. Because the statute uses the word "before," it resolves any temporal "tie" in favor of the secured party. Therefore, BAMCO's lien in any seized asset will never arise earlier than ("before") MegaBank's moment of perfection in that asset. This leaves MegaBank with priority in all of the seized collateral (whether "pre-lawsuit" or "post-lawsuit"), **making Answer (A) the correct answer and Answer (B) and Answer (C) incorrect answers.**

    Answer (C) also is incorrect because it erroneously suggests that priority turns on what happens during a specific forty-five-day period. No such period is mentioned in section 9-317(a).

    Answer (D) is incorrect because section 9-317(a) does not distinguish between involuntary and voluntary lien creditors, and no other Article 9 priority rule does so, either.

145.   **Answer (B) is the correct answer.** Under section 9-317(a)(2), the general rule used to resolve priority disputes between lien creditors and secured parties, Ima's lien will enjoy priority if AMC's security interest was unperfected on September 13, when Ima's lien encumbered the violin. AMC provided seller financing, and the violin secures repayment of its purchase price, so AMC's security interest is a purchase-money security interest under section 9-103. If Timmy Zee uses the violin in a manner that makes it a "consumer good," then AMC's PMSI is automatically perfected at the moment of attachment. *See* § 9-309(1). Therefore, if Timmy Zee uses the violin primarily for personal, family, or household purposes, AMC has priority in the violin with no regard to if or when it filed a financing statement. Answer (B) contemplates this situation, **making Answer (B) the correct answer.**

    Answer (D) is incorrect because it erroneously suggests that AMC must file a financing statement in order to have priority in the violin, if the violin is a consumer good. AMC need not file at all, because Article 9 provides for automatic perfection of purchase-money security interests in consumer goods.

What if Timmy Zee is a professional musician and uses the violin as "equipment," rather than a consumer good? AMC still enjoys purchase-money status, but its security interest will not be automatically perfected on attachment. Instead, AMC must perfect by filing (absent possession). Under the baseline priority rule, Ima's lien has priority if AMC has not filed its financing statement by September 13, the date of Ima's lien. Mindful, though, that purchase-money sellers "sell today and file tomorrow," the drafters of Article 9 offer some protection against the risk that a "lien" will encumber the collateral after the security interest attaches but before the secured party files. Section 9-317(a)(2) defers to this purchase-money exception by directing the reader to subsection (e), which awards priority to a security interest that (i) attaches before the lien arises, (ii) enjoys purchase-money status, and (iii) is perfected by a financing statement filed no later than twenty days after the debtor receives delivery of the collateral. The problem states that AMC retained an enforceable security interest in the violin, so attachment occurred no later than September 5 (and perhaps as early as September 1), before Ima's lien arose on September 13. And AMC's security interest is a purchase-money security interest, as already noted. Answer (A) suggests AMC will win if it files on September 28, but that date is more than twenty days after Timmy Zee takes possession of the violin on September 5, so **Answer (A) is an incorrect answer.** Answer (C) suggests that Ima will win if AMC files on September 24. But that filing date is timely because it is not later than twenty days after Timmy Zee's possession date of September 5. That filing date favors AMC, not Ima, **making Answer (C) an incorrect answer.**

146.   **Answer (C) is the correct answer.** Because a search against "Quantum Technologies" will not reveal Omega Bank's earlier filing against "ZeeTech," the name change has rendered the earlier filing seriously misleading. *See* § 9-506(c). Therefore, the earlier filing will perfect Omega Bank's security interest in collateral acquired before the name change and within four months thereafter, but not its security interest in collateral acquired by ZeeTech/Quantum more than four months after the name change. *See* § 9-507(c). Quantum acquired Item #1 on April 15, within four months of the name change in February. But Quantum acquired Item #2 on July 15, more than four months after the name change in February. Therefore, Omega Bank's original filing continues to perfect its security interest in Item #1, but it does not perfect a security interest in Item #2.

Meredith did not become a "lien creditor" with respect to Item #1 until August. Omega Bank had a perfected security interest in Item #1 on the purchase date of April 15, and its interest in Item #1 remained perfected, notwithstanding the name change. Therefore, Omega Bank's security interest is not subordinate to Meredith's lien under section 9-317(a)(2). Instead, Omega Bank has priority in Item #1, **making Answer (B) an incorrect answer.**

Meredith did not become a "lien creditor" with respect to Item #2 until August. Omega Bank's earlier filing is not effective to perfect its security interest in Item #2 for reasons discussed above. Therefore, Omega Bank's unperfected security interest in Item #2 is subordinate to Meredith's lien, giving Meredith priority in Item #2. **Answer (A), then, is incorrect.**

In summary, Omega Bank has priority in Item #1, and Meredith has priority in Item #2.

Answer (C) says as much, **making Answer (C) the correct answer.**

Answer (D) is incorrect because the facts provide sufficient information to resolve the priority dispute in both pieces of equipment.

147. Under section 9-323(b), the sheriff should pay $110,000 to Bank and $10,000 to Hannah. That statute makes Bank's security interest subordinate to Hannah's property interest "to the extent that the security interest secures an advance made more than 45 days after [Hannah] becomes a lien creditor." Rephrased, Bank's security interest enjoys priority with respect to all advances funded on or before the forty-fifth day after Hannah became a lien creditor (this forty-five-day period is absolute and is not shortened if the secured creditor acquires knowledge of the competing lien during the period). Hannah became a lien creditor on September 20, so advances funded by Bank on or before November 4 — $50,000 on September 1, $35,000 on October 1, and $25,000 on November 1 — are entitled to priority. The $20,000 advanced on November 15 is not protected because it was funded more than forty-five days after Hannah became a lien creditor. So Bank is entitled to receive $110,000 (covering its first three advances), and Hannah is entitled to receive the remaining $10,000.

Observe that Bank cannot take advantage of the post-forty-five-day protection offered by section 9-323(b)(1) and (b)(2) because Bank had knowledge of Hannah's lien as early as October 15 (before the forty-five-day period ended) and did not fund the advances pursuant to a prior commitment entered into without knowledge of the lien.

148. Yes, the assumptions permit Bank to receive the entire $120,000. Bank's agreement to loan $150,000 to Debtor in one or more advances means that all of the advances were funded "pursuant to commitment," a phrase defined in section 9-102(a)(68). Even though Bank is not obligated to fund an advance if an Event of Default exists, the advances are funded "pursuant to commitment." This is so because the definition of "pursuant to commitment" is met even if "a subsequent event of default or other event not within the secured party's control has relieved or may relieve the secured party from its obligation." Because Bank funded the four advances pursuant to commitment, all of the advances are protected against Hannah's competing $75,000 claim under section 9-323(b)(2) because the commitment was entered into on September 1, before Bank discovered Hannah's competing claim in October. As all of Bank's advances enjoy priority, the sheriff should pay the entire $120,000 to Bank.

149. **Answer (D) is the correct answer.** Redbird Bank's filing on January 18, 2007, is effective for five years. *See* § 9-515(a). Redbird Bank can continue the effectiveness of its original filing by timely filing a continuation statement within the last six months of the five-year period. *See* § 9-515(d). In this case, that six-month period is roughly July 19, 2011, through January 18, 2012. **Answer (A) is incorrect** because a continuation statement filed on July 10, 2011, is premature and, therefore, ineffective (even if recorded by the clerk). *See* § 9-510(c). **Answer (B) is incorrect** because a continuation statement filed on January 24, 2012, is too late and, therefore, ineffective (even if recorded by the clerk). *Id.*

The difference between Answer (C) and Answer (D) is that Redbird Bank wins under the former only if it timely files a continuation statement, whereas Redbird Bank wins under the latter even if it never files a continuation statement. Section 9-515(c) addresses the effect of a filing that lapses because the secured party fails to timely file a continuation statement. On the assumption that the secured party is perfected solely by its original filing, its security interest becomes unperfected prospectively. This does not concern Redbird Bank, as its filing was effective when Bradford Industries became a lien creditor in December 2011. Section 9-515(c) also states that Redbird Bank's security interest becomes unperfected retroactively "against a purchaser of the collateral for value." Section 1-201 defines "purchaser" and "purchase" in a manner that requires a party to acquire a property interest in a "voluntary transaction." Lien creditors, by definition, acquire their property interests by judicial process, an involuntary transaction. Therefore, Bradford Industries fails to quality as a "purchaser of the collateral for value." This means that Redbird Bank's security interest will become unperfected if it fails to file a continuation statement, but it will continue to enjoy priority against a lien creditor whose property interest (or "lien") arises while Redbird Bank's original filing was effective. That is the case under the facts. Given that Bradford Industries is an involuntary creditor whose behavior is not dictated by the filing system, the result seems only fair. Redbird Bank need not file a continuation statement to preserve its priority against Bradford Industries. Redbird Bank has priority even if it never files a continuation statement. *See* § 9-515 cmt. 3 (Example 2). Therefore, **Answer (C) is an incorrect answer and Answer (D) is the correct answer.**

150. **Answer (B) is the correct answer.** The section that resolves priority disputes between secured parties (Fidelity Bank) and lien creditors (Heather) is section 9-317(a)(2). That section states that the rights of a holder of an Article 9 security interest are subordinate to the rights of "a person that becomes a lien creditor before the earlier of the time: (A) the security interest or agricultural lien is perfected; or (B) one of the conditions specified in Section 9-203(b)(3) is met and a financing statement covering the collateral is filed." The magical date is June 25, when Heather became a lien creditor. On that date, Fidelity Bank did not yet have a security interest in any assets of Mockingbird Industries. Its security interest did not attach until July 1, when Mockingbird authenticated the security agreement and Fidelity Bank gave value in the form of a loan commitment. Because Fidelity Bank had previously filed its financing statement, its security interest became perfected on the attachment date of July 1. Fidelity Bank fails to enjoy priority under section 9-317(a)(2)(A) because its perfection date of July 1 is after June 25, the date on which Heather acquired her lien. And Fidelity Bank fails to enjoy priority under section 9-317(a)(2)(B), even though it filed its financing statement in early June (before Heather acquired her lien on June 25), because *none* of the "agreement" conditions specified in section 9-203(b)(3) (in most cases, the authentication of a security agreement that adequately describes the collateral) were in place on June 25 (Mockingbird Industries did not authenticate the security agreement until July 1). Fidelity Bank's security interest does not enjoy priority. That result makes sense under the general principle of *nemo dat* (you can only give that which you have). Fidelity Bank acquired a security interest that was subject to Heather's lien because the lien arose before the security interest attached. The only answer that takes this into account is Answer (B), **making Answer (B) the correct answer.**

Answer (A) is incorrect because a financing statement filed before the lien arises, without more, is insufficient to give priority to the filer.

Answer (C) is incorrect, and a red herring, because an "all assets" filing is permitted. *See* § 9-504(2). Recall, however, that such a supergeneric collateral description is not acceptable in the security agreement. *See* § 9-108(c). Also remember that an "all assets" filing cannot expand the collateral beyond the description found in the security agreement. *See* § 9-504 cmt. 2 (last paragraph). Perhaps rephrased, a filing cannot perfect a security interest that never attaches.

Answer (D) is incorrect because claiming a PMSI will not help Fidelity Bank under these facts. Sometimes priority does turn on the PMSI status of the security interest under section 9-317(e), but that statute requires the PMSI to attach *before* the lien arises (with perfection occurring thereafter). Here, Heather's lien arose before Fidelity Bank's security interest attached. Therefore, even if Fidelity Bank held a PMSI, it would lose the dispute.

151. **Answer (C) is the correct answer.** "Commercial financing security" refers to "(i) paper of a kind ordinarily arising in commercial transactions, (ii) accounts receivable, (iii) mortgages on real property, and (iv) inventory." 26 U.S.C. § 6323(c)(2)(C). Accounts and inventory are expressly mentioned, **making Answers (A) and (D) incorrect answers.** Chattel paper ordinarily arises in commercial transactions, **making Answer (B) incorrect.** Equipment is not mentioned in the definition, **making Answer (C) the correct answer.**

152. **Answer (C) is the correct answer.** Under the Federal Tax Lien Statutes (26 U.S.C. §§ 6321–6323), advances funded after the IRS files its tax lien notice may enjoy priority if the secured party funded the advances (i) within the forty-five-day period following the filing date of the tax lien notice *and* (ii) without knowledge of the tax lien notice. 26 U.S.C. § 6323(c)(2)(A), (d). The IRS filed its tax lien notice on August 1, so the forty-five-day period ended on September 15. But Bank discovered the tax lien filing on August 21, within the forty-five-day period. So only advances funded prior to discovery are protected. Those advances aggregate $900,000, **making Answer (C) the correct answer and Answers (A), (B), and (D) incorrect answers.**

Appreciate that, unlike section 9-323(b), the forty-five-day period under the Federal Tax Lien Statutes is not absolute. The period can be terminated by the secured party's knowledge of the competing tax lien, and the period cannot be extended if the debtor and the secured party have entered into a binding commitment without knowledge of the competing tax lien.

153. **Answer (A) is the correct answer.** As used by ZinnMark Fashions (a clothing retailer), the dresses and shoes are inventory, a type of commercial financing security. 26 U.S.C. § 6323(c)(2)(C)(iv). So **Answer (B) is incorrect.** Bank's discovery of the tax lien notice does terminate the forty-five-day period of protection for advances funded after the tax lien notice is filed. 26 U.S.C. § 6323(c)(2)(A). But Bank's discovery of the tax lien notice does not terminate the forty-five-day period of protection for collateral acquired by the debtor after the tax lien notice is filed. 26 U.S.C. § 6323(c)(2)(B). So **Answer (C) is incorrect.** (The difference is justified because Bank's knowledge can affect its own funding decision but not necessarily the debtor's purchasing activity.) Because the collateral is commercial financing security and was timely acquired on September 7 (within forty-five days following the filing of the tax lien notice on August 1), Bank's security interest enjoys priority, **making Answer (A) the correct answer. Answer (D) is incorrect**, as the relevant forty-five-day period of protection commences on the date of the tax lien filing, not the date of the assessment.

154. **Answer (D) is the correct answer.** The computers, in the hands of a business that sells clothing, are equipment, which is a type of collateral not included within the definition of "commercial financing security." 26 U.S.C. § 6323(c)(2)(C). But the definition of "commercial financing security" becomes relevant only with respect to collateral acquired by the debtor

after the IRS files its tax lien notice. ZinnMark Fashions acquired these machines on July 25, before the IRS filed its tax lien notice on August 1. So the fact that the collateral is not "commercial financing security" has no effect on priority, **making Answer (A) an incorrect answer. Answer (B) is incorrect** because the tax lien filing date, not the tax assessment date, dictates priority. And **Answer (C) also is incorrect.** If anything, Bank's lack of knowledge at the time of purchase should favor Bank, not the IRS.

155. **Answer (D) is the correct answer.** Section 9-601 states: "After default, a secured party has the rights provided in this part." Most, if not all, provisions in Part 6 (§ 9-601 through § 9-628) mention "default." Therefore, understanding its meaning is rather important. The likely places to find a definition are sections 1-201 and 9-102, but neither section defines "default." Therefore, **Answer (A) and Answer (B) are incorrect answers.** The next place the reader might look is in section 9-601 itself. But that statute also does not define the term, so **Answer (C) is an incorrect answer.** That leaves Answer (D). As noted in section 9-601 cmt. 3, "this Article leaves to the agreement of the parties the circumstances giving rise to a default." The term, then, is defined by the parties, and they should memorialize their understanding and agreement in the security agreement or one of the other loan papers, **making Answer (D) the correct answer.**

156. **Answer (A) is the correct answer.** Section 9-610(a) authorizes the secured party to dispose of collateral after default. The statute does not restrict that remedy to collateral in the secured party's possession. In fact, some collateral is intangible (e.g., accounts, general intangibles, intellectual property, etc.) and is not subject to possession. So **Answer (A) is the correct answer.** The statute also does not condition disposition on the perfected or unperfected status of the security interest, so **Answer (B) is incorrect.**

Answer (C) is incorrect. Section 9-601(a) gives statutory rights and remedies to the secured party while preserving its contractual rights and remedies. Section 9-601(c) tells the secured party that its statutory and contractual rights and remedies "are cumulative and may be exercised simultaneously." Therefore, the secured party need not first exhaust its rights and remedies in the collateral before exercising its contractual rights and remedies, **making Answer (C) an incorrect answer.**

Answer (D) is incorrect. While the former version of Article 9 did not expressly permit partial strict foreclosures, the current version of Article 9 leaves no such doubt. Section 9-620(a) states that "a secured party may accept collateral in full or partial satisfaction of the obligation it secures." Therefore, **Answer (D) is an incorrect answer.**

157. **Answer (A) is the correct answer.** An "account debtor," as defined by section 9-102(a)(3) means "a person obligated on an account, chattel paper, or general intangible." For example, a person who buys inventory from a debtor and pays with a credit card is an "account debtor" on the "account." Section 9-607(a)(1) permits the secured party, after default, to "notify an account debtor . . . to make payment . . . to or for the benefit of the secured party." Section 9-607(c) requires the secured party to "proceed in a commercially reasonable manner" if it "undertakes to collect from . . . an account debtor." Therefore, **Answer (A) is the correct answer.**

Answer (B) is incorrect because section 9-607 does not require the debtor to be in default for any specific period of time before the secured party can exercise collection rights.

Answer (C) and Answer (D) are incorrect because section 9-607 does not require the secured party to have a perfected security interest or the senior security interest. In fact, the section acknowledges that junior creditors can exercise collection rights. *See* § 9-607 cmt. 5.

158.   **Answer (C) is the correct answer.** Section 9-609(a)(1) permits a secured party, after default, to take possession of collateral. Under section 9-609(b)(2), the secured party may take possession of collateral "without judicial process, if it proceeds without breach of the peace." The statute provides no other conditions, **making Answer (C) the correct answer.** **Answer (A) is incorrect** because Tim's primary use (e.g., consumer good or equipment) is irrelevant. **Answer (B) is incorrect** because the statute provides no threshold dollar amount. And **Answer (D) is incorrect** because the statute does not require the secured party to give the debtor a timely warning of an impending repossession. In fact, any such requirement would likely encourage the debtor to hide, secure, immobilize, or damage the collateral, frustrating the secured party's statutory rights.

159.   **Answer (B) is the correct answer.** What constitutes a "breach of the peace" may vary among the jurisdictions, but a review of the case law suggests that a court will often find that the secured party breached the peace if it ignored a debtor's objection and continued with the taking. *See, e.g., Fulton v. Anchor Sav. Bank*, 452 S.E.2d 208, 213 (Ga. Ct. App. 1994); *First and Farmers Bank v. Henderson*, 763 S.W.2d 137, 140 (Ky. Ct. App. 1988); *Hester v. Bandy*, 627 So.2d 833, 840–41 (Miss. 1993); *Hollibush v. Ford Motor Credit Co.*, 508 N.W.2d 449, 453–55 (Wis. Ct. App. 1993). A debtor whose objections are ignored is likely to continue to object and perhaps take more forceful, and physical, action, perhaps leading to an unfortunate result for one or both parties. Therefore, to minimize the likelihood of incurring liability for action that may be deemed a breach of the peace, a secured party should cease the repossession and immediately leave the area if the debtor is present and objects. **Answer (B), then, is the correct answer.**

Answer (A) is incorrect because section 9-603(b) makes inapplicable section 9-603(a)'s language (which allows parties to agree on certain standards) to efforts to define breach of the peace. As a consequence, any attempt by the parties to contractually agree on what behavior constitutes breach of the peace is not enforceable.

Answer (C) is incorrect because section 9-602(6) renders unenforceable any contract provision that attempts to waive the secured party's duty to avoid breaching the peace.

Answer (D) is incorrect because a secured party can be liable for the actions of its independent contractors. "In considering whether a secured party has engaged in a breach of the peace . . . courts should hold the secured party responsible for the actions of others taken on the secured party's behalf, including independent contractors engaged by the secured party to take possession of collateral." *See* § 9-609 cmt. 3. *See also Clark v. Associates Comm. Corp.*, 877 F. Supp. 1439, 1443–49 (D. Kan. 1994); *Sammons v. Broward Bank*, 599 So. 2d 1018, 1019–21 (Fla. Dist. Ct. App. 1992); *Robinson v. Citicorp Nat'l Servs., Inc.*, 921 S.W.2d 52, 54–55 (Mo. Ct. App. 1996); *Mauro v. General Motors Acceptance Corp.*, 626 N.Y.S.2d 374, 376–77 (1995); *Williamson v. Fowler Toyota, Inc.*, 956 P.2d 858, 860–62 (Okla. 1998); *McCall v. Owens*, 820 S.W.2d 748, 751–52 (Tenn. Ct. App. 1991); *MBank El Paso, N.A. v. Sanchez*, 836 S.W.2d 151, 152–54 (Tex. 1992).

160.   **Answer (D) is the correct answer.** The fact that the car is parked on Tim's driveway —

private property — does not trigger a breach of the peace (assuming Repo Company has free access to the car and is not opening gates, fences, garage doors, etc.), so **Answer (A) is an incorrect answer.** *See, e.g., Butler v. Ford Motor Credit Co.*, 829 F.2d 568, 568 (5th Cir. 1987) (removing truck from driveway); *Raffa v. Dania Bank*, 321 So. 2d 83, 84 (Fla. Dist. Ct. App. 1975) (removing car from driveway); *Pierce v. Leasing Int'l, Inc.*, 235 S.E.2d 752, 755 (Ga. Ct. App. 1977) (removing car from open garage attached to residence); *Laurel Coal Co. v. Walter E. Heller & Co.*, 539 F. Supp. 1006, 1007 (W.D. Pa. 1982) (removing bulldozer after cutting chain used to lock fence); *Henderson v. Security Nat'l Bank*, 140 Cal. Rptr. 388, 391 (Ct. App. 1977) (removing car after breaking lock on garage door). Owners of motor vehicles often leave personal items in a parked and locked vehicle, and rarely would those items fall with the collateral description found in the security agreement. If those personal items prevented the secured party from repossessing the car, then owners in default could easily frustrate the creditor's ability to exercise one of its most valuable remedies. Alternatively, the creditor might be forced to remove the personal items from the car and just leave them nearby, extending the time necessary to seize the vehicle (increasing the likelihood of a confrontation or altercation) while exposing the debtor to additional loss of personal property. The law should not, and does not, approve either result, **making Answer (B) an incorrect answer.** Instead, the law permits the secured party to take the car and any non-collateral contents therein, but it provides the debtor with a remedy for conversion if the non-collateral contents are damaged. Additionally, the secured party cannot use the non-collateral contents as leverage to extract payment from the debtor. Instead, the secured party must make the non-collateral contents available to the debtor once the vehicle is secure. *See, e.g., Larranaga v. Mile High Collection & Recovery Bureau, Inc.*, 807 F. Supp. 111, 112 (D.N.M. 1992) (finding creditor liable for conversion of personal property in repossessed vehicle in absence of any contractual language); *Ford Motor Credit Co. v. Herring*, 589 S.W.2d 584, 586–87 (Ark. 1979) (holding contract terms did not shield creditor from liability for intentionally withholding personal items in repossessed vehicle from debtor who demanded return after creditor had secured possession of vehicle); *Southern Indus. Sav. Bank v. Greene*, 224 So.2d 416, 417–18 (Fla. Dist. Ct. App. 1969) (concluding creditor was liable for losing cash and jewelry hidden in trunk of repossessed car); *Jones v. General Motors Acceptance Corp.*, 565 P.2d 9, 12 (Okla. 1977) (stating contractual provision authorizing seizure of personal items in repossessed vehicle did not save creditor from liability for wrongful retention). Therefore, **Answer (D) is the correct answer and Answer (C) is an incorrect answer.**

161. **Answer (B) is the correct answer.** Section 9-623 extends the right to redeem collateral not just to the debtor, but also to other parties, including a "secondary obligor" as defined by section 9-102(a)(71). Robert is a guarantor, a common example of a secondary obligor. Therefore, Robert can redeem the collateral, **making Answer (A) an incorrect answer.** Because future scheduled payments have been properly accelerated, the redemption price is $11,400, rather than the single missed payment of $400. *See* § 9-623(b) and cmt. 2. Therefore, **Answer (B) is the correct answer.** Section 9-623 does not condition the exercise of redemption rights on any specific dollar amount of secured debt, so **Answer (C) is an incorrect answer.** Section 9-624(c) does permit a debtor and a secondary obligor to waive their redemption rights, but that waiver must be authenticated by the waiving party after default. A waiver clause found in the security agreement, presumably authenticated by Robert before Tim defaults, is not enforceable, **making Answer (D) an incorrect answer (first reason).** Furthermore, a redemption waiver is not enforceable in a "consumer-goods

transaction" as defined in section 9-102(a)(24). The secured debt is the purchase price of the car, which Tim uses primarily as a consumer good, so the transaction is a consumer-goods transaction. This means that Robert cannot waive his redemption rights, **making Answer (D) an incorrect answer (second reason).**

162. **Answer (A) is the correct answer.** As a general rule, a secured party may propose to forgive all of the debt (a "full" strict foreclosure) or just part of the debt (a "partial" strict foreclosure). *See* § 9-620(a). But section 9-620(g) prohibits a partial strict foreclosure in a "consumer transaction" as defined by section 9-102(a)(26) (perhaps because most consumers would be shocked to learn that they remain liable for any part of the debt after losing possession of the collateral). The secured debt is the purchase price of the car (which is the collateral), and Tim uses the car primarily as a consumer good, so the transaction is a consumer transaction. This means that Dealer cannot propose a partial strict foreclosure, **making Answer (A) the correct answer.**

Answer (B) is incorrect because the magical statutory percentage which triggers a forced disposition is 60%, rather than 50%. *See* § 9-620(e). (The drafters thought that at some level of repayment the consumer would benefit from a forced disposition, perhaps thinking that the sale proceeds would yield a surplus when compared to the amount of the debtor's built-up equity in the collateral. They picked 60%. Given how quickly automobiles depreciate, however, query whether a forced disposition at any level of repayment will yield a surplus.)

Answer (C) is incorrect. Section 9-621(b) obligates Dealer to send its proposal to Robert (a secondary obligor) only if Dealer is proposing a partial strict foreclosure. Robert has an interest in reviewing the terms of a partial strict foreclosure because he remains liable for the debt that is not forgiven. But Robert has no remaining liability if Dealer proposes a full strict foreclosure, so the statute dispenses with any requirement to notify Robert of such terms.

Answer (D) is incorrect because a debtor's silence can, after a period of time, be deemed consent to a secured party's proposal. *See* § 9-620(c)(2)(C). Note, however, that silence cannot create consent to a partial strict foreclosure (presumably because some debt would remain after any such consent).

163. **Answer (A) is the correct answer.** Any time a statute imposes a notice duty, the reader should determine whether the duty focuses solely on the giving of notice or also on the receiving of notice. Section 9-611 addresses this issue in subsection (b), which says that "a secured party . . . shall send . . . a reasonable authenticated notification of disposition." The secured party complies with this notice duty by merely sending the notice. The notice may be effective, even if the debtor never receives it. Therefore, **Answer (A) is the correct answer.** Appreciate, though, that litigation may trigger an investigation into why the notice was not received, and Article 9 acknowledges that in some cases the secured party may be under a duty to "try again." *See* § 9-611 cmt. 6.

As noted in the previous paragraph, the notice must be "authenticated," a term that accommodates written and electronic forms, but not oral communications. Therefore, **Answer (B) is an incorrect answer.**

A notice sent at least ten days prior to the earliest time of disposition meets the safe harbor of section 9-612, but the ten-day period is "not a minimum requirement." *See* § 9-612 cmt. 3.

A notice sent less than ten days prior to the earliest time of disposition may comport with the contractual agreement of the parties or otherwise be commercially reasonable. Therefore, **Answer (C) is an incorrect answer.**

Article 9 does not require the notice to be notarized, even if the secured debt exceeds a specific amount. Therefore, **Answer (D) is an incorrect answer.**

164. Yes, Dealer should order a UCC search report before it sells the piano. Section 9-611(b) requires Dealer to send a disposition notice to the recipients listed in section 9-611(c). Those recipients include "any other secured party . . . that, 10 days before the notification date, held a security interest in . . . the collateral perfected by the filing of a financing statement." Because the list of intended recipients includes parties that have filed a financing statement against the piano, Dealer must order a UCC search report to discover those filings and the names of parties who may be entitled to notice. Absent the search report, Dealer may fail to send a notice to a party otherwise entitled to it, triggering litigation.

165. **Answer (B) is the correct answer.** Section 9-613 (applicable because this is *not* a consumer-goods transaction) provides the information that Dealer should include in its disposition notice. Section 9-613(1)(D) says that the notice should state "that the debtor is entitled to an accounting." Therefore, **Answer (B) is the correct answer.** If the transaction was a consumer-goods transaction, then Dealer's notice must remind the Resort that it remains liable for any deficiency remaining after the sale. *See* § 9-614(1)(B). But that reminder is not required by section 9-613, so **Answer (A) is an incorrect answer.** Section 9-613(1)(E) requires the notice to mention "the time and place of a public disposition or the time after which any other disposition is to be made." The facts mention that Dealer will sell the piano to a private buyer, rather than at a public sale, so the notice must mention the "time after which" the sale will take place but need not mention the precise date of sale. Therefore, **Answer (C) is an incorrect answer.** And while section 9-614(1)(C) requires a reminder of redemption rights, section 9-613(1) does not, **making Answer (D) an incorrect answer.**

166. **Answer (C) is the correct answer.** Former Article 9 did not clearly articulate what would happen to a deficiency claim arising from a disposition that was not commercially reasonable. So courts developed three responses over time. One response, the "absolute bar rule," favored the debtor by completely barring recovery of any deficiency, regardless of the severity of the breach or the resulting harm. Another response permitted the debtor to counterclaim for, and recover, any damages that it could prove resulted from the creditor's non-compliance. And a third response was a presumption that compliance would have generated proceeds equal to the debt (and thus no deficiency). The presumption was rebuttable, so the secured party could offer evidence that compliance would have generated proceeds less than the unpaid debt, still leaving a deficiency that the creditor should recover. Revised Article 9 adopts this so-called "rebuttable presumption rule." *See* § 9-626(a) and cmt. 3. Under this test, the court should enter a deficiency judgment of $3,700, calculated by subtracting the proceeds generated from a commercially reasonable disposition ($8,300) from the unpaid debt ($12,000), and **making Answer (C) the correct answer.** Because the "absolute bar rule" is inapplicable and Dealer offered proof rebutting the statutory presumption, **Answer (A) is incorrect.** The "rebuttable presumption rule" requires a determination of the amount of proceeds generated by a commercially reasonable disposition, not necessarily the fair market value (remember, nonjudicial foreclosures are distress sales that attract bargain hunters). So **Answer (B)**, calculated by subtracting the

fair market value ($9,500) from the unpaid debt ($12,000), **is incorrect**. And **Answer (D) is incorrect** because Dealer's own evidence revealed that a commercially reasonable disposition might have generated proceeds in excess of $8,000.

167. **Answer (D) is the correct answer.** This problem presents questions of the relationship between junior and senior creditors after default. First, did Henry have the right to seek replevin? Yes, notwithstanding any other interests in the property, Henry at least had attachment (a signed security agreement adequately describing the collateral, rights in the collateral, and the presence of value). As such, under section 9-203, his interest was enforceable. Under section 9-609, enforceable security interests (or "attached" security interests) can be enforced, after default, by repossession, which is what Henry did by his replevin action (and the replevin action is not a substitute for a court-ordered levy and execution sale; it simply determines the party with superior rights to possession).

Henry then conducts a non-complying foreclosure sale. Henry failed to comply with Article 9 because he did not send notice to the debtor (as mandated by section 9-611(c)), and by failing to advertise the sale he did not proceed in a commercially reasonable manner (as required by section 9-610(b)). These actions, however, probably only affect the deficiency that Q Corporation, Inc., may owe. The focus of this question, in part, is the effect on Beth's security interest.

Beth also appears to have an enforceable security interest. She also appears to be perfected: she has filed a financing statement in the same appropriate place as Henry, and her filing provides the debtor's legal name (the name mandated by section 9-503). Henry's filing, however, utilized the debtor's trade name. Moreover, Henry's listing of only "Q Corp." is "seriously misleading," rendering his filing ineffective and leaving him unperfected. Under section 9-506(c), "[i]f a search of the records of the filing office under the debtor's correct name, using the filing office's standard search logic, if any, would disclose a financing statement that fails sufficiently to provide the name of the debtor in accordance with Section 9-503(a), the name provided does not make the financing statement seriously misleading." Our situation is the converse: Henry's financing statement indexed under "Q Corp." would not be returned in a search under the true name. This means that Henry's filing is seriously misleading, and hence ineffective. The fact that a search under Q Corporation, Inc. (the correct name under section 9-503) would not turn up a filing showing just "Q Corp." is what makes the filing seriously misleading (sort of like the difference, as Mark Twain would have noted, between "lightning" and "lightning bug").

What is the consequence of this? Beth had the superior property interest. Her security interest was perfected, and Henry's security interest was unperfected. Beth, then, enjoys priority under section 9-322(a)(2). As a consequence, when Henry refused to turn over possession when Beth requested it, he thereafter maintained possession contrary to Beth's rights. This usually results in a conversion action. *See* § 9-609 cmt. 5. This means that Answers (C) and (D) are potentially correct. (Answer (A) can be easily dismissed. Henry's botched foreclosure does not affect Beth's rights against the debtor, so the debtor, Q Corporation, Inc., still owes the original $15,000, **making Answer (A) an incorrect answer.** Answer (B) does not mention conversion, and thus while correct as far as it goes, does not go far enough. Thus,

Answer (B) is not the correct answer.)

But what about Beth's rights against the innocent purchaser, Sarah? It is a fundamental premise of foreclosure that the sale extinguishes the interest of the person conducting the sale as well as all interests junior to it. *See* § 9-617(a). Senior interests are not affected (which explains why senior creditors do not share in the distribution of foreclosure proceeds under section 9-615(a)). So, effectively, Sarah has become a new debtor since she now owns the collateral. Beth may thus pursue the property in Sarah's hands, but nothing else that Sarah owns. She will get, against Sarah, the value of the property, but must stop when her debt of $15,000 is satisfied. Because Answer (C) omits the option to pursue Sarah,

Answer (C) is not the best answer. Answer (D) is the most complete answer and, therefore, the correct answer.

168. **Answer (B) is the correct answer.** Because Simon and his family use the horse for recreational pleasure, the horse is a "consumer good" as defined in section 9-102(a)(23). When collateral is a consumer good, First Bank must send its notice only to the debtor and any secondary obligor. *See* § 9-611(c). Simon, who owns the horse that is serving as collateral, is the debtor under section 9-102(a)(28)(A). Rachel, the guarantor on First Bank's loan, is a secondary obligor under section 9-102(a)(71)(A). So **Answer (B) is the correct answer. Answer (A) is underinclusive and incorrect.** First Bank can send its notice to other parties, such as Remington Farms and Second Bank. But Article 9 does not require First Bank to do so. Because of that, and the fact that Answers (C) and (D) do not indicate that Rachel must be sent notice, **Answers (C) and (D) are incorrect.**

169. First Bank should distribute the remaining $55,000 according to the payout scheme found in section 9-615(a). Under that statute, First Bank must remit proceeds to *subordinate* creditors who have provided to First Bank an authenticated demand for proceeds. Remington Farms, who gave written demand, is not a subordinate creditor. True, it never filed a financing statement. But Remington Farms, who engaged in seller financing, can claim a purchase-money security interest (§ 9-103(a), (b)(1)) in a consumer good, so its security interest is automatically perfected on attachment (§ 9-309(1)), giving it priority under section 9-322(a) over the competing claims of other subsequent secured creditors like First Bank and Second Bank. Therefore, Remington Farms is not a subordinate creditor and cannot claim any of the proceeds. (Remington Farms remains protected, however, because its senior security interest survives the disposition. *See* § 9-617(a) (discharging the security interests of the foreclosing creditor and *subordinate* creditors).) Second Bank is a subordinate creditor. However, Second Bank is not entitled to any proceeds because First Bank never received from Second Bank an authenticated demand for proceeds. Therefore, all remaining proceeds revert to the debtor, Simon, as "surplus" under section 9-615(d).

170. **Answer (D) is the correct answer.** Under 11 U.S.C. § 362(d), a court shall grant relief from the stay if (i) BigBank's security interest is not adequately protected (11 U.S.C. § 362(d)(1)) or (ii) Karen has no equity in the vehicle and the vehicle is not necessary to an effective reorganization (11 U.S.C. § 362(d)(2)) — and since this is a Chapter 7 liquidation, it is a given that the vehicle is not necessary for an effective reorganization. Under 11 U.S.C. § 362(g)(1), BigBank (as the party requesting relief) will have the burden of proof on Karen's equity in the vehicle, and under 11 U.S.C. § 362(g)(2), Karen (the party opposing the relief) has the burden of proof on all other issues, including the issue of adequate protection. This allocation of proof is correctly stated in **Answer (D), making it the correct answer and Answers (A), (B), and (C) incorrect answers.**

171. **Answer (D) is the correct answer.** The automatic stay is "automatic" and does go into effect regardless of whether any alleged violator of the stay knows or should know about it. But Answer (C) indicates that not only will the court find a violation — which did occur — but will award damages for that violation. While the operation of the stay is automatic — here resulting in rendering Yost's actions null or giving Henry the absolute right to nullify them — damages require more. Section 362(k) requires a "willful violation of the stay." If one exists, then "an individual injured by any willful violation of a stay provided by this section shall recover actual damages, including costs and attorneys' fees, and, in appropriate circumstances, may recover punitive damages." 11 U.S.C. § 362(k)(1). Here, when Yost applied the account's balance to the loan, it did not have notice of Henry's individual filing. Any violation of the stay, then, would not be "willful," and no damages would flow. **Answer (C) is thus incorrect.** But once Henry calls Yost and tells it that he had commenced a bankruptcy case, Yost had actual notice of the filing, and its actions thereafter in refusing to release the funds constituted a separate and independent violation of the stay — at a minimum, it was exercising control over estate property in violation of Section 362(a)(3). For that violation, Yost may be liable in damages for actual loss, including in some circuits, emotional distress damages. *See Sternberg v. Johnson*, 595 F.3d 937 (9th Cir. 2009). Because the statute limits damages to the time period after it learned of Henry's filing, it limits recovery to the period of Yost Bank's "willful" violation — its inaction in the face of a void or voidable act — **making Answer (D) the correct answer.**

    Answer (A) is incorrect because section 9-109(d)(13) only excludes "deposit account[s] in consumer transaction[s]." Under section 9-102(a)(26)(i), however, a "consumer transaction" is one in which "an individual incurs an obligation primarily for personal, family, or household purposes." Here, the facts state that the loan was incurred for business purposes, and thus the security interest is within Article 9, thus negating the premise of the answer.

    Answer (B) is incorrect because Yost Bank acted after it received actual notice of the existence of the stay; bankruptcy law does not require formal notice be given for consequences to attach. Once it received Henry's telephone call, it acted at its peril by proceeding as if nothing had occurred. In short, Yost could not rely on the fact that it did not get proper notice; the fact that it received actual notice was sufficient for its later actions to be deemed "willful."

172. **Answer (A) is the correct answer.** Because the trustee cannot set aside the security interests of either creditor, this problem is merely an Article 9 priority dispute. MedCo, a seller-financer, is claiming a purchase-money security interest in the kidney dialysis machine under section 9-103(a) and (b)(1). Because MedCo filed its financing statement on August 25, within twenty days after delivering the machine to Clinic on August 9, MedCo's security interest in the machine enjoys priority under section 9-324(a). Bank's security interest in Clinic's remaining equipment enjoys priority under section 9-322(a)(1) because Bank filed its financing statement on July 7, before MedCo filed its financing statement on August 25. Clinic owes $80,000 to MedCo, and the kidney dialysis machine has a value of $90,000. Under Section 506(a) of the Bankruptcy Code, a creditor has a secured claim to the extent of the value of its security, so MedCo has an $80,000 secured claim. Clinic owes $120,000 to Bank, and Bank's claim is secured in an amount equal to the remaining collateral: $60,000. Under Section 506(a), if a secured creditor's debt is more than the value of the collateral, the creditor has an unsecured claim for the deficiency. The balance of Bank's claim, $60,000, is thus an unsecured claim. So Bank has a $60,000 secured claim and a $60,000 unsecured claim, and MedCo has an $80,000 secured claim. This result is found in **Answer (A), making it the correct answer and Answers (B), (C), and (D) the incorrect answers.**

173. **Answer (C) is the correct answer.** Normally the act of filing a post-petition financing statement violates the automatic stay. 11 U.S.C. § 362(a)(4), (5). But post-petition perfection is permitted by 11 U.S.C. § 362(b)(3) if "the trustee's rights and powers are subject to such perfection under section 546(b) of this title." Under 11 U.S.C. § 546(b)(1), a trustee's rights and powers are subject to any Article 9 provision that permits perfection to be effective against a lien creditor that acquired its lien prior to perfection. The applicable Article 9 provision is section 9-317(e), which permits a purchase-money creditor to enjoy priority over the competing (and prior) claim of a lien creditor if the purchase-money creditor's interest is perfected no later than the twentieth day after the debtor receives possession of the collateral. As Dealer (a seller-financer) can claim a purchase-money security interest in the refrigerator under section 9-103(a) and (b)(1), and because Dealer timely filed its financing statement, Dealer can invoke the protection afforded by section 9-317(e). Therefore, Dealer did not violate the automatic stay by filing its financing statement after Restaurant filed its bankruptcy petition.

Answer (A) is incorrect because the refrigerator is equipment, and a purchase-money security interest is automatically perfected only in consumer goods. § 9-309(1). **Answer (B) is incorrect** because only individuals can exempt property from the estate. 11 U.S.C. § 522(b) (indicating that "an individual debtor" may exempt property). And **Answer (D) is incorrect** because Chapter 7 is a liquidation chapter, not a reorganization chapter.

174. **Answer (C) is the correct answer.** Standing alone, an after-acquired property clause is ineffective to encumber post-petition collateral. 11 U.S.C. § 552(a). The Bankruptcy Code, however, does recognize security interests in post-petition proceeds of prepetition collateral. 11 U.S.C. § 552(b)(1). The purpose of Section 552(b) is to free up assets needed by the bankrupt debtor to secure post-petition financing in favor of a creditor that will insist on a first-position security interest in unencumbered collateral. It is also a recognition that no

new value is extended by virtue of a security interest obtained solely due to an after-acquired property clause.

Under Section 552(b), Bank has a security interest in inventory worth $400,000 to $450,000 calculated as follows: $300,000 (collateral which existed on the petition date) + $100,000 (admitted proceeds of prepetition collateral) + perhaps $50,000 (depends on whether the post-petition accounts were generated by the sale of pre-petition inventory). The $50,000 allocable to the sale of Google stock does not represent prepetition collateral or its proceeds, and thus is not included. As to accounts, Bank has a security interest in accounts worth $350,000 to $400,000 calculated as follows: $250,000 (collateral existed on the petition date) + $100,000 (proceeds of prepetition collateral) + perhaps $50,000 (the post-petition inventory may have been acquired with cash proceeds of prepetition accounts, and thus would be proceeds of proceeds, which Section 552(b) also recognizes). The $50,000 allocable to the donated equipment does not represent prepetition collateral or its proceeds. So Bank has a security interest in accounts and inventory that aggregate $750,000 to $850,000, **making Answer (C) the correct answer and Answers (A), (B), and (D) incorrect answers.**

175. **Answer (A) is the correct answer.** The strong-arm clause, a moniker given to 11 U.S.C. § 544(a)(1), gives the trustee the status of a hypothetical lien creditor as of the petition date, together with the rights and powers associated with that status, including the right to "avoid any transfer of property of the debtor" that could be avoided by such a lien creditor as of the petition date. This gives the trustee no independent rights; it only gives the trustee the powers that state law gives lien creditors generally. Working in tandem with section 9-317(a)(2), the strong-arm clause permits the trustee to avoid any security interest that is unperfected on the petition date, **making Answer (A) the correct answer. Answers (B) and (C) — both incorrect —** quote language from the actual and constructive fraud tests of the fraudulent transfer provision, 11 U.S.C. § 548(a). And **Answer (D), also incorrect,** is a reference to 11 U.S.C. § 522(f), which permits a consumer debtor to avoid certain judicial liens on, and non-possessory, non-purchase-money security interests in, property that otherwise would be exempt in the absence of the encumbrance.

176. **Answer (B) is the correct answer.** Under 11 U.S.C. § 544(a)(1), also known as the "strong-arm clause," the trustee can "avoid any transfer of property of the debtor" (which includes a security interest) that could be avoided by a hypothetical lien creditor on the date of the petition. And under section 9-317(a)(2), a security interest is subordinate to the property rights of a lien creditor (e.g., the bankruptcy trustee) if, when the lien arises, the security interest is not perfected (or, in less frequent situations, when perfection has not occurred solely because the secured party has not given value when the lien arises). Taken together, these two statutes permit the trustee to destroy any security interest that is unperfected on the petition date. Therefore, you must determine whether Secured Party's security interest was perfected on September 13.

Debtor is a Delaware corporation, making it a "registered organization" under section 9-102(a)(70). Therefore, to the extent that Secured Party is relying on a financing statement for perfection, it must file the financing statement in Delaware. *See* §§ 9-301(1), 9-307(e). Secured Party is perfected in Answer (A) because it filed its financing statement in Delaware. That is the proper place to file, not because the collateral was in Delaware, but because Delaware is the law under which Debtor was created. The collateral location is irrelevant, so no subsequent filing in Illinois is required. Secured Party remained perfected on the petition date in the Illinois collateral by the Delaware filing, so the trustee cannot avoid the security interest under 11 U.S.C. § 544(a)(1), **making Answer (A) an incorrect answer.**

Under section 9-305(c)(1), Secured Party should have filed its financing statement in Delaware to perfect a security interest in investment property. Instead, Secured Party filed in the state where the stock certificate was located (Georgia), a mistake that left Secured Party unperfected on the petition date. Therefore, the trustee can avoid Secured Party's unperfected security interest under 11 U.S.C. § 544(a)(1), **making Answer (B) the correct answer.**

For reasons already mentioned, Secured Party is perfected in Debtor's Texas-based inventory by the Delaware filing. Normally a post-petition filing is ineffective because it violates the automatic stay under 11 U.S.C. § 362(a)(4). But subsection (a) is expressly subject to subsection (b). And 11 U.S.C. § 362(b)(3) permits a post-petition filing "to the extent that the trustee's rights and powers are subject to such perfection under section 546(b) of this title." Under that section, the trustee's avoiding powers "are subject to any generally applicable law that — (A) permits perfection of an interest in property to be effective against an entity that acquires rights in such property before the date of perfection." The "generally applicable law" is section 9-317(e), which permits a secured party to perfect its purchase-money security interest after the lien creditor obtains a competing property interest and yet enjoy priority over that competing property interest. Secured Party timely perfected its purchase-money security interest and can invoke the protection afforded by section 9-317(e). Therefore, the post-petition filing did not violate the automatic stay and is effective to prevent the trustee from avoiding the security interest under 11 U.S.C. § 544(a)(1). So **Answer (C) is an incorrect answer.**

And Secured Party's security interest in the bank account became perfected by "control" under section 9-104(a)(1) at the moment of attachment and remained perfected on the petition date. Thus, the trustee cannot avoid the security interest under 11 U.S.C. § 544(a)(1), and **Answer (D) is an incorrect answer.**

177. **Answer (B) is the correct answer.** This question focuses on fraudulent transfers and their effect on the transfer of property (so if you are not covering fraudulent transfers in your course, ignore this question). Under the law of fraudulent transfers, a transfer may be set aside notwithstanding compliance with various formalities. It can be set aside in two situations: the first is if the debtor made the transfer with the intent to hinder, delay, or defraud his or her creditors; the second is if the transfer is for less than a reasonably equivalent value and the transferor, after the transfer, is left in a poor financial state such as insolvency.

Given the power of fraudulent transfer law to override other formalities, **Answer (A) is incorrect.** Similarly, since fraudulent transfers look at the intent or the financial state of the debtor/transferor, the financial state of the recipient is irrelevant. That **excludes Answer (C) as a correct answer.**

Since this was a gift transaction, with no expectation that Sally would recover or reclaim the car, it does not appear to be a transaction that creates a security interest, and thus filing a financing statement would do no good, and this **eliminates Answer (D) as an answer.**

This leaves Answer (B). Under section 2(b) of the Uniform Fraudulent Transfer Act, if a creditor can show that the transferor/debtor was not paying his or her debts as they become due, then a presumption of insolvency is created. Insolvency, in turn, is otherwise defined as having more liabilities than assets. But it is up to the debtor/transferor to show that he or she was not insolvent; if the debtor does not make that showing, then he or she will be assumed to be insolvent.

But in addition to a bad financial state such as insolvency, the creditor must show that there was a lack of reasonably equivalent value for the transaction. Here, in a gift transaction, not only is there a lack of reasonably equivalent value, but there is no value given. With both insolvency and a lack of reasonably equivalent value, the transaction may be set aside for the benefit of Sally's creditors. Thus **Answer (B) is correct.**

178. **Answer (C) is the correct answer.** This fact pattern presents the classic leveraged buyout, which can be held to be a fraudulent transfer. *See Boyer v. Crown Stock Dist., Inc.*, 587 F.3d 787 (7th Cir. 2009); *Official Comm. of Unsecured Creditors of Tousa, Inc. v. Citicorp North Am., Inc. (In re TOUSA, Inc.)*, 422 B.R. 783, 866 (Bankr. S.D. Fla. 2009). But before we can get to that conclusion, the question is structured so that we have to assess the transaction under both preference and fraudulent transfer law.

Note first that, from the perspective of Article 9, Fred's security interest is valid and properly perfected. The security agreement describes a broad range of collateral, using Article 9 terms as is permitted by section 9-108. The financing statement uses an "all assets" description as is permitted by section 9-504. And the financing statement is filed in Delaware, where GI is located for purposes of Article 9 under section 9-307. But this question points out that more than Article 9 has to be consulted when the debtor has filed a bankruptcy petition.

Is there a preference or a fraudulent transfer? First, preference law requires a "transfer," and fraudulent transfer law will set aside certain transfers. Transfers are defined very broadly in the Bankruptcy Code. Under the Bankruptcy Code, the term "transfer" "means — (A) the creation of a lien; (B) the retention of title as a security interest; (C) the foreclosure of a debtor's equity of redemption; or (D) each mode, direct or indirect, absolute or conditional, voluntary or involuntary, of disposing of or parting with — (i) property; or (ii) an interest in property." 11 U.S.C. § 101(54). Here, the transfer is the transfer of a security interest from GI to Fred; this transaction gave property rights to Fred.

But preferences require that the transfer be "to or for the benefit of a creditor," 11 U.S.C. § 547(b)(1), and "for or on account of an antecedent debt owed by the debtor before such transfer was made," 11 U.S.C. § 547(b)(2). Here, there is no indication that the creation of the security interest was for anything but the debt created simultaneously with the sale of the GI stock. Thus, the transfer cannot be a preference, because there appears to be no antecedent debt, thereby **disqualifying Answers (B) and (D).**

Is it a fraudulent transfer? In addition to transactions made with the actual intent to hinder, delay, or defraud (which does not seem to be present here), fraudulent transfers include transfers that are made for less than a reasonably equivalent value, *and* which either rendered the debtor insolvent (or nearly so) or were made at a time at which the debtor was insolvent (or nearly so). 11 U.S.C. § 548(a)(1)(B).

Was the transfer for a "reasonably equivalent value"? Probably not. GI, as a separate entity with separate creditors, did not receive anything in return for the grant of a security interest in its assets. It is as if it guaranteed Alice's debt and received nothing in return. (Note: most gift transactions, or transactions without consideration such as the payment of dividends, will be made for less than a reasonably equivalent value.)

Was GI insolvent or nearly so when it granted the security interest? The test for constructively fraudulent transfers under 11 U.S.C. § 548(a)(1)(B) requires *both* a lack of reasonably equivalent value and a shaky or insolvent financial state. Specifically, 11 U.S.C. § 548(a)(1)(B) requires one of the three adverse financial states;[1] namely that the debtor: "(I) was insolvent on the date that such transfer was made or such obligation was incurred, or became insolvent as a result of such transfer or obligation; (II) was engaged in business or a transaction, or was about to engage in business or a transaction, for which any property remaining with the debtor was an unreasonably small capital; or (III) intended to incur, or believed that the debtor would incur, debts that would be beyond the debtor's ability to pay as such debts matured." Insolvency, under the Bankruptcy Code, is a balance sheet test. It requires a "financial condition such that the sum of such entity's debts is greater than all of such entity's property, at a fair valuation." 11 U.S.C. § 101(32).

While there is not enough information here to find without question that GI was insolvent (no financial information at all is given), the speedy decline of GI and its inability to attract any new capital given Fred's security interest probably means that GI was insolvent (no one would lend on its assets in a junior position) or that it had "unreasonable small capital" (since it could not raise any based on its other assets). Given the likelihood of a colorable fraudulent transfer action, **Answer (A) is incorrect, leaving Answer (C) as the correct answer.**

179. **Answer (C) is the correct answer.** First Bank is perfected in all collateral. The facts give the value of that collateral as $6,000,000. What is the secured claim in bankruptcy? That is determined by 11 U.S.C. §§ 506(a)(1) and 506(b). Under 11 U.S.C. § 506(a)(1), "[a]n allowed claim of a creditor secured by a lien on property in which the estate has an interest, . . . is a secured claim to the extent of the value of such creditor's interest in the estate's interest in such property." This states that the secured claim has a maximum value of $6,000,000, the value of the collateral. Thus, **Answer (A) is incorrect.**

We also know that bankruptcy will not give First Bank more than its state law claim. That means that we figure out what the debt is under state law, and that also is a maximum value. Here, we know that there is at least $5,000,000 in principal outstanding. Thus, the claim is at least $5,000,000. Is it more? Under state law, that is, under Article 9, First Bank was careful to note that attorneys' fees were also debts that would be secured by the collateral. If First Bank had not indicated that its attorneys' fees were part of the obligation secured, they would just be unsecured claims (that is, not secured by the collateral).

Knowing that interest continues to accrue under state law, we now know that **Answer (B) is incorrect**, since the $5,000,000 answer does not account for any accrued interest and attorneys' fees. Whether these additional amounts — the accrued interest and attorneys' fees — will be added to the secured claim in bankruptcy is a function of 11 U.S.C. § 506(b). That section states that "[t]o the extent that an allowed secured claim is secured by property the value of which . . . is greater than the amount of such claim, there shall be allowed to the

---

[1] The 2005 amendments added a fourth condition to Section 548(a)(1)(B). Item (IV) does not relate to the financial condition of the debtor; rather, it states, as a condition of equal relevance, that the debtor: "(IV) made such transfer to or for the benefit of an insider, or incurred such obligation to or for the benefit of an insider, under an employment contract and not in the ordinary course of business."

holder of such claim, interest on such claim, and any reasonable fees, costs, or charges provided for under the agreement or State statute under which such claim arose."

So in cases such as First Bank's, in which the agreement provides for attorneys' fees and costs, post-petition interest and reasonable attorneys' fees and costs will accrue post-petition and be added to the secured claim. First Bank will not get more than its actual claim, **making Answer (D) an incorrect answer. That leaves Answer (C) as the correct answer.**

180. **Answer (A) is the correct answer.** Here, the changed fact is the reduced value of the collateral. For all the reasons listed in the preceding answer, the secured claim in bankruptcy cannot exceed the value of the collateral. Thus, it is irrelevant, for purposes of calculating the secured claim, what the amount secured by the debt would be under state law. Under 11 U.S.C. § 506(a)(1), then, the secured claim is limited to the value of the collateral, or $4,000,000. **The only answer consistent with this answer is Answer (A), making Answers (B), (C), and (D) incorrect.**

181. **Answer (D) is the correct answer.** This question again involves fraudulent transfer law. Here, there were transfers to Diablo (the foreclosure) and to Larry's, Inc. (the foreclosure sale). Under 11 U.S.C. § 548(a)(1)(A), a trustee may avoid any transfer made or obligation incurred within two years of the petition date if the transaction was made with the intent to hinder, delay, or defraud creditors. (Before 2005, the lookback period was only one year.) Since the lookback period is now two years, **Answer (A) is incorrect.**

It is also irrelevant that Larry's, Inc. may have been solvent. The actual intent standard of Section 548(a)(1)(A) applies notwithstanding the financial condition of the debtor at the time of the transaction. The law only looks at the intent with which the transaction was made. As a result, **Answer (C) is incorrect.**

That leaves Answer (B), which focuses on Diablo's intent, and Answer (D), which focuses on Larry's intent. Under Section 548(a)(1)(A), the intent of the recipient of the transfer is irrelevant. Their intent may affect their defenses, but it does not factor into the basic elements of the cause of action. As a consequence, **Answer (B) is incorrect.** As to Answer (D), a corporation's or LLC's intent is the intent of its owners or officers engaged in the transaction, and the intent specified in Section 548 is in the alternative: the trustee need only establish an intent to hinder, or an intent to delay, or an intent to defraud to prevail. Indeed, Section 4(b)(11) of the Uniform Fraudulent Transfer Act states that a badge of fraud — that is, a set of facts from which one can infer proscribed intent — exists if "the debtor transferred the essential assets of the business to a lienor who transferred the assets to an insider of the debtor." *See also Voest-Alpine Trading USA Corp. v. Vantage Steel Corp.*, 919 F.2d 206, 212 (3d Cir. 1990). As a result, **Answer (D) is correct.**

It also may be the case that the transaction left Larry's, LLC with unreasonably small capital. Since it received dollar for dollar reduction in debt — which is value under Section 548(d) — it likely received reasonably equivalent value, although some courts might collapse the transaction.

This answer can be answered affirmatively under state law as well — the Uniform Fraudulent Transfer Act (enacted in forty-four states) provides for a four-year statute of repose and all of the essential elements of avoidance as Section 548 of the Bankruptcy Code. The bankruptcy trustee has access to such law under Section 544(b) of the Bankruptcy Code.

182.   **Answer (C) is the correct answer.** Under 11 U.S.C. § 547(e), a transfer cannot occur until the debtor acquires rights in the encumbered property. Debtor acquired rights in the Item on the sale date, June 8, under UCC § 2-501(1)(b) ("identification occurs . . . when goods are shipped, marked, or otherwise designated by the seller as goods to which the contract refers"). As Bank had previously filed a financing statement, its security interest in the Item became perfected on June 8. That is the date of transfer. **Answers (A) and (B) are incorrect** because Debtor did not, at either of those times, have any rights in the Item. And **Answer (D) is incorrect** because Debtor need not have possession in order to have sufficient rights in the Item to use it as collateral.

183.   **Answer (A) is the correct answer.** Under 11 U.S.C. § 547(b), the trustee can attack as voidable preferences "any transfer of an interest of the debtor in property." Angela's payment of $500 is a transfer, as is Elliott's conveyance of a security interest in his investment portfolio. But neither Angela nor Elliott is the "debtor." Kirk, the party in bankruptcy, is the debtor. Therefore, because the transfers were made by non-debtor parties, the transfers cannot be attacked by the trustee as voidable preferences. There was no "transfer of an interest of the debtor in property." **Answers (B), (C), and (D) are all incorrect** because they suggest that Angela's payment of $500, Elliott's grant of a security interest, or both, can be attacked as voidable preferences.

As easy as this requirement seems to be, students should be very careful when dismissing a preference analysis solely because the transfer did not come from the debtor. For example, the requirement that the transfer be of property of the estate has not stopped courts from recharacterizing a transaction when the effect, but not the letter, of the transaction is to transfer property that would have been property of the estate. This can be seen when someone assumes the debt of another as part of the purchase price for assets (as when a buyer of a business's assets agrees to assume the existing business lease). Payments on that assumed debt from and after the transfer, while made directly from the non-bankrupt buyer, are held to be indirectly made by the bankrupt debtor, since the assumption is part of the consideration the debtor received. This was summarized by the Seventh Circuit as follows:

> In those cases in which courts have held that a preference was given in the context of an asset sale, there is a fairly direct, traceable link between the consideration given for the debtor's assets and the funds used to pay the creditor. For instance, a debtor may sell its assets to a third party, and, as part of the purchase agreement, the third party may agree to assume the debtor's liabilities. When the third party subsequently pays a creditor of the debtor, courts have allowed the bankruptcy trustee to recover the payment as a preference. *See* [Mordy v. Chemcarb, Inc. (*In re* Food Catering & Housing, Inc.), 971 F.2d 396, 397–98 (9th Cir. 1992)]; Sommers v. Burton (*In re* Conard Corp.), 806 F.2d 610, 611–12 (5th Cir. 1986). In such cases, the third party's

assumption of the debtor's debt is consideration for the sale of the debtor's assets. *See In re* Food Catering, 971 F.2d at 398. The debtor effectively transferred to the creditor its right to receive a portion of the sale price equal to the amount of the debt. *See In re* Conard Corp., 806 F.2d at 612. The result is the same when, instead of transferring the money directly to the creditor, the third party deposits the money into an escrow account over which the debtor has no control. *See In re* Interior Wood, 986 F.2d at 231. Nor does the result change when the third party, rather than the debtor, specifies which creditor will receive the funds paid into the escrow account. *See* Feltman v. Bd. of County Comm'rs of Metro. Dade County (*In re* S.E.L. Maduro (Florida), Inc.), 205 B.R. 987, 992–93 (Bankr. S.D. Fla.1997).

Warsco v. Preferred Technical Group, 258 F.3d 557, 565 (7th Cir. 2001).

184. **Answer (D) is the correct answer. Answer (A) is incorrect** because the presumption can be rebutted by the secured party. **Answer (B) is incorrect** because 11 U.S.C. § 547(g) places the burden of proving non-avoidability of the transfer on the secured party. **Answer (C) also is incorrect.** For example, debtor borrows money on July 1, and the security interest attaches on July 3 and is perfected on July 25. Because the security interest is perfected within thirty days of attachment, the attachment date is the date of the transfer under 11 U.S.C. § 547(e)(2). But the debt date of July 1 remains antecedent (or prior) to the transfer date of July 3. So **Answer (C) is incorrect.** And **Answer (D) is correct** under 11 U.S.C. § 550(c). This position was reaffirmed by the addition of Section 547(i) in 2005. The effect of Sections 547(i) and 550(c) is to permit lenders to extract guaranties from insiders (almost all guaranties tend to be executed by insiders) without worrying that its preference period exposure will be extended from ninety days to one year.

185. **Answer (B) is the correct answer.** The "substantially contemporaneous exchange" exception, codified at 11 U.S.C. § 547(c)(1), can preserve any type of transfer, so **Answer (A) is incorrect.** The "enabling loan" exception," found at 11 U.S.C. § 547(c)(3), preserves only security interest transfers, **making Answer (C) incorrect.** The "floating lien" exception of 11 U.S.C. § 547(c)(5) preserves only security interest transfers in specific types of collateral, so **Answer (D) is incorrect.** But the "ordinary course of business" exception, codified at 11 U.S.C. § 547(c)(2), preserves only transfers "in payment of a debt," **making Answer (B) the correct answer.**

186. **Answer (C) is the correct answer.** The "floating lien" exception of 11 U.S.C. § 547(c)(5) permits the secured party to preserve its perfected security interest in inventory and accounts as of the petition date if the deficiency as of the petition date is not less than the deficiency on the later of (i) the date on which the secured creditor first gave value and (ii) the first day of the preference period (generally the ninetieth day before the petition date). But the security interest on the petition date is voided to the extent that the deficiency on the petition date is less than the deficiency calculated on the earlier date. The statute requires knowledge of the debt amount and the collateral value on two, and only two, dates. One date is the petition date; the other date is the later of the two dates described above. Debt amounts and collateral values on other dates are irrelevant.

In this problem, the deficiency on the petition date of October 1 is $200,000 (debt of $2 million and collateral worth $1.8 million). The ninetieth day preceding October 1 is approximately July 1. But Bank did not loan money until July 16, so this later date is the date on which the other comparative deficiency is calculated. That deficiency is $300,000 (debt of $2.0 million and collateral worth $1.7 million). Comparing the two deficiencies reveals that Bank has improved its position by $100,000 (the deficiency decreased from $300,000 to $200,000). This amount is subtracted from the collateral value on October 1 ($1.8 million), leaving Bank with a perfected security interest in collateral worth $1.7 million (**making Answer (C) the correct answer and Answers (A), (B), and (D) incorrect answers**).

187. **Answer (C) is the correct answer.** Here, we have a non-purchase-money security interest in a consumer good — the security interest in the television was not given as part of its purchase. As such, Friendly had only an unperfected security interest in the television. Being unperfected, however, does not mean unenforceable; indeed, attachment alone is sufficient for the security interest to be enforced. So Friendly could repossess the goods. It had that right under section 9-609, and it accomplished the repossession without a breach of the peace. Therefore, **Answer (D) is incorrect.**

Friendly's sale, however, is not in accordance with Article 9. It does not give proper notice under section 9-611(c), and the process of sale is likely not commercially reasonable under section 9-610(b), given its timing and the ultimate purchaser. But that may not matter, if the teller who purchased the set paid an amount equal to its fair market value. Moreover, such actions would affect Friendly's deficiency, not the sale itself.

Thus, the focus should be on Friendly's receipt of the $2,500. **Answer (B) is incorrect** because the sale has already occurred. The strong-arm power of 11 U.S.C. § 544(a)(1) that gives the trustee the status of a lien creditor only matters with respect to property that the debtor still has at the time of the bankruptcy filing. That leaves Answer (A) — under which Friendly keeps the money — and Answer (C) — which requires a preference analysis.

Is the receipt of the $2,500 preferential? Here, our determination that Friendly's security interest was unperfected matters. Friendly meets all of the requirements for a preference. It is a transfer (that it was involuntary does not matter) to a creditor (Friendly) on account of an antecedent debt (the $5,000 loan) within ninety days of the filing, and which, if Friendly were allowed to keep it, would allow it to receive a better dividend than other unsecured creditors (if there is a 10% dividend, then Friendly will collect $2,750 on its loan ($2,500 from the sale, and $250 in the form of a 10% dividend on the $2,500 deficiency). Had it not repossessed the goods, it would have received only $500 (10% of the $5,000 debt). Since there are no applicable defenses under 11 U.S.C. § 547(c), this means that Friendly will have to turn over the $2,500 it received, **making Answer (C) the correct answer and Answer (A) the incorrect answer.**

188. **Answer (D) is the correct answer.** The only transfer in Answer (A) is the loan repayment. But the loan was repaid by Debtor's brother, not the bankrupt party (Debtor). Therefore, the loan repayment does not represent a "transfer of an interest of the debtor in property" under 11 U.S.C. § 547(b), **making Answer (A) an incorrect answer. Answer (B) also is incorrect.** Dealer is fully secured at all times (the collateral is always worth at least $80,000 — the amount of the original credit). Because Dealer is fully secured, Debtor's loan repayment of $35,000 does not permit Dealer to receive more than it would under a Chapter 7 liquidation if the payment had not been made. If Dealer keeps the $35,000 it will file a proof of claim for $45,000, a fully secured claim. If Debtor never made the $35,000 payment, then Dealer will file a proof of claim for $80,000, also a fully secured claim. In both instances Dealer is repaid in full. Therefore, the trustee cannot satisfy 11 U.S.C. § 547(b)(5), **making**

Answer (B) incorrect. Answer (C) is incorrect because the transfer occurred on May 1, a date that falls outside the ninety-day preference period preceding the petition date of August 15. 11 U.S.C. § 547(b)(4)(A). **Answer (D) is correct** because all elements of 11 U.S.C. § 547(b) are present. The transfer is Debtor's grant of a security interest to Finance Company (a pre-petition creditor) in early February, within the ninety-day period preceding the petition date of April 25. And the transfer permits Finance Company to receive more than it would in a Chapter 7 liquidation without the security interest. If Finance Company keeps the security interest, it will file a proof of claim for $10,000, a fully secured claim. But if Debtor never grants the security interest, Finance Company will file a proof of claim for $10,000 — an unsecured claim. So the transfer does favor Finance Company by converting an unsecured claim to a secured claim (the type of behavior that the voidable preference statute seeks to condemn).

189.   **Answer (C) is correct.** First, the payment is preferential under 11 U.S.C. § 547(b) — it is a transfer, of property of the debtor, made within ninety days of the filing, at a time when the debtor was (presumed) insolvent (*see* § 547(f)), and, because the creditor is undersecured, it enables the creditor to receive more than it would had the payment not been made and the debtor's assets distributed under chapter 7 (*see* § 547(b)(5)). Because the creditor is unsecured, the payment is deemed applied to the undersecured portion of the claim, and since that portion is unsecured by definition, the payment/transfer is preferential. As a result, **Answer (A) is incorrect.**

The answer then turns on whether the bank can prove a defense, and the defense most applicable here is the ordinary course of business defense found in Section 547(c)(2). Before 2005, this defense required five elements: (1) the debt was incurred in the ordinary course of business of the debtor; (2) the debt was incurred in the ordinary course of business of the transferee; (3) the transfer was made in the ordinary course of business of the debtor; (4) the transfer was made in the ordinary course of business of the transferee; and (5) the transfer was made according to ordinary business terms. In 2005, Congress significantly changed the defense. Now it only has three elements. The first two are the same as before: (1) the debt was incurred in the ordinary course of business of the debtor; and (2) the debt was incurred in the ordinary course of business of the transferee. The third element, however, collapses the final three elements of the pre-2005 statute: (3) the transfer (i) was made in the ordinary course of business of the debtor and the transferee; *or* (ii) was made according to ordinary business terms.

Here, the facts state that there was nothing unusual about the creation of the debt. The only question is whether Ladle's collection practices, being different than the industry norm, matter. And it appears that they do not. The clerk pays the amount owed with a regular check, which would seem to be within "ordinary business terms." **That means that Answer (C) is correct.**

Answer (B) is incorrect because notwithstanding the physical presence of the collector sent, the facts state that no breach of the peace occurred, and that the collector was civil and well-behaved at all times. Moreover, so long as the payment was made on ordinary business terms, the manner in which collection was made does not matter.

Answer (D) is incorrect for the same reason. So long as the transfer — here the payment — was made according to ordinary business terms, the defense protects the transferee. The result might be different if the payment was demanded and made in cash or by wire transfer, since those might not qualify as ordinary business terms. But then the practices of both the debtor and the bank would be at issue as to whether such form of demand and payment were in the ordinary course of business of the debtor and the bank.

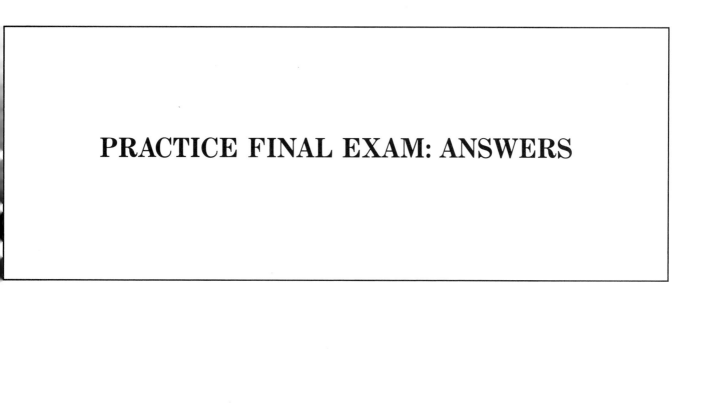

PRACTICE FINAL EXAM: ANSWERS

190. **Answer (C) is the best answer.** A purchase-money security interest (often referred to as a "PMSI" (pronounced by some as "pim-zee")) is defined at section 9-103(b)(1) as a "security interest in goods . . . (1) to the extent that the goods are purchase-money collateral with respect to that security interest." (Alternative methods of obtaining a PMSI are found in subsections (b)(2) and (b)(3), which are irrelevant to this problem.) Under this definition, a creditor can claim a PMSI only in goods. **Answer (B), then, is incorrect** because capital stock is "investment property" under section 9-102(a)(49), and "investment property" is excluded from the definition of "goods" under the last sentence of section 9-102(a)(44). Answers (A), (C), and (D) remain viable answers, however, because a TV, a snowmobile, and a comic book collection are all examples of "goods."

Continuing with the definition, the collateral (the goods) must be "purchase-money collateral," defined in section 9-103(a)(1) as "goods . . . that secures a purchase-money obligation incurred with respect to that collateral." A "purchase-money obligation" is defined at section 9-103(a)(2) as "an obligation of an obligor incurred as all or part of the price of the collateral [often referred to as seller financing] or for value given to enable the debtor to acquire rights in or the use of the collateral if the value is in fact so used [often referred to as third-party financing]." **Answer (A) is incorrect** because the SmallBank loan is not a "purchase-money obligation." SmallBank did not engage in seller financing, and its loan did not "enable the debtor to acquire rights in or the use of the collateral." Karen, the debtor, already owned the TV.

Answer (D) is not the best answer because Friendly Finance cannot be confident that its loan was a "purchase-money obligation." Friendly Finance did not engage in seller financing. And because Friendly Finance wired the funds directly into Gordon's account (rather than to the seller), Friendly Finance may have difficulty proving that its money was "in fact so used" when Gordon pays for the comic book collection three weeks later. Depending on the account balance prior to the wire transfer, the subsequent activity in the account, and the applicable method of tracing (FIFO — funds first in are first out; LIFO — funds last in are first out), Friendly Finance may or may not have a PMSI. But these issues do not exist under **Answer (C), which is the best answer.** Winterpark Motors has engaged in seller financing, its extension of credit is a "purchase-money obligation," and the snowmobile is "purchase-money collateral." Winterpark Motors' failure to properly perfect its security interest may prove fatal in a priority dispute with another creditor (or the loss of the security interest in a bankruptcy). But a creditor need not be perfected to claim a PMSI under section 9-103.

191. **Answer (B) is the correct answer.** Section 9-104(a) provides three ways in which Lender can achieve "control" of BAMCO's savings account maintained with Prosperity Bank. The first option, which gives "control" to a secured party that is also the financial institution that maintains the account, is not available to Lender because a third party — Prosperity Bank — maintains the savings account. The second option is available to Lender, though. It

requires Lender, BAMCO, and Prosperity Bank to authenticate a record in which Prosperity Bank agrees to honor Lender's instructions to liquidate the savings account without BAMCO's further consent. The third option permits Lender to obtain "control" if it becomes Prosperity Bank's "customer" on the deposit account (an option which is not explored in this question, but which could be satisfied if account records at Prosperity Bank were revised in a manner that named Lender as the owner (or perhaps co-owner with BAMCO) of the savings account). Note that Lender's "control" need not be exclusive. Lender will have "control" of the savings account even if BAMCO retains deposit and withdrawal rights on the savings account. *See* § 9-104(b).

With this background in mind, a review of the options reveals that **Answer (B) is correct.** All three parties have executed the agreement, which gives Lender the right to liquidate the account without BAMCO's further consent. Lender has achieved "control" under the second option above (§ 9-104(a)(2)), **making Answer (B) the correct answer.** BAMCO's retention of withdrawal rights above a specific minimum account balance does not negate "control."

Answer (A) is incorrect because the action taken fails to satisfy any of the three statutory options. The security agreement satisfies the "security agreement" requirement for attachment (*see* § 9-203(b)(3)(A)), but it falls short of establishing "control."

Answer (C) is incorrect because "control" requires a three-party agreement, and Prosperity Bank is not a party to this agreement.

Answer (D) is incorrect and is a nonsense answer. If Lender was a "bank" at which BAMCO maintained its savings account (i.e., the secured party and the financial institution were the same entity), then Lender would have automatic "control" under section 9-104(a)(1). But because Prosperity Bank maintains the savings account, Lender's status as a "bank" is irrelevant.

192. **Answer (C) is the correct answer.** A security interest attaches to collateral "when it becomes enforceable against the debtor." § 9-203(a). A security interest becomes "enforceable" when value has been given, the debtor has rights (or power to transfer rights) in the collateral, and a security agreement is in place between the parties. *See* § 9-203(b). Notice that section 9-203(b) is a conjunctive statute; all three requirements must be satisfied. (The security agreement requirement can be satisfied in any of four ways; section 9-203(b)(3) is written disjunctively.) So the security interest in the X-Ray machine attached when the last of the three requirements was met.

Clinic did not acquire the machine until July 9, so the security interest could not attach any earlier. Therefore, **Answer (A) is incorrect.**

Clinic did not authenticate the security agreement until July 11, so the security interest did not attach when Clinic acquired the machine on July 9. Therefore, **Answer (B) is incorrect.**

Bank certainly gave value, but when? Possibilities include July 1 (when Bank committed to making the loan), July 8 (when Clinic requested the initial advance), and July 14 (when Bank funded the advance). The answer is found in section 1-204, which defines "value." Under subsection (1), Bank gave value when it entered into a "binding commitment to extend credit . . . whether or not drawn upon." (Alternatively, Bank's binding commitment satisfied subsection (4), which defines "value" as "any consideration sufficient to support a simple contract.") So Bank gave value as early as July 1. Bank also gave value on July 14, but the earlier date of July 1 also is correct, so **Answer (D) is incorrect.**

Because Clinic authenticated the security agreement on July 11, after it acquired the machine on July 9 and after Bank gave value on July 1, the security interest attached on July 11 (the date on which the last of the three elements is satisfied). Therefore, **Answer (C) is the correct answer.**

193. **Answer (C) is the correct answer.** Borrowing from the previous answer, Clinic authenticated the security agreement on July 11 and Bank gave value as early as July 1. Clinic acquired rights in the MRI machine on July 12. So Bank's security interest in the machine attached on that date (**making Answer (C) the correct answer). Answers (A) and (B) are incorrect answers** because Clinic had not yet acquired rights in the MRI machine by the dates mentioned in those answers. **Answer (D) is incorrect** because all three attachment requirements were satisfied no later than July 12, an earlier date.

Comparing the answers to this and the previous question reveals an important point: the three requirements of attachment under section 9-203(b) can occur in any order. But the security interest will not attach until all three requirements are in place. Additionally, note that while the filing date of the financing statement may dictate the *perfection* date, it has no bearing on the *attachment* date.

One of your authors uses the following memory device to remember the elements of attachment: RAVE (R = rights in the collateral; A = agreement; and V = value; when all three are met, the security interest attaches, or becomes E = Enforceable).

194. **Answer (B) is the correct answer.** Under section 9-203(b)(3)(A), the written security agreement must include a real estate description "if the security interest covers timber to be cut." Timber is mentioned in **Answer (B), making it the correct answer.** No other collateral requires an accompanying real estate description in order to create an enforceable security interest, so **Answers (A), (C), and (D) are incorrect answers.**

Observe, though, that in addition to timber to be cut, fixtures (Answer (A)) and minerals (Answer (B)) may prompt the secured party to file a fixture filing, which *does require* a real estate description. *See* § 9-502(b)(3).

195. The trustee should invoke Bankruptcy Code § 544(a)(1) (sometimes called the "strong-arm" clause) and avoid Finance Company's unperfected security interest in the piano (and effectively convert Finance Company's alleged secured claim into an unsecured claim in Lauren's bankruptcy). Rather than admitting mere forgetfulness in filing, Finance Company may invoke the automatic perfection afforded by section 9-309(1) to a PMSI in a consumer good. Lauren plays the piano for personal enjoyment and wants her children to take piano lessons. Therefore, she is using the piano primarily for a personal, family, or household purpose, making the piano a "consumer good" as defined in section 9-102(a)(23). But Finance Company's security interest in the piano is not a PMSI under section 9-103 because the credit it extended to Lauren is not a "purchase-money obligation" under section 9-103(a)(2). The credit given did not enable Lauren to acquire any rights in the piano; she already had acquired all of the rights in the piano (albeit with funds borrowed from her parents) earlier in the year. (*See* § 9-103 cmt. 3 (last paragraph).) As the security interest is not a PMSI, Finance Company cannot rely on automatic perfection. Finance Company has not filed or taken any other steps to perfect its security interest, so it is unperfected. As a result, the trustee can avoid the security interest.

196. **Answer (D) is the correct answer.** Section 9-301(1) dictates that Lender should file its financing statement where the debtor is "located." Section 9-307 discusses where a debtor is "located." Section 9-307(b)(1) says that a human debtor is located at the individual's primary residence. In Answer (D), the debtor is a human and lives in Chicago. Therefore, Lender should file its financing statement in Illinois, **making Answer (D) the correct answer.** True, the collateral will be located in Virginia. But the location of the collateral is irrelevant.

In Answer (C), the debtor is a human who lives in Michigan but operates, as a sole proprietorship, a business in Chicago. The law does not treat a human and the sole proprietorship as separate legal entities. Therefore, Lender should file its financing statement in Michigan (where the human debtor lives), rather than in Illinois (the location of the business and the collateral), **making Answer (C) an incorrect answer.**

A corporation is an example of a "registered organization" as defined in section 9-102(a)(70). Section 9-307(e) says that a registered organization is located in the state of its organization. Therefore, **Answer (B) is incorrect** because Lender should file its financing statement in Texas (the debtor is a Texas corporation), rather than in Illinois (the location of the debtor's chief executive office and tangible business property).

A general partnership is not a registered organization. *See* § 9-102 cmt. 11. Therefore, section 9-307(b), rather than 9-307(e), dictates the location of the general partnership. Section 9-307(b) says that an organization is located at its place of business (if it has only one place of business) or chief executive office (if it has multiple places of business). The debtor is a general partnership in Answer (A), and it does business in several states. But the facts fail to mention where the partnership maintains its chief executive office. Without this information, Lender cannot be sure where to file, **making Answer (A) possibly wrong, and therefore not the best answer.**

197. **Answer (A) is the correct answer.** The collateral, two or more stock certificates, is investment property. Section 9-305 states some general rules regarding perfection of security interests in investment property. Subsection (a) states a general rule applicable to security certificates: a secured party should perfect its security interest under the law of the jurisdiction where the certificate is located. As MegaCorp keeps the two stock certificates at its chief executive office in Salt Lake City, then it appears that Zion Finance should file its financing statement in Utah, **making Answer (C) the correct answer.** But the rules of section 9-305(a) are subject to subsection (c). And that subsection states that if a secured party intends to perfect its security interest in investment property by filing (rather than some other method, such as control), then the secured party should file its financing statement in the jurisdiction where the debtor is located. In this problem, the debtor is MegaCorp, a Delaware corporation and, therefore, a "registered organization" under section 9-102(a)(70). A registered organization is located in the state of its incorporation. *See* § 9-307(e). So Zion Finance should file its financing statement in Delaware, **making Answer (A) the correct answer.** A filing elsewhere (e.g., Utah, Arizona, New Mexico, etc.) is ineffective, **making Answers (B), (C), and (D) incorrect answers.**

198. **Answer (D) is the correct answer.** This question tests your knowledge of two filing problems, and whether those problems have any effect on the continued effectiveness of the filings. The first problem arises when the clerk erroneously indexes the filing, frustrating the intended notice function of the filing. Section 9-517 places the risk of clerk error (and the resulting non-disclosure) on the searcher, rather than the filer, by stating: "The failure of the

filing office to index a record correctly does not affect the effectiveness of the filed record." This means that Dealer's PMSI remains perfected by its mis-indexed filing (a risk that is borne by Canyon Bank and other searchers). (This potential filing problem is just one of many reasons why a filer should order a search report a few days after filing to confirm that its filing has indeed been properly recorded.)

The second problem arises when the debtor changes its name in a manner that leaves the filing seriously misleading because a search against the new name will not disclose the filing indexed under the original name. This problem offers such a name change: the debtor changed its name from "Phoenix Healthcare, Inc." to "Arizona Healthcare, Inc." — a change that is seriously misleading because the filing by Integrity Finance against the earlier name was not disclosed when Canyon Bank ordered a search against the debtor under its new name. The effect of this seriously misleading name change is found in section 9-507(c), which states that the filing remains effective to perfect Integrity Finance's security interest in collateral acquired by the debtor before the name change and within four month thereafter, but the filing will not perfect a security interest in collateral acquired by the debtor more than four months after the name change.

In summary, then, Dealer remains perfected, and Integrity Finance remains perfected in collateral acquired prior to — and within four months after — the name change (but unperfected in collateral acquired thereafter). **Answer (A) is incorrect**, because both creditors are perfected (in whole or in part). Answer (B) correctly states that Dealer remains perfected, but it incorrectly concludes that Integrity Finance is not perfected at all, **making Answer (B) incorrect.** Answer (C) correctly states that Dealer remains perfected, but it erroneously states that Integrity Finance is perfected only in collateral acquired by the debtor prior to the name change, **making Answer (C) incorrect. Answer (D) is correct** because it paraphrases our summary from above: Dealer remains perfected, and Integrity Finance remains perfected in collateral acquired by the debtor prior to, and within a few months after, the name change.

199. **Answer (B) is the correct answer.** Meredith is offering as collateral her partnership interest in the law firm, which operates as a general partnership. Her partnership interest is not tangible, but rather intangible. The basic classifications covering intangibles are accounts, deposit accounts (which we can exclude because Meredith is not offering her savings account, checking account, etc.), general intangibles (which includes payment intangibles and software), and in some cases investment property. The term "contract right" may properly describe the bundle of rights that Meredith holds through her partnership interest. That term, while popular under former versions of Article 9, no longer is used as a type of collateral. Therefore, **Answer (D) is incorrect.** But the other three options remain viable and require further discussion.

Is the partnership interest an account? No, it is not really a right to payment; it is an ownership interest coupled with a right to receive a certain percentage of profits. Is it investment property? Investment property is defined in section 9-102(a)(49) as a "security," which in turn is defined in section 8-102 (incorporated via section 9-102(b)), as "except as otherwise provided in Section 8-103, . . . an obligation of an issuer or a share, participation, or other interest in an issuer or in property or an enterprise of an issuer." This looks like a partnership interest might be a "security" (and hence investment property), but we have to check section 8-103. And that is where the maze stops: section 8-103(c) states that "[A]n interest in a partnership or limited liability company is not a security unless it is dealt in or traded on securities exchanges or in securities markets, its terms expressly provide that it is a security governed by this Article, or it is an investment company security." Meredith's interest is not traded, and because it is a law firm partnership, it is not an "investment company security." Since the partnership agreement fails to mention the Uniform Commercial Code or any of its Articles, the law firm has not exercised its "opt-in" to Article 8.

We have eliminated accounts — so **Answer (A) is incorrect.** And we have eliminated investment property — so **Answer (C) is incorrect.** Because the partnership interest fails to fit into any other collateral type, it must fall within the catchall category and be a "general intangible," a term that section 9-102(a)(42) defines by excluding every other collateral type. For this reason, **Answer (B) is the correct answer.**

200.   **Answer (C) is the correct answer.** Section 9-301(1) informs Gotham Bank that it should file its financing statement where the debtor is located. Meredith is the debtor. Section 9-307(b)(1) says that a human debtor is located at her primary residence. Meredith lives in Connecticut, so Gotham Bank should file its financing statement against Meredith in Connecticut. For this reason, **Answer (C) is the correct answer.**

    Answer (A) is incorrect because Meredith, rather than the law firm, is the debtor, and it is the location of Meredith, not the law firm, that dictates the filing location.

    Answer (B) is incorrect because Meredith is located where she resides (Connecticut), not where she works (New York).

    Answer (D) is incorrect as a nonsense answer. The only way to perfect a security interest in a general intangible (excluding contrary federal or non-UCC state law) is by filing a financing statement.

201.   **Answer (B) is the correct answer.** The photocopier and the cash represent proceeds of the furniture under section 9-102(a)(64)(A) ("whatever is acquired upon the sale . . . of collateral"). The refrigerator also represents proceeds because Article 9 does not limit proceeds to "first generation" proceeds (but the tracing burden becomes more difficult with each subsequent generation). Peachtree Bank has an enforceable security interest in Foxx Furniture's inventory of furniture, so section 9-203(f) awards Peachtree Bank with an enforceable security interest in proceeds (and proceeds of proceeds) "as provided by Section 9-315," notwithstanding any omission of magical words (such as "proceeds") from the loan papers. Under section 9-315(a), Peachtree Bank's security interest attaches to "identifiable" proceeds. The facts stipulate that Peachtree Bank can satisfy its tracing burden, so it has an enforceable security interest in the photocopier and the refrigerator. Therefore, **Answer (D) is incorrect** because it erroneously suggests that Peachtree Bank has no security interest in the refrigerator.

    Under section 9-315(c), the security interest in proceeds is perfected if the security interest in the original security interest was perfected. Peachtree Bank perfected its security interest in the inventory of furniture by filing a financing statement, so its security interest in the proceeds also is perfected. The perfection afforded by section 9-315(c) is temporary, though, and is limited to the twenty-day period following the date on which the security interest attaches to the proceeds. Foxx Furniture received the photocopier and the cash, and used the cash to purchase the refrigerator, approximately two months ago, so the twenty-day period of perfection has expired as of today, unless Peachtree Bank can extend the perfection by satisfying one of the options found in section 9-315(d). Subsection (d)(2) can be easily eliminated from consideration because neither the photocopier nor the refrigerator are "cash proceeds" as defined in section 9-102(a)(9). Subsection (d)(1) will protect the photocopier because: a financing statement covers the original collateral (furniture inventory), a financing statement filed in the same office will perfect a security interest in the proceeds (the photocopier), and the photocopier was not acquired by Foxx Furniture with cash proceeds. Peachtree Bank passes the first two requirements with respect to the refrigerator, but it fails the third requirement because Foxx Furniture purchased the refrigerator with cash proceeds. Peachtree Bank has taken no other action to perfect a security interest in the refrigerator (such as amending its original financing statement or filing a new financing statement), so the temporary perfection of its security interest in the refrigerator has expired.

In summary, then, as of today (a date after the twenty-day period referenced in section 9-315(c)), Peachtree Bank has a perfected security interest in the photocopier, and an unperfected security interest in the refrigerator. Therefore, **Answer (B) is correct. Answer (A) is incorrect** because the security interest in the refrigerator is unperfected, and **Answer (C) is incorrect** because the security interest in the photocopier is perfected.

202. **Answer (B) is the correct answer.** The act of commingling proceeds with non-proceeds does not automatically destroy a secured party's ability to "identify" some or all of the assets as its collateral. Article 9 permits the secured party to identify the proceeds "by a method of tracing, including application of equitable principles, that is permitted under law other than this article with respect to commingled property of the type involved." § 9-315(b)(2). A common "equitable principle" is the "lowest intermediate balance rule." § 9-315 cmt. 3. Under the lowest intermediate balance rule, (i) the creditor can claim an interest in commingled assets identified as proceeds, (ii) non-proceeds are considered used by the debtor before proceeds, and (iii) proceeds that are used by the debtor are not deemed replenished with subsequently commingled non-proceeds.

When the problem involves a bank account, it is helpful to run a daily balance and identify that part of the total balance that represents proceeds. The following is a summary of the bank activity:

Date	Balance	Proceeds
6/1	7,000	3,000
6/6	2,000	2,000
6/8	8,000	8,000
6/15	13,000	8,000
6/18	11,000	8,000
6/22	15,000	12,000
6/24	9,000	9,000
6/26	11,000	9,000

Because the ending number in the "proceeds" column is $9,000, **Answer (B) is the correct answer and Answers (A), (C), and (D) are incorrect answers.**

203. **Answer (D) is the correct answer.** Section 544(a)(1) of the Bankruptcy Code, often referred to as "the strong-arm clause," permits the bankruptcy trustee to successfully challenge and avoid (or set aside) an Article 9 security interest that is unperfected on the petition date. First, then, we must determine whether Bamco has an enforceable security interest in the

bikes under section 9-203. For attachment to occur, Bamco must give value. It did so by selling the bikes to TBN on credit. Also, TBN must have rights in the bikes. It acquired rights in the bikes at the time of purchase. Finally, TBN must authenticate a security agreement that describes the bikes. TBN never authenticated a formal security agreement. But the note will suffice. TBN did execute the note, which described the bikes. The note also included a "title reservation" clause, which, under the UCC, gives Bamco a security interest in the bikes. *See* §§ 1-201(b)(35) (penultimate sentence in definition of "security interest"), 2-401(1). Because all three elements of attachment exist, Bamco has an enforceable security interest in the bikes. Bamco perfected that security interest by filing its financing statement in Arizona. Arizona, rather than Nevada (or elsewhere), is the correct filing location because section 9-301(1) tells Bamco to file where the debtor is located. TBN is a corporation and, therefore, a registered organization under section 9-102(a)(70). A registered organization is deemed located under section 9-307(e) in its state of creation. TBN is chartered under Arizona law, so that is its location. Therefore, Bamco filed its financing statement in the correct state. Its security interest in the bikes is perfected as of the petition date, so the bankruptcy trustee cannot challenge Bamco's security interest under the strong-arm clause of the Bankruptcy Code. For these reasons, **Answer (D) is the correct answer and Answer (A) is an incorrect answer.**

Answers (B) and (C) suggest that the answer turns on the location of the bikes. But the answer turns on whether Bamco filed its financing statement in the proper place, which is dictated by the location of the debtor, not the location of the collateral. Therefore, **Answers (B) and (C) are incorrect.**

204.   **Answer (A) is the correct answer.** The strong-arm clause (Bankruptcy Code § 544(a)(1)) allows the bankruptcy trustee to avoid a security interest that is unperfected on the petition date. Therefore, analysis turns on whether Bamco's security interest in the various assets was perfected when TBN filed its bankruptcy petition in late June.

The ten checks and the $1,000 account receivable represent "proceeds" under section 9-102(a)(64)(A) ("whatever is acquired upon the sale . . . of collateral"). Under section 9-203(f), Bamco's enforceable security interest in TBN's bicycle inventory gives it "rights to proceeds provided by Section 9-315." Under that section, Bamco's security interest attaches to the checks and the receivable if they are "identifiable" proceeds. The facts trace the checks and the receivable to bikes sold by Bamco to TBN, so the checks and receivable are "identifiable" proceeds. Under section 9-315(c), the security interest in all of these proceeds is perfected because the security interest in the bikes (the original collateral) was perfected (by a financing statement). This automatic perfection is only temporary for twenty days and terminates thereafter unless perfection continues under subsection (d). Seven of the checks arose from sales within twenty days of the petition date, so Bamco's security interest in those checks is perfected as of the petition date. But the other three checks, and the receivable, all arose from sales more than twenty days before the petition date. Therefore, Bamco's security interest in those proceeds is unperfected as of the petition date unless Bamco can extend the perfection under section 9-315(d). It can do so with respect to the three checks because checks are "cash proceeds" under section 9-102(a)(9), and subsection (d)(2) extends perfection beyond the twenty-day period of subsection (c) to "cash proceeds." The receivable is an example of an "account" under section 9-102(a)(2) and is not a "cash proceed." Therefore, Bamco cannot extend perfection under subsection (d)(2). It can, however, extend perfection under subsection (d)(1) because: a filing covers the original collateral (the bikes), a filing in the same office will perfect a security interest in the proceeds (an account), and there are no intervening cash proceeds. As a result, Bamco has a perfected security interest in the $1,000 receivable as of the petition date.

In summary, then, Bamco's security interest in all ten checks and the $1,000 receivable is perfected as of the petition date. Therefore, the trustee's challenge under the strong-arm clause of the Bankruptcy Code will be unsuccessful. This means that **Answer (A) is correct and Answers (B), (C), and (D) are incorrect.**

205. **Answer (B) is the correct answer.** The baby furniture represents proceeds (of proceeds) of the piano. The cashier's check, marked with Gwen's indorsement, will facilitate Dealer's tracing burden, making the baby furniture "identifiable proceeds" in which Dealer can claim an enforceable security interest under section 9-315(a)(2). Therefore, **Answer (A) is incorrect.** Normally the security interest in proceeds is automatically (albeit temporarily) perfected for twenty days under section 9-315(c). But that brief period of perfection is available only if the security interest in the original collateral was perfected. Dealer did file a financing statement against Gwen and the piano in Colorado, where Gwen was "located" (at that time) under section 9-307(b)(1). But Gwen later moved to Indiana, a different state. This change in jurisdiction required Dealer to file a new financing statement in Indiana within four months after the relocation if it wanted to maintain continuous and uninterrupted perfection. *See* § 9-316(a)(2). The facts do not indicate that Dealer took any filing action in response to Gwen's relocation, so its security interest is unperfected both prospectively and retroactively. *See* § 9-316(b). This means that Dealer cannot invoke section 9-315(c). Its security interest in the baby furniture is unperfected, **making Answer (B) the correct answer and Answers (C) and (D) incorrect answers.**

Gwen's relocation from Colorado to Indiana would have no bearing on the perfected status of Dealer's security interest in the grand piano if Dealer could rely on the alternative method of automatic perfection available to purchase-money creditors (and the facts bestow that status on Dealer). But claiming a PMSI is insufficient. The collateral must be a consumer good. *See* § 9-309(1). Gwen uses the piano in her studio to generate her earnings. Therefore, the piano is equipment, not a consumer good (*see* § 9-102(a)(23)). This label frustrates Dealer's ability to rely on automatic perfection of its PMSI.

206. For reasons discussed above, Dealer can claim an enforceable security interest in the baby furniture as identifiable proceeds of the piano. Is it perfected, though? If so, for how long? A search against "Markell" will not reveal Dealer's filing against "Zinnecker," so Gwen's name change has rendered Dealer's filing seriously misleading under section 9-506. But Dealer obtained its enforceable security interest in the piano before Gwen changed her name, so Dealer's filing remains effective against the piano under section 9-507(c)(1). Therefore (and unlike the previous analysis), Dealer enjoys the automatic perfection afforded by section 9-315(c) in the proceeds for twenty days. The cash is gone, so the focus is on the continued perfection of Dealer's security interest in the baby furniture beyond the twenty-day period. Given that the facts do not suggest that Dealer has taken any further filing action, Dealer's only hope is to successfully navigate the three requirements of section 9-315(d)(1). Dealer did file a financing statement against Gwen and the piano (equipment), and it would file a financing statement in the same place to perfect a security interest in baby furniture (consumer goods). But Gwen purchased the baby furniture with intervening cash proceeds, so the third condition of the three-part test fails. Therefore, Dealer's perfection of its

security interest in the baby furniture will lapse at the end of the twenty-day period.

207. The contents of an effective fixture filing are summarized in section 9-502(b). A fixture filing must include the same information as a regular financing statement. It also must (i) state that it covers fixtures, (ii) state that it is to be filed in the real estate records, (iii) provide a description of the real estate, and (iv) provide the name of the record owner of the real estate if the debtor does not have a recorded interest. Furthermore, section 9-501(a)(1) dictates that a fixture filing be filed in the real estate records where the real estate is located (often referred to as a "local filing" or a "county filing"), whereas section 9-501(a)(2) mandates that a standard financing statement be filed in a central filing office (and thus the term, "central filing") in the state where the debtor is located (*see* § 9-301(1)).

208. **Answer (D) is the correct answer.** The priority rules concerning fixture disputes are found in section 9-334. The default rule is found in subsection (c), which awards priority to Fidelity Finance (the real estate encumbrancer) unless ZinnCo can claim priority under another subsection. ZinnCo has engaged in seller financing, so it can claim a purchase-money security interest in the chandelier under section 9-103(a) and (b)(1). And Fidelity Finance's interest in the real estate arose in March, before the chandelier became a fixture in October. Therefore, ZinnCo's security interest in the chandelier enjoys priority if it files a fixture filing no later than the twentieth day "after the goods become fixtures." § 9-334(d). The chandelier became a fixture on October 18, so a fixture filing on or before November 7 is timely. Therefore, if ZinnCo files its fixture filing on November 5, its security interest in the chandelier enjoys priority over the competing claim asserted by Fidelity Finance, **making Answer (D) the correct answer.**

   Answer (C) is incorrect because it erroneously states that the timeliness of a fixture filing is dictated by the purchase date of the chandelier (October 1), rather than the date on which the chandelier becomes a fixture (October 18).

   The chandelier has been installed at Meredith's home, making it a consumer good. ZinnCo has provided seller financing, so its PMSI is eligible for automatic perfection under section 9-309(1), **making Answer (A) an incorrect answer.** No provision of Article 9 terminates this automatic perfection when the consumer good becomes a fixture, so **Answer (B) is incorrect.**

209. ZinnCo's security interest in the chandelier enjoys priority over the competing claim asserted by Buzz Norton. Section 9-334(e) awards priority to a "perfected security interest in fixtures" over "a conflicting interest of an encumbrancer" if "(3) the conflicting interest is a lien on the real property obtained by legal or equitable proceedings after the security interest was perfected by any method permitted by this article." ZinnCo can satisfy the three conditions of this priority rule. First, the chandelier is installed in Meredith's residence, so the chandelier is a consumer good; and ZinnCo provided seller financing, so ZinnCo is a purchase-money creditor. Therefore, ZinnCo's PMSI in the chandelier is automatically perfected (a "method permitted by this article"). Second, Norton's lien on the residence and chandelier arose from his successful lawsuit, a "legal proceeding." And third, Norton's lien arose on October 10, after ZinnCo's security interest attached and became automatically perfected on October 1. Therefore, notwithstanding the absence of any standard filing or fixture filing, ZinnCo's automatically perfected PMSI in the chandelier enjoys priority over Norton's competing judgment lien.

210. **Answer (C) is the correct answer.** This three-party dispute can be broken down into three separate two-party disputes (Dealer v. Bank, Bank v. parents, and parents v. Bank). As the following analysis reveals, no clear winner emerges. Instead, the facts illustrate the "circular priority" conundrum, where each party enjoys priority over one other party but does not enjoy priority over the other party (think "rock, paper, scissors").

Dealer's standard financing statement perfected its security interest under section 9-501(a)(2). Jennifer's parents perfected their security interest under section 9-501(a)(1) by filing a fixture filing. And Bank's interest arose from the mortgage that it recorded.

The competing property interests of Dealer and Jennifer's parents arose under Article 9, rather than real estate law. Therefore, the applicable priority rule is not found in section 9-334, but in section 9-322(a). Dealer filed and perfected its interest earlier than did Jennifer's parents, so Dealer wins this two-party dispute.

Bank's interest arose under its mortgage, so section 9-334 will resolve its disputes with Dealer and Jennifer's parents. Bank enjoys priority over Dealer under section 9-334(c) because Bank is a real estate encumbrancer and Dealer is claiming an interest in fixtures. No exception applies (Dealer never filed a fixture filing, and the fixture is not readily removable). But because Jennifer's parents filed a fixture filing that perfected their security interest before Bank recorded its mortgage, Jennifer's parents enjoy priority over Bank under section 9-334(e)(1).

In summary, then, Dealer beats Jennifer's parents, Jennifer's parents defeat Bank, and Bank enjoys priority over Dealer. Everyone is a winner. But everyone is a loser, too. We are not quite sure how a court will resolve this dilemma. But the correct answer among the four options will be the answer that recognizes no party will lose to, or have priority over, the other two parties. Answer (C) is the only answer that does so, so **Answer (C) is the correct answer.** The other three answers erroneously suggest that a party suffers two defeats or enjoys two victories, **making Answers (A), (B), and (D) incorrect answers.**

211. **Answer (B) is the correct answer.** Item #1 was an asset acquired by Lauren and later transferred to Eastman Photography, a separate legal entity. Lender did not authorize this asset transfer, so its security interest in the item continues under the general rule of section 9-315(a) (no exception applies). And the security interest remains perfected against Eastman Photography under section 9-507 by the original financing statement filed against Lauren. Because Lender's interest in Item #1 remains perfected, **Answer (D) is incorrect.** Lauren did not transfer Items #2 and #3 to Eastman Photography. Instead, Eastman Photography acquired those items from another party. Therefore section 9-315(a) does not apply (it applies only to transferred assets). Because the facts state that Eastman Photography is a "new debtor," Lender has an enforceable security interest in Items #2 and #3 under section 9-203(d) and (e). Under section 9-508, the original financing statement filed against Lauren is effective to perfect the security interest in assets acquired by Eastman Photography, subject to a significant exception. If the difference between the name of the original debtor ("Lauren Eastman Jefferson") and the new debtor ("Eastman Photography") is seriously misleading, then the original financing statement will not perfect a security interest in assets acquired by Eastman Photography more than four months after it became bound under the original security agreement. The difference in names appears to be seriously misleading under section 9-506(c) because a search against "Eastman Photography" is not likely to reveal the prior filing against "Jefferson, Lauren Eastman." Therefore, the original financing

statement is ineffective to perfect a security interest in Item #3, which Eastman Photography purchased on November 1, more than four months after Eastman Photography became a new debtor in June. The original financing statement is effective, however, to perfect a security interest in Item #2, which Eastman Photography acquired on September 15, within the four-month period. Because Lender has a perfected security interest in Items #1 and #2 but not Item #3, **Answer (B) is the correct answer. Answer (A) is incorrect** (the answer is overinclusive because it includes Item #3). And **Answer (C) also is incorrect** (the answer is underinclusive because it excludes Item #2).

212. Lauren's incorporation of her business under Delaware law means that Eastman Photography is located, for filing purposes, in Delaware. *See* §§ 9-301(1), 9-307(e). Lender must be concerned that this change in location may adversely impact the continued effectiveness of its California filing under section 9-508. Section 9-316(a)(3) addresses this concern, and tells Lender that its California filing remains effective for one year following the date on which Lauren transferred the collateral to her Delaware corporation. The question asks for analysis as of December 15, a date within one year of the transfer date in June. Therefore, the decision to incorporate in Delaware, rather than in California, has no effect (yet) on the perfected status of its security interest in the transferred asset: Item #1.

But what about the non-transferred assets, Items #2 and #3, which the Delaware corporation acquired on its own from a third party (rather than Lauren)? Article 9 does not provide an answer that is obvious from any particular statute. But an examination of section 9-508 cmt. 4 (the sentence beginning "Moreover,"), and the "example" cross-referenced at the end of cmt. 4, reveals this result: Lender's filing in California is never effective to perfect its security interest in any non-transferred collateral acquired by the corporate entity.

Bottom line: If Lauren incorporates her business in California, Lender has a perfected security interest in Items #1 and #2 but not Item #3, and if Lauren incorporates her business in Delaware, Lender (for the moment, anyway) has a perfected security interest in Item #1 but not Items #2 and #3.

213. **Answer (B) is the correct answer.** Lender's perfected security interest in Item #1 enjoys priority over Bank's perfected security interest under section 9-325 because Eastman Photography acquired Item #1 subject to the security interest created by Lauren (*see* § 9-315(a)) and that security interest remained perfected when Eastman Photography acquired Item #1 (*see* § 9-507). So **Answer (A) is incorrect.** Lender and Bank each have a perfected security interest in Item #2. Because Bank has filed against Eastman Photography and Lender has filed only against Lauren, Bank's interest enjoys priority under section 9-326(a). Thus, **Answers (C) and (D) are incorrect. Answer (D) also is incorrect** because Bank's perfected security interest in Item #3 enjoys priority over Lender's unperfected security interest under the general rule that a perfected security interest trumps an unperfected security interest. § 9-322(a)(2).

214. The answer remains the same, although the analysis concerning Item #2 is different. For reasons explained in the narrative response above, Bank's filing in California never perfects its security interest in non-transferred assets acquired by the Delaware entity. Therefore, Lender continues to enjoy priority in Item #2 not under section 9-326(a), but under the "perfected beats unperfected" rule of section 9-322(a)(2). The analysis for Items #1 (for the moment, anyway) and #3 is unaffected by Lauren's decision to incorporate her business under Delaware, rather than California, law. But Bank could lose a future priority dispute

over Item #1 if it fails to take timely action in Delaware as mandated by section 9-316(b).

215.   **Answer (D) is the correct answer.** The court should enter a declaratory judgment awarding priority to Second Bank. To continue its priority (under the general "first to file or perfect" rule of section 9-322(a)(1)) after January 10, 2007, First Bank needed to file a continuation statement within the six-month period ending on the last date of the five-year period of the filing's effectiveness (§ 9-515(d)). That six-month period started on July 10, 2011, and ended on January 10, 2012. But First Bank filed its continuation statement on July 5, 2011 — a date five days *before* the start of the six-month period that began on July 10, 2011 — so its continuation statement was ineffective (§ 9-510(c)) even though the statement was recorded. As a result, First Bank's security interest became unperfected on January 10, 2012, and "is deemed never to have been perfected as against a purchaser of the collateral for value" (§ 9-515(c)). Second Bank falls within the definition of "purchaser" (§ 1-201) and presumably gave value (a loan). Therefore, Second Bank's perfected security interest enjoys priority over First Bank's unperfected security interest (*see* § 9-322(a)(2)) as soon as the effectiveness of First Bank's original financing statement lapsed, **making Answer (D) the correct answer.**

Answer (A) is incorrect because First Bank does not have priority.

Answer (B) is incorrect because First Bank does not have priority, and Second Bank's security interest remains perfected. Its original filing remains effective through at least part of August 2013, and the facts end in March 2013, so the absence of a continuation statement is a red herring, as is Second Bank's knowledge of First Bank's security interest and previous filing.

Answer (C) is incorrect because First Bank's security interest became unperfected when the effectiveness of its original filing lapsed at the end of its five-year period.

216.   **Answer (B) is the correct answer.** A security interest in investment property can be perfected by filing. § 9-312(a). So John's financing statement perfected his security interest in the stock certificate. A security interest in investment property also can be perfected by taking delivery of it. § 9-313(a). Therefore, Heather perfected her security interest in the stock certificate when she took delivery of it. John filed in October, before Heather took delivery in November, so he would seem to have priority under the general "first to file or perfect" rule of section 9-322(a). But as noted in section 9-322(a) and (f), this general priority rule is subject to other priority rules, including those in section 9-328 concerning investment property. If the Waldorf stock certificate was issued to Sharon in bearer form (issued to "bearer" or in blank), then Heather would have "control" of the certificate under section 8-106(a) by taking delivery of it. Perfection by control trumps perfection by filing. § 9-328(1). But the certificate may have been issued in registered form (issued in Sharon's name). Taking delivery of a certificate in registered form, without more, does not give Heather control. See § 8-106(b) (requiring delivery plus either indorsement or registration). So it is possible, without knowing more facts, that Heather does not have control of the Waldorf stock certificate even though she has taken delivery. And without control, she cannot invoke the priority rule of section 9-328(1). Even so, though, Heather enjoys priority under section 9-328(5). That section states: "A security interest in a certificated security in registered form which is perfected by taking delivery . . . and not by control . . . has priority over a conflicting security interest perfected by a method other than control." John perfected by filing, not by control. Therefore, the rule applies and Heather enjoys priority, **making Answer (B) the correct answer.**

Answer (A) is incorrect because a secured party that takes delivery of a stock certificate trumps a security interest perfected by filing, even if the filing occurred prior to the delivery.

Answer (C) is incorrect because Heather enjoys priority if she takes delivery, whether the stock certificate is issued in bearer form or registered form.

Answer (D) is incorrect because Heather may not have control of the stock certificate if it is issued in registered form. Delivery alone does not suffice. *See* § 8-106(b).

217. **Answer (B) is the correct answer.** Doubleday Finance's search against the debtor's current legal name of "Home Run Collectibles" has failed to reveal Cooperstown Bank's previous filing against "The Card Shop." Therefore, under section 9-506(c), the debtor's name change has caused Cooperstown Bank's financing statement to become seriously misleading. Nevertheless, its filing against "The Card Shop" remains effective to perfect a security interest in baseball cards acquired by the debtor (i) prior to the name change and (ii) within four months after the name change (§ 9-507(c)) — even if the perfected or unperfected status is examined (as in this problem) on a date long after the four-month period has concluded. The debtor acquired Card #1 on June 5, within four months after the name change on March 20, so the original filing remains effective to perfect Cooperstown Bank's security interest in Card #1. The debtor acquired Card #2 on July 25 and Card #3 on October 1. These two dates fall outside the four-month period that concluded on or about July 20. Therefore, Cooperstown Bank's filing does not perfect its security interest in those two Cards. Cooperstown Bank remains perfected in Card #1 by its filing, so it has priority in Card #1 under the "first to file or perfect" rule of section 9-322(a)(1) because it filed in January, and Doubleday Finance filed in August. But Doubleday Finance has priority in Cards #2 and #3 under the "perfected beats unperfected" rule of section 9-322(a)(2). Doubleday Finance perfected its security interest in all of the baseball cards, but Cooperstown Bank's security interest in Cards #2 and #3 is unperfected because the debtor's name change has rendered the filing seriously misleading and those two cards were acquired by the debtor more than four months after the name change. These perfection and priority results are correctly stated in Answer (B), **making Answer (B) the correct answer and Answers (A), (C), and (D) incorrect answers.**

218. **Answer (D) is the correct answer.** The lease is chattel paper under section 9-102(a)(11) because it is a lease of specific goods (the photocopier) and memorializes the lessee's monetary obligations ($400 each month, for three years). The lease represents identifiable proceeds of the unit of inventory. Therefore, Fidelity Bank has a security interest in the lease under sections 9-203(f) and 9-315(a)(2). Fidelity Bank's security interest is automatically perfected for twenty days from the date of attachment under section 9-315(c). Perfection of the security interest in the lease continues thereafter under section 9-315(d)(1) because Fidelity Bank filed a financing statement against the inventory, the lease is chattel paper under section 9-102(a)(11) and a filing against inventory is made in the same office as a filing against chattel paper, and the lease was not acquired with cash proceeds. But even though Fidelity Bank's security interest in the lease is perfected, CommCorp's interest enjoys priority under either section 9-330(a) (applicable if Fidelity Bank claims an interest in the lease "merely as proceeds of inventory") or section 9-330(b) (applicable if Fidelity Bank claims an interest in the lease "other than merely as proceeds of inventory"). (For a discussion of the distinction, see PEB Commentary #8.) The lease is chattel paper, and CommCorp is a "purchaser" under section 1-201(b)(30) (one who takes by "purchase" — a

voluntary transaction — section 1-201(b)(29)). CommCorp appears to have acted in good faith, has taken possession of the lease pursuant to a transaction in the ordinary course of its business, and has given new value for the lease. The lease does not appear to "indicate that it has been assigned to an identified assignee (e.g., Fidelity Bank) other than the purchaser," so CommCorp enjoys priority if subsection (a) applies. And CommCorp enjoys priority if subsection (b) applies because knowledge of Fidelity Bank's financing statement does not give CommCorp "knowledge that the purchase violates the rights of the secured party [Fidelity Bank]." *See* § 9-330 cmt. 6. Because CommCorp enjoys priority, notwithstanding Fidelity Bank's perfected status, **Answer (D) is the correct answer.**

Answer (A) is incorrect because Article 9 applies to sales of chattel paper. *See* § 9-109(a)(3).

Answer (B) is incorrect because section 9-330 awards priority to CommCorp, notwithstanding Fidelity Bank's perfected status in the lease as a proceed of inventory.

Answer (C) is incorrect. A suggestion that priority may turn on resolution within a particular twenty-day period is a hint that perhaps a secured party's automatic, but temporary, perfection under section 9-315(c) in proceeds does not extend beyond that brief period. But the preceding analysis reveals that Fidelity Bank can extend its perfection beyond the twenty-day period by navigating section 9-315(d)(1).

219. **Answer (D) is the correct answer.** The presumption is that TNB enjoys priority in both disputes, under section 9-322(a)(1), as the first filer. TNB filed its financing statement in 2010, Dealer filed in June 2011, and ZinnMark Press filed in August 2012. Section 9-322(a), though, by its own language, defers to other applicable priority rules found in the section or elsewhere in the 9-300 series. Dealer will invoke the superpriority exception for equipment financers in section 9-324(a), and ZinnMark Press will invoke the superpriority exception for inventory financers in section 9-324(b). Each provided seller financing and can claim a PMSI under section 9-103 in the goods they sold on credit. Each perfected their PMSI by filing a financing statement. Therefore, both may be eligible for superpriority.

Dealer, the equipment financer, enjoys superpriority if it filed its financing statement no later than twenty days after delivering the photocopiers to Barnaby's Bookstores. Delivery occurred on June 5, and filing took place on June 23. The filing is timely (barely), so Dealer has superpriority in the photocopiers. The fact that Dealer ordered a UCC search report that revealed TNB's earlier filing is irrelevant, as is Dealer's failure to give notice of its PMSI to TNB. Prudence always dictates a search, but section 9-324(a) imposes no notice obligation on the purchase-money creditor.

ZinnMark Press, the inventory financer, must satisfy more rigorous standards. First, it must be perfected in the books before Barnaby's Bookstores receives the shipment. ZinnMark perfected by filing on August 13, and the books were not delivered until August 19. ZinnMark must also send notice of its PMSI to TNB, which must receive the notice before Barnaby's Bookstores receives the shipment. ZinnMark sent notice on August 11, and TNB received the notice on August 17, before the shipment delivery date of August 19. Finally, the notice must meet specific substantive requirements, which the facts state were satisfied. ZinnMark Press has met all conditions, so its PMSI in the book shipment enjoys superpriority over TNB's security interest.

In summary, then, TNB loses both priority disputes to the purchase-money creditors, **making Answer (D) the correct answer and Answers (A), (B), and (C) incorrect answers.**

220.   **Answer (D) is the correct answer.** Dealer enjoyed superpriority in the photocopier under section 9-324(a). Therefore, his superpriority extends to all identifiable proceeds, in whatever form, including a cashier's check. **Answer (D), then, is the correct answer and Answers (A), (B), and (C) are incorrect answers.**

221.   **Answer (B) is the correct answer.** ZinnMark enjoyed superpriority in the shipment of books under section 9-324(b). That section extends superpriority to "identifiable cash proceeds [that] are received [by Barnaby's Bookstores] on or before the delivery of the inventory to a buyer." "Cash proceeds" under section 9-102(a)(9) include cash and checks. Therefore, ZinnMark (rather than TNB) enjoys priority if the Law School paid cash, or delivered a teller's check, at the time of purchase, **making Answer (C) and Answer (D) incorrect answers.** Swiping a debit card creates a cash proceed (either as an electronic entry in a "deposit account" or under the "or the like" language of the definition prior to the electronic entry), so ZinnMark (rather than TNB) enjoys priority if the Law School paid for its purchase with a debit card. Therefore, **Answer (B) is the correct answer.**

Depending on its language, a promissory note could create chattel paper, an instrument, or an account. In each case, though, the promissory note will not be a cash proceed. Therefore, ZinnMark does not have superpriority in the note under the language quoted near the opening of this paragraph. Section 9-324(b) does extend superpriority to proceeds in the form of chattel paper and instruments, but only if the purchase-money creditor has possession of the proceeds and otherwise satisfies the conditions of section 9-330. Here, Barnaby's Bookstores has possession of the promissory note, so 9-324(b) will not extend superpriority to the note. Therefore, TNB (rather than ZinnMark) will have priority in the note, **making Answer (A) an incorrect answer.**

222.   **Answer (C) is the correct answer.** Dealer's enforceable security interest in the piano is perfected, notwithstanding its failure to file a financing statement. Dealer provided seller financing, so it has a PMSI under section 9-103. Timmy Zee plays the piano for personal enjoyment and relaxation, so in his hands the piano is a consumer good under section 9-102(a)(23). Because Dealer has a PMSI in a consumer good, its security interest became automatically perfected on attachment, under section 9-309(1).

Timmy Zee sold the piano to First Church, offering seller financing, so its enforceable security interest also is a PMSI under section 9-103. It perfected its security interest by filing a financing statement within two weeks after First Church took delivery, so Timmy Zee can indeed allege superpriority over Dealer, an earlier filer, under section 9-324(a). But that makes no sense, does it? A debtor should not be able to obtain a security interest in collateral that primes a security interest perfected by a financing statement previously filed by the debtor's own creditor. Section 9-325 comes to Dealer's rescue and achieves the logical result. Subsection (a) subordinates Timmy Zee's PMSI to Dealer's security interest because (i) debtor First Church acquired the piano subject to Dealer's security interest (*see* § 9-315(a)(1)), (ii) Dealer's security interest was perfected (automatically) when debtor First Church acquired the piano, and (iii) Dealer's perfection has not lapsed. Subsection (b) triggers application of subsection (a) because a contrary result (Timmy Zee enjoying priority under section 9-324(a)) otherwise would result. So Dealer has priority over Timmy Zee.

Both Dealer and Timmy Zee have priority over First Church. Section 9-201 offers the general rule that security interests are effective against purchasers of the collateral. That rule is subject to several exceptions, none of which protect First Church. Section 9-315(a) is of no help, as Timmy Zee did not have Dealer's consent to sell the piano. First Church cannot invoke section 9-320(a) because it is not a buyer in the ordinary course of business; Timmy Zee was not in the business of selling pianos. Nor can First Church invoke section 9-320(b) because it is using the piano as equipment, not as a consumer good. Both creditors are perfected (one automatically, one by filing), so First Church finds no solace in section 9-317(b). Absent any exception, First Church acquired the piano subject to security interests held by Dealer and Timmy Zee.

The mediator, then, should resolve the priority dispute in this order: Dealer, then Timmy Zee, then First Church. This result is stated in Answer (C), **making Answer (C) the correct answer and Answers (A), (B), and (D) incorrect answers.**

223. The liquidator should pay $35,000 to Dealer and the remaining $5,000 to First Bank. Dealer offered seller financing for $50,000 and held a purchase-money security interest in the imaging machine to secure repayment of that amount. First Bank offered third-party financing by releasing its security interest in the trade-in, freeing up equity valued at $25,000. First Bank held a purchase-money security interest in the imaging machine to secure repayment of that amount. (The new imaging machine also secures all previous loans, but that interest is not a PMSI.) Both creditors are perfected by filed financing statements (First Bank filed long before delivery on March 23, 2010, and dealer filed on April 10, within twenty days after the delivery date), so each can claim the superpriority awarded to purchase-money creditors by section 9-324(a). In such a situation, section 9-324(g)(1) applies and awards priority to Dealer, the seller (which holds "a security interest securing an obligation incurred as all or part of the price of the collateral"), rather than First Bank, the third-party financer (which holds "a security interest securing an obligation incurred for value given to enable the debtor to acquire rights in or the use of collateral"). (See section 9-324 cmt. 13 for policy reasons.) As the party with priority, Dealer has the first claim to the proceeds. Its unpaid debt is $35,000 (MolarCorp has paid $15,000 of the $50,000), so the liquidator should pay that amount to Dealer. It should pay the $5,000 balance to First Bank to apply against its unpaid purchase-money debt of $20,000 (MolarCorp has paid $5,000 of the $25,000).

224. The liquidator should remit at least $20,000 — and perhaps the entire $40,000 — to First Bank (and no more than $20,000 to Willie Floss). The actual distribution will depend on when Willie Floss filed his financing statement. The facts state that he filed his financing statement "within a month" after Dealer delivered the imaging machine to MolarCorp. If Willie Floss's filing date is more than twenty days after the delivery date, then Willie Floss cannot invoke the superpriority afforded to purchase-money creditors by section 9-324(a), and First Bank is entitled to the entire $40,000 under the general "first to file or perfect" rule of section 9-322(a)(1). If, however, Willie Floss filed his financing statement not more than twenty days after the delivery date, then he can invoke the superpriority afforded to purchase-money creditors by section 9-324(a). Even so, First Bank also can invoke the same provision, up to the amount of its third-party financing (originally $25,000, now paid down to $20,000). In this situation, where neither purchase-money creditor was the seller, section 9-324(g)(2) applies and awards priority under the general rule of section 9-322(a). Under that rule, First Bank enjoys priority because it filed its financing statement in 2010, long before Willie Floss filed his financing statement in 2011. As the party with priority, First Bank receives the first $20,000 (the amount of its unpaid *purchase-money* debt), and Willie Floss gets the remaining

$20,000 (leaving it with a $15,000 unsecured claim).

225.   Dealer is entitled to the all of the proceeds, until its secured debt is paid in full. This question involves a priority dispute in an "accession." Section 9-102(a)(1) defines an "accession" as "goods that are physically united with other goods in such a manner that the identity of the original goods is not lost." The bus and the seats retained their respective identities after the seats were installed. Therefore, from BusCo's perspective, the bus is an "accession"; from Dealer's perspective, the seats are "accessions." *See* § 9-335 cmt. 3. Normally, priority in the liquidation proceeds is dictated by rules found outside section 9-335. *See* § 9-335(c). But an exception exists if the accession becomes part of a whole that is subject to certificate-of-title laws. Such is the case here, where the collateral involves a bus. In this instance, section 9-335(d) subordinates the interest in the accession (the seats) to the interest in the whole (the bus). Therefore, the sales proceeds should be distributed first to Dealer until its secured debt is paid, with any remaining proceeds paid to BusCo for application against its secured debt.

The drafters explain this result as follows: "It enables a secured party to rely upon a certificate of title without having to check the UCC files to determine whether any components of the collateral may be encumbered. The subsection imposes a corresponding risk upon those who finance goods that may become part of goods covered by a certificate of title." § 9-335 cmt. 7.

226.   **Answer (A) is the correct answer.** This question involves a priority dispute in an "accession." Section 9-102(a)(1) defines an "accession" as "goods that are physically united with other goods in such a manner that the identity of the original goods is not lost." The frame and the tapestry each retained their identity after the frame was affixed to the tapestry. Therefore, from Framed Again!'s perspective, the tapestry is an "accession"; from Gilmore Artworks' perspective, the frame is an "accession." *See* § 9-335 cmt. 3. The collateral does not involve a certificate of title, so priority in the liquidation proceeds is dictated by rules found outside section 9-335. *See* § 9-335(c).

Determining which priority rule resolves the dispute between the two creditors requires knowing whether their security interests are perfected and qualify for purchase-money status. Both creditors hold a purchase-money security interest under section 9-103; Gilmore Artworks offered seller financing for the tapestry, and Framed Again! offered seller financing for the frame. Both creditors perfected their interests by filing. Framed Again! filed its financing statement on June 15, more than twenty days after returning the framed tapestry to Bruce on May 23. Therefore, Framed Again! cannot claim the superpriority afforded to its PMSI by section 9-324(a). This leaves Gilmore Artworks with priority under the basic "first to file or perfect" rule of section 9-322(a)(1) because it filed its financing statement in April or May, and Framed Again! did not file until June 15. The trustee, then should distribute the entire $6,500 to Gilmore Artworks to be applied against its unpaid $7,500 debt, leaving no remaining proceeds for Framed Again! This distribution is found in Answer (A), **making Answer (A) the correct answer and Answers (B), (C), and (D) incorrect answers.**

(Answer (B) would have been correct if Framed Again! had filed its financing statement no later than twenty days after delivering the framed tapestry to Bruce on May 23, which would have entitled Framed Again! to claim superpriority under section 9-324(a)).

227. **Answer (D) is the correct answer.** Muscles Bank does not have a PMSI because its funds were not used by BAM to acquire any additional rights in the UniFlex machines. BAM had acquired all of the property rights in the machines a few weeks earlier, using funds borrowed from its majority shareholder, Brenda Mahan. That loan was unsecured, so Muscles Bank cannot argue that it bought an earlier PMSI position. And the facts do not suggest that BAM, Mahan, and Muscles Bank collectively contemplated, at the time of purchase, that BAM intended to quickly replace Mahan's unsecured financing with Muscles Bank's secured financing. *See generally* § 9-103 cmt. 3 ("The concept of 'purchase-money security interest' requires a close nexus between the acquisition of collateral and the secured obligation. Thus, a security interest does not qualify as a purchase-money security interest if a debtor acquires property on unsecured credit and subsequently creates the security interest to secure the purchase price."). Therefore, **Answer (A) is an incorrect answer.** Absent a PMSI, Muscles Bank cannot claim superpriority under section 9-324(a), so the date of its filing is irrelevant, **making Answer (B) and Answer (C) incorrect answers.** Therefore, Fitness Finance wins the priority dispute under section 9-322(a)(1) because its filing date (2009) is earlier than Muscles Bank's filing date (2010), **making Answer (D) the correct answer.**

228. **Answer (C) is the correct answer.** When collateral is covered by a certificate of title statute, then that statute dictates the means of perfection. It is as if compliance with the certificate of title statute is the equivalent of filing a financing statement. *See* § 9-311(b). Thus, AutoFinance was perfected in the Camaro when Lauren sold it to Integrity Motors, and under sections 9-315(a) and 9-201(a), its interest continued in the Camaro. This is so regardless of whether Lauren paid any or all of the $8,500 to AutoFinance. Thus, **Answer (D) is incorrect.**

Beta Bank also was perfected in the Camaro when Integrity Motors bought the car from Lauren, even though it filed a financing statement against the inventory rather than noting its lien on the Camaro's certificate of title. Section 9-311(d) allows a secured party to perfect its security interest in motor vehicles by filing a financing statement, if (as here) the motor vehicles are held by the debtor as inventory (rather than equipment or a consumer good). But even though Beta Bank has a perfected security interest in the Camaro, it loses a priority dispute with AutoFinance, a previously perfected secured party, under section 9-322(a)(1). Thus, **Answer (B) is incorrect.**

Bruce is a "buyer in ordinary course of business" from Integrity Motors under section 1-201(b)(9). Therefore, under section 9-320(a), he will acquire the Camaro free of any security interest created by his seller, Integrity Motors. Unfortunately for Bruce, that is only Beta Bank; Integrity Motors had nothing to do with the creation of the security interest granted by Lauren to AutoFinance. So **Answer (A) is an incorrect answer.** With no rule or statute to cut off or eliminate AutoFinance's interest, it will prevail in a replevin action, **making Answer (C) the correct answer.** (In the real world, Integrity Motors would have breached the implied warranty of title found in Article 2 and would be personally liable to Bruce for any losses. But such a warranty is only as sound as Integrity Motors is, and if Integrity Motors is in default to Beta Bank, then its unsecured promises may not be worth much.)

229. **Answer (A) is the correct answer.** BAMCO never consented to the sale, so unless another provision favors Billy, BAMCO will win the dispute in reliance on sections 9-201(a) and 9-315(a). Billy cannot win under section 9-320(a). He is not a "buyer in ordinary course of

business" as defined in section 1-201(b)(9) because Joe's routine business is lawn maintenance, not selling tractors. Therefore, **Answer (B) is incorrect.** Also, Billy cannot invoke the protection afforded to buyers under section 9-320(b) because Joe used the tractor in his lawncare business, making it equipment, rather than a consumer good (also, BAMCO filed a financing statement in Georgia). Therefore, **Answer (C) is incorrect.** Because BAMCO's security interest survives the disposition under section 9-315(a), its original filing (against Joe in Georgia) continued to perfect its security interest in the tractor under section 9-507(a). True, Billy is "located" in Alabama, and BAMCO filed in Georgia where Joe had been "located," so there has been a change in the debtor's location. But the question asks for a resolution as of July 15, a date within any grace period mentioned in either section 9-316(a)(2) (four months, triggered by Joe's relocation to Alabama in April) or section 9-316(a)(3) (one year, triggered by Joe's sale to Billy in May). So as of July 15, the dispute resolution date, BAMCO's security interest remains perfected, **making Answer (D) an incorrect answer.** Billy cannot successfully invoke any buyer-protection statute, so BAMCO wins its conversion lawsuit in reliance on sections 9-201(a) and 9-315(a), **making Answer (A) the correct answer.**

230. Billy will win the conversion lawsuit if it is resolved as of September 10. Joe moved to Alabama in April, triggering a change in the debtor's "location" and a corresponding filing duty under section 9-316(a)(2). Any date in April precedes September 10 by more than four months. BAMCO's failure to file a new financing statement in Alabama leaves its security interest in the tractor unperfected not just prospectively, but also retroactively (because Billy is a "purchaser of the collateral for value"). As section 9-316(b) treats BAMCO as if it were never perfected, Billy can rely on the protection afforded to buyers by section 9-317(b) because he had no knowledge of Joe's transaction with BAMCO. For these reasons, Billy wins the lawsuit if it is resolved as of September 10.

231. BAMCO will win a conversion lawsuit that is resolved as of September 10, if BAMCO filed a financing statement in Alabama against Joe and the tractor on June 15. Joe moved to Alabama in April, triggering a change in the debtor's "location" and a corresponding filing duty under section 9-316(a)(2). BAMCO's filing on June 15 is timely, as it falls within the four-month window. Billy can no longer successfully invoke section 9-317(b), or any other buyer-protection provision. Therefore, BAMCO wins its conversion lawsuit, relying on sections 9-201(a) and 9-315(a). (Appreciate that this result may seem odd, given that BAMCO's filing on June 15 follows the date on which Joe sold the tractor to Billy. That sale triggers section 9-316(a)(3), which provides a one-year grace period during which BAMCO must file in Alabama against Billy.)

232. Billy wins the conversion lawsuit under these revised facts. Joe, the original debtor, was located in Georgia. He sold the collateral to Billy, who acquired the tractor subject to BAMCO's security interest under sections 9-201(a) and 9-315(a). Billy became a debtor, but he is a debtor located in Alabama, not Georgia. This transaction has triggered a change in jurisdiction addressed by section 9-316(a)(3). Under that provision, BAMCO had one year (from the date of the asset transfer) in which to file a financing statement in Alabama against Billy. BAMCO failed to do so, under the revised facts. Therefore, BAMCO's security interest in the tractor became unperfected not just prospectively, but also retroactively (because Billy was a "purchaser of the collateral for value"). As section 9-316(b) treats BAMCO as if

it were never perfected, Billy can rely on the protection afforded to buyers by section 9-317(b) because he had no knowledge of Joe's transaction with BAMCO. For these reasons, Billy wins the lawsuit under the revised facts.

233. **Answer (C) is the correct answer.** Meredith used funds provided by Knight Finance to acquire the chess set, which she used primarily for personal, family, or household purposes. Therefore, Knight Finance has a PMSI in the chess set, a consumer good. As a result, Knight Finance can rely on automatic perfection of its enforceable security interest under section 9-309(1). Its failure to file a financing statement does not preclude perfection.

Knight Finance, relying on section 9-315(a), can argue that its security interest in the chess set survived Meredith's sale, unless another provision leads to a contrary result in favor of the buyer. Section 9-317(b) offers protection to a buyer if the security interest is unperfected when the buyer takes possession. Knight Finance, though, continues to enjoy automatic perfection of its security interest. Section 9-320(a) protects buyers in the ordinary course of business, but the facts are less than clear that Meredith (an astronaut) is in the business of buying and selling chess sets. Section 9-320(b) applies only if the goods are consumer goods in the hands of both the seller and the buyer. Here, Meredith may have used the chess set as a consumer good, but the buyer has purchased the chess set for its inventory. Absent any exception, then, the merchant has acquired the chess set subject to a perfected security interest held by Knight Finance. Therefore, **Answer (D) is an incorrect answer** because it erroneously suggests that Knight Finance has no superior claim to the chess set.

What about Knight Finance's claim to the $10,000, deposited by Meredith into her checking account? The $10,000 was proceeds under section 9-102(a)(64) and would remain so, even after Meredith deposited the amount into her checking account. Knight Finance can claim a security interest in proceeds, but only those that are "identifiable." *See* § 9-315(a)(2). The most common form of tracing funds that are deposited (and commingled with non-proceeds) into a deposit account is the lowest intermediate balance rule. That rule assumes that the first funds expended from the account are *not* proceeds; it is as though the existing balance is oil and the proceeds deposited are water; the water will sink to the bottom and the oil will float to the top. Any withdrawals of liquid will thus be first from the "oil," or non-proceeds. And if the secured party can "identify" the cash proceeds under the rule, its security interest is perfected for twenty days under section 9-315(c) and thereafter under section 9-315(d)(2).

Following Meredith's deposit, the account balance fell to zero at some point. This means that Meredith has spent the entire $10,000 of proceeds. It also means that Meredith's subsequent deposits had to be from non-proceeds, and, under the lowest intermediate balance rule, no identifiable cash proceeds remain in the account. As a result, Knight Finance has no claim to any money in Meredith's checking account, **making Answer (A) an incorrect answer.**

Answers (B) and (C) differ in whether Knight Finance has a perfected security interest in the comic book. Since there was $5,000 in Meredith's account immediately before she deposited the $10,000, and she paid for the comic book with a $12,000 check drawn on the account three days later, it is possible — although by no means a certainty — that she purchased the comic book, in part, with proceeds (a low of $1 and a high of $10,000, depending the account balance fluctuations during that brief period of time). If none of the $12,000 represents proceeds, then Knight Finance has no claim to the comic book, **making Answer (C) the correct answer.** Assume, though, that some of the $12,000 represents proceeds. To that extent, Knight Finance has an enforceable security interest in the comic book. That interest is perfected for twenty days under section 9-315(c). Perfection will not continue thereafter, however. Knight Finance cannot invoke section 9-315(d)(1) because it relied on automatic financing, rather than filing a financing statement, and any security interest in the comic book arises from Meredith's use of cash proceeds. It cannot invoke section 9-315(d)(2) because the comic book is not a "cash proceed." And Knight Finance has taken no other action to perfect its security interest in the comic book. Therefore, to the extent that it can claim a security interest in the comic book, that interest is unperfected on the petition date. This allows the bankruptcy trustee to claim a superior interest under the "strong-arm" clause of the bankruptcy code (*see* Bankruptcy Code § 544(a)(1), which generally allows the bankruptcy trustee to avoid security interests that are unperfected on the petition date), **making Answer (B) an incorrect answer.**

In summary, Knight Finance has a superior claim to the chess set, but not the comic book or any part of Meredith's checking account. **Answer (C), then, is the correct answer.**

234.   **Answer (D) is the correct answer.** Nevada Bank has a perfected security interest in the pool table before the sale. Hannah's only hope is that she has acquired the pool table free of that perfected security interest under section 9-320(a), which favors buyers in the ordinary course of business. Section 1-201(b)(9) defines "buyer in ordinary course of business." In part, the definition states: "Only a buyer that takes possession of the goods *or has a right to recover the goods from the seller under Article 2* may be a buyer in ordinary course of business." (Emphasis added.)

Hannah did not take possession of the pool table, but she otherwise met all the requirements: she acted in good faith and without knowledge that her purchase violated Nevada Bank's property rights; she also bought from someone in the business of selling goods of the kind bought (pool tables) and in the ordinary course of business (no odd terms). The definition says that Hannah may be a buyer in the ordinary course if she "has a right to recover the goods from the seller under Article 2," even though she lacks possession. Therefore, Answer (B) is not an absolute truth, **making Answer (B) an incorrect answer.** Whether Hannah has any rights against ZinnCo is governed by sections 2-502 and 2-716, the two sections of Article 2 that give buyers property rights sufficient to maintain possessory actions for the goods being purchased.

Section 2-502(1) protects "a buyer that has paid a part or all of the price of the goods." Because the facts do not indicate that Hannah made any payment before Nevada Bank seized the store and its contents, section 2-502 is inapplicable. Nor will Hannah find solace in section 2-716(1), which provides Hannah with the remedy of specific performance "if the goods are unique or in other proper circumstances." The facts specifically indicate that Hannah did not buy a unique pool table, as she shopped around and bought a model, sold by a competitor, from ZinnCo because ZinnCo offered a better price. And fungible goods do not provide "other proper circumstances."

Section 2-716(3) also provides Hannah with a right of replevin (a right to possession) generally and without regard to the type of collateral "if after reasonable effort the buyer is unable to effect cover for such goods." Again, since the model is generally available, Hannah will be able to cover under section 2-712(1), and thus she is not entitled to this generally available right of replevin.

Finally, section 2-716(3) also provides that a right of replevin exists for consumer goods (such as the pool table as Hannah intends to use it) "upon acquisition of a special property, even if the seller . . . failed to deliver." Whether Hannah acquired a "special property" is, in turn, determined by section 2-501, which states that a special property is obtained by "identification to the contract," which in the absence of an agreement on that point, occurs "(a) when the contract is made if it is for the sale of goods already existing and identified; [or] (b) if the contract is for the sale of future goods . . . when goods are shipped, marked or otherwise designated by the seller as goods to which the contract refers." Here, the contract does not identify a specific pool table, and thus the matter will be determined by the statutory defaults in section 2-501(1). With respect to section 2-501(1)(a) and (b), ZinnCo did not set aside or otherwise identify a particular pool table for Hannah, waiting instead to select one when she returned. As a result, no pool table was identified to the contract. Hannah thus has no special property, and no right to replevin under section 2-716(3).

Absent possession, and without any remedy under section 2-502 or section 2-716, Hannah does not qualify as a "buyer in the ordinary course," **making Answer (A) an incorrect answer.** Therefore, she cannot acquire the pool table free of Nevada Bank's perfected security interest under section 9-320(a), and no other provision of Article 9 (e.g., sections 9-320(b) and 9-317(b)) is applicable. While Nevada Bank could have contractually consented to inventory sales in the ordinary course of ZinnCo's business in its security agreement, which would have terminated Nevada Bank's security interest under section 9-315(a) upon signing the sales contract with Hannah, the security agreement is silent on this point, thus making Hannah's rights congruent with and subject to section 9-320(a). No statute expressly protects "good faith purchasers for value," so **Answer (C) is an incorrect answer.** The only statute that remains is section 9-201, which favors Nevada Bank against the world (including Hannah).

If Hannah had paid all or part of the purchase price to ZinnCo before Nevada Bank closed the store and seized its contents, Hannah could have qualified as a buyer in the ordinary course of business and claimed priority under section 9-320(a). She also could have prevailed if ZinnCo had put a "sold" sign, with Hannah's name on it, on one of the pool tables. But she failed to make any such payment, and ZinnCo failed to set aside or otherwise designate a pool table for her. For those reasons, Nevada Bank has priority and **Answer (D) is the correct answer.**

235. **Answer (B) is the correct answer.** Bank's advance that it funded on June 1, before BAM became a lien creditor on June 15, is entitled to priority. The degree of protection afforded to Bank's future advances is found in section 9-323(b). Under that section, Bank's future advances (i.e., advances funded after a party becomes a lien creditor) are protected if Bank funds the advance (i) within the forty-five-day period after the party becomes a lien creditor, (ii) without knowledge of the lien, or (iii) pursuant to a commitment entered into without knowledge of the lien. This means that Bank's advances that were funded on June 20, July 8, and July 25 are entitled to priority because those advances were funded within the forty-five-day period following the date (June 15) when BAM became a lien creditor. (Notice that the forty-five-day period is absolute. It is not shortened by the secured party's knowledge of the lien — as Bank so learned on July 15.) Bank's advance funded on August 5 is not entitled to priority. Bank funded that advance outside the forty-five-day period, with knowledge of the lien, and not pursuant to any commitment. So Bank is entitled to $105,000 ($35,000, plus $15,000, plus $20,000, plus $35,000), with the balance of $25,000 payable to BAM. This result is found in **Answer (B), making it the correct answer and Answers (A), (C), and (D)**

incorrect answers.

236.   Under section 9-323(b), all of Bank's advances (including the $10,000 advance funded on August 5, outside the forty-five-day period) are protected because Bank funded them "pursuant to commitment" (defined in section 9-102(a)(68)) entered into on June 1 without knowledge of the lien. Therefore, the sheriff should award the first $115,000 to Bank, and the remaining balance of $15,000 to BAM.

237.   **Answer (D) is the correct answer.** This question requires analysis of three priority disputes: First Bank v. Ima, Ima v. Second Bank, and Second Bank v. First Bank. In each instance, the party first named will win its dispute. Rephrased, First Bank beats Ima. Ima beats Second Bank. And Second Bank beats First Bank. This is an example of circular priority (a variation of the "rock, paper, scissors" game), with no clear winner.

First Bank filed its original financing statement on August 10, 2007. First Bank filed its continuation statement on February 5, 2012, outside the six-month window mandated by section 9-515(d). Therefore, the continuation statement, notwithstanding its appearance in the search report, is ineffective to continue First Bank's original filing. *See* § 9-510(c). This leaves First Bank unperfected prospectively, so Second Bank has priority over First Bank under section 9-322(a)(2) (perfection trumps unperfection). First Bank continues to enjoy priority over Ima, however, because Ima's lien arose during the five-year period (and after First Bank acquired its initial priority against Ima under section 9-317(a)(2)), and section 9-315(c) renders First Bank unperfected retroactively only against "a purchaser of the collateral for value." Ima is not a "purchaser" under section 1-201 because she did not acquire her property interest in the collateral by a voluntary transaction, but rather by judicial process. Therefore, First Bank's security interest (although now unperfected) continues to enjoy priority over Ima's judgment lien under section 9-317(a)(2) because First Bank's security interest was perfected when Ima's lien attached to the collateral. *See* § 9-515 cmt. 3. Finally, Ima enjoys priority over Second Bank because Ima's lien arose in July 2012, months before Second Bank's security interest attached in September 2012. *See* § 9-317(a)(2).

In summary, then, First Bank enjoys priority over Ima, who enjoys priority over Second Bank, who enjoys priority over First Bank. Answer (D) is the only answer that correctly states this result, **making Answer (D) the correct answer and Answers (A), (B), and (C) incorrect answers.**

238.   **Answer (B) is the correct answer.** In addition to the information found in section 9-613(1), a disposition notice in a consumer-goods transaction also must include "(B) a description of any liability for a deficiency of the person to which the notification is sent; (C) a telephone number from which the amount that must be paid to the secured party to redeem the collateral under Section 9-623 is available; and (D) a telephone number or mailing address from which additional information concerning the disposition and the obligation secured is available." § 9-614(1). The only answer with information required by the quoted passage is Answer (B), **making Answer (B) the correct answer. Answer (A) is incorrect.** Although Article 9 permits the debtor to attend a public disposition and purchase the collateral, the notice need not mention that the debtor may do so. The notice need not describe the nature of the default, so **Answer (C) is incorrect.** And **Answer (D) also is incorrect.** Article 9 does not provide the debtor with any statutory right to a strict foreclosure (a process by which the secured creditor retains the collateral and forgives all or part of the secured debt).

239. **Answer (B) is the correct answer.** Section 9-611(c) states that BankTwo must send its disposition notice to the debtor, any secondary obligor, and any other secured party that has filed a financing statement against the Asset. BAMCO owns the Asset, making it the debtor. BankOne and BankThree hold perfected security interests in the Asset (by filing, the only logical assumption). Therefore, BAMCO, BankOne, and BankThree are entitled to notice, **making Answer (B) the correct answer and Answer (D) an incorrect answer.** ZinnCorp is a borrower and a primary obligor on the $1 million loan from BankOne, but it is not a debtor (or a secondary obligor) because it has no property rights in the Asset (owned by its subsidiary, BAMCO). *See* § 9-102, cmt. 2.a. Therefore, ZinnCorp is not entitled to notice of the disposition. For this reason **Answer (A) and Answer (C) are incorrect answers.**

240. The $2 million is allocated according to the distribution scheme in section 9-615. First, under section 9-615(a)(1), BankTwo can recover its repossession and disposition-related expenses if they are "reasonable" (these expenses include attorney fees and legal expenses "to the extent provided for by agreement and not prohibited by law"). Second, under section 9-615(a)(2), BankTwo receives $400,000 — the amount of its secured debt. Third, under section 9-615(a)(3), BankThree receives $300,000 as a holder of a security interest that under section 9-322(a) is subordinate to the security interest of BankTwo — but only if BankTwo received from BankThree an "authenticated demand for proceeds before distribution of the proceeds is completed." And fourth, under section 9-615(d)(1), the remaining amount (the "surplus") should be returned to BAMCO (the debtor, as owner of the Asset). (Observe that BankOne, the senior creditor, does not share in the proceeds distribution under section 9-615(a), for a reason explained in the next answer.)

241. The answer is found in section 9-617(a). Under subsection (a)(1), the foreclosure sale transfers all of BAMCO's property interest in the Asset to the successful buyer. Under subsection (a)(2), the foreclosure sale terminates BankTwo's security interest. And under subsection (a)(3), the foreclosure sale terminates the subordinate security interest held by BankThree, whether or not BankThree shared in the proceeds distribution under section 9-615(a)(3). But the foreclosure sale does not discharge the senior security interest held by BankOne (which is the statutory protection that BankOne receives in lieu of sharing in the proceeds under section 9-615(a)). Instead, BankOne's security interest survives the sale.

242. As noted in the answer to the previous question, BankOne's security interest survives the foreclosure sale. Therefore, Buyer acquired the Asset subject to a $500,000 encumbrance. Buyer has thus paid too much for the Asset because its current fair market value, if unencumbered, is only $2 million. Buyer has suffered an immediate loss (at least on paper) of $500,000, because the value of the Asset, as encumbered, is only $1.5 million (this loss is calculated as follows: $2 million fair market value if unencumbered – [$2 million purchase price +$500,000 security interest]). If the unencumbered Asset's fair market value had been more than $2.5 million, Buyer would have received a bargain. For example, Buyer can show a profit (at least on paper) of $400,000 if the fair market value of the unencumbered Asset had been $2.9 million (this gain is calculated as follows: $2.9 million fair market value if unencumbered – [$2 million purchase price +$500,000 security interest]).

243. **Answer (D) is the correct answer.** Section 9-610(b) imposes on Dealer the duty to conduct any disposition in a "commercially reasonable" manner. Section 9-602(7) prohibits Dealer from waiving or varying that duty, **making Answers (A) and (B) incorrect answers.** Notwithstanding the statutory prohibition against waiver or variance of the duty of

commercial reasonableness, section 9-603(a) permits Dealer and its customers to "determine by agreement the standards measuring the fulfillment of . . . the duties of a secured party under a rule stated in Section 9-602 if the standards are not *manifestly* unreasonable" (emphasis added). Therefore, **Answer (D) is the correct answer and Answer (C) is an incorrect answer.**

Whether a standard is unreasonable, manifestly unreasonable, or unconscionable must be determined by specific facts. Therefore, it is possible that courts may not reach uniform results in their conclusions, and their conclusions could be shaped by a variety of factors, including the nature of the transaction and the sophistication and negotiating strength of the parties. Even so, Dealer is encouraged to utilize section 9-603 in an attempt to define the contours of "commercial reasonableness," if for no other reason than to reduce the likelihood of litigation on (or to guide a court in its review of) Dealer's compliance with section 9-610(b).

244.   **Answer (A) is the correct answer.** A secured party may repossess collateral without judicial process, "if it proceeds without breach of the peace." § 9-609(b)(2). This duty cannot be waived or varied by the parties. § 9-602(6). Nor can the parties attempt to define the contours of acceptable behavior through standards (even if the standards are not manifestly unreasonable). § 9-603(b). Therefore, the self-serving provision in the standard form of security agreement will not shield Otto's Auto's from liability for any breach of the peace, **making Answer (B) an incorrect answer.**

The overwhelming number of courts have held that the duty to avoid breaching the peace cannot be delegated; therefore, a secured party will incur liability for any breach of the peace by an independent contractor. *See, e.g., Clark v. Associates Commercial Corp.*, 877 F. Supp. 1439 (D. Kan. 1994); *MBank El Paso, N.A. v. Sanchez*, 836 S.W.2d 151 (Tex. 1992); *see also* § 9-609 cmt. 3 ("In considering whether a secured party has engaged in a breach of the peace . . . courts should hold the secured party responsible for the actions of others taken on the secured party's behalf, including independent contractors engaged by the secured party to take possession of collateral."). Therefore, the fact that Towtruck Tim, an independent contractor, repossessed the vehicle should not protect Otto's Autos from liability for any breach, so **Answer (D) is not the best answer.** The speed and silence with which Towtruck Tim repossessed the vehicle no doubt reduced the likelihood of a confrontation with Keith or a nearby neighbor. But the absence of a confrontation does not necessarily prevent a breach of the peace. Most courts have held that a creditor breaches the peace if it removes collateral from a restricted area. *See, e.g., Henderson v. Security National Bank*, 140 Cal. Rptr. 388 (Ct. App. 1977) (removal of car after breaking lock on garage door); *Bloomquist v. First National Bank*, 378 N.W.2d 81 (Minn. Ct. App. 1985) (removal of collateral from business premises after entering cracked, but taped, window and opening garage door secured by deadbolt lock). Given the well-deserved sanctity afforded by courts to a person's home, the locked or unlocked status of the garage should be irrelevant if the garage door is closed. Indeed, the very act of opening the closed door may be a breach of the peace (if not a violation of the local criminal code). Therefore, **Answer (C) is not the best answer.** Instead, **Answer (A) is the best (and therefore the correct) answer.** If a court does find that the repossession triggered a breach of the peace, Otto's Autos may be liable. And courts have not hesitated in awarding punitive damages in appropriate cases. *See, e.g., Chrysler Credit Corp. v. Turner*, 553 So.2d 64 (Ala. 1989) ($15,000); *Williamson v. Fowler Toyota, Inc.*, 956 P.2d 858 (Okla. 1988) ($15,000). Opening a garage door, even though unlocked, may merit such an award to discourage similar conduct.

245. **Answer (C) is the correct answer.** This question combines elements of bankruptcy and Article 9. Under bankruptcy law, a secured creditor's rights are entitled to adequate protection. 11 U.S.C. §§ 362(d), 361 (illustrations of adequate protection). Section 362(d) determines adequate protection. It provides that a secured creditor may receive relief from the automatic stay if its interests are not adequately protected, § 362(d)(1), or if the debtor does not have an equity in the collateral and if the collateral is not necessary for an effective reorganization, § 362(d)(2). There are two other grounds under paragraphs (3) and (4) of section 362(d), but they do not apply here since HCI is not a single asset debtor (§ 362(d)(3)), nor do the facts suggest fraud (§ 362(d)(4)).

Here, **Answer (B) is incorrect** because it is incomplete. A lack of equity (which occurs when the debt exceeds the value of the collateral, as it would here if the accounts had a value less than the debt of $1 million) only justifies stay relief if it is also the case that the property is not necessary for an effective reorganization. Here the accounts are likely necessary cash flow for the company, and the second requirement is not met.

Whether HCI continues making monthly payments is irrelevant to adequate protection; while such an offer might constitute sufficient adequate protection, it is certainly not necessary. **Answer (D) is thus incorrect.**

That leaves Answers (C) and (A). Whether "accounts" covers future accounts is an issue resolved by non-Article 9 common law — usually contract law. *See* § 9-108 cmt. 3. Accounts, however, by their nature are not durable and turn over frequently in a business. There is thus some common sense to implying an after-acquired property provision to protect the parties' reasonable expectations, which can be gleaned, if not determined, by the use of "all" to qualify accounts. As a result, although it is a close call, **Answer (A) is incorrect.**

That leaves Answer (C). This answer precludes relief under Section 362(d)(2) as it states that the accounts are necessary for an effective reorganization. It also likely precludes relief under Section 362(d)(1) in that HCI is offering adequate protection by offering an interest in post-petition accounts (cut off by the operation of Section 552(a) of the Bankruptcy Code to the extent that "all accounts" is determined to imply an after-acquired property clause). If there is no appreciable decline in business, the granting of a post-petition lien in accounts is generally held to adequately protect the secured creditor as it keeps their total collateral value stable. As a result, **Answer (C) is correct.**

246. **Answer (D) is the correct answer.** When an individual files a Chapter 13 bankruptcy petition, a stay goes into effect not only as to the debtor in the bankruptcy case, but also as to any codebtor on any consumer debt. Under these facts, Sally's daughter signed the note, and thus for bankruptcy purposes, Sally is a codebtor. As such, "a creditor may not act, or commence or continue any civil action, to collect all or any part of a consumer debt of the debtor from any individual that is liable on such debt with the debtor, or that secured such debt." 11 U.S.C. § 1301(a). As such, Drive Bank may not repossess the car (an "act . . . to collect"), may not telephone Sally (same), and may not file an action for replevin ("commence . . . any civil action"). **Answers (A), (B), and (C) are thus incorrect. This leaves Answer (D) as the correct answer.**

247. **Answer (D) is the correct answer.** An undersecured creditor — one whose debt exceeds the value of any collateral — holds two claims in bankruptcy: a secured claim equal to the value of the collateral and an unsecured claim equal to any deficiency. 11 U.S.C. § 506(a). Unlike oversecured creditors, an undersecured creditor is not entitled to any interest accrued post-

petition, or any attorneys' fees spent post-petition. As a consequence, **Answers (A) and (B) are incorrect.**

While a secured creditor is entitled to a distribution on its secured claim, it is also entitled to a distribution on its unsecured deficiency claim. As a result, **Answer (C) is incomplete and incorrect**, given the fact that **Answer (D) is complete, and thus correct.**

248. **Answer (D) is the correct answer.** Under Section 1129(b)(2)(A) of the Bankruptcy Code, bankruptcy courts may confirm plans over the dissent of secured creditors if the plans provide for property that has a present value equal to the allowed amount of the secured creditor's claim. "Property" has been construed to mean a promise of payments over time that have a present value equal to the allowed amount of the claim, and a promise to repay an amount at a market rate of interest accomplishes this requirement. Here, the plan does exactly this — it promises a stream of payments over time, that the debtor can make (a separate feasibility requirement of Section 1129(a)(11)), that have a present value equal to BigBank's claim. As a result, **Answer (D) is correct.**

Answer (A) is incorrect because the contract rate, 12%, is irrelevant; so long as the prevailing market rate is offered, then the stream of payments has a present value equal to the principal amount of the debt. **Answer (B) is incorrect** because a creditor may not be paid more than what it is owed, even if its collateral exceeds that amount. **Answer (C) is incorrect** because the original maturity date is immaterial given the debtor's compliance with the other requirements of Section 1129(b)(2)(A). As a result, a bankruptcy debtor may impose upon a secured creditor a loan with a non-consensual rate of interest (so long as it is a market rate of interest) and for a period well beyond the original maturity date of the secured obligation.

249. **Answer (B) is the correct answer.** A preference under Section 547 of the Bankruptcy Code requires: a transfer of an interest of the debtor in property (here, the $2 million payment); made on account of an antecedent debt (that is, a debt that existed at the time of the transfer, which here is met by the fact that LargeBanc was owed $5 million); made while the debtor was insolvent; made within ninety days of the filing (met here since it was made one month prior to filing); allowed the recipient to do better than it would have if the transfer had not been made and the debtor had filed a Chapter 7 bankruptcy petition (present here, assuming insolvency, since the bank in a Chapter 7 without the transfer would have received $2.5 million (the value of the painting) and an unsecured dividend on its $2.5 deficiency. If not avoided, the bank will receive or keep $4.5 million (the $2.5 million painting, and the $2 million payment), and an unsecured dividend for its $500,000 deficiency.

This analysis is independent of how the bank was perfected; the only thing that matters is whether it was perfected. Thus, possession of the painting is irrelevant to the $2 million payment, and thus **Answer (A) is incorrect.** Similarly, the relationship between the value of the collateral and the amount of the payment is irrelevant (the relevant relationship is whether the *total debt* is less than the collateral's value; if that is the case, then the transfer fails the "chapter 7" test of Section 547(b)(5), as the creditor would ultimately receive the same amount — the full amount of its claim — if it was oversecured regardless of whether the $2 million payment was made or not). As a consequence, **Answer (D) is incorrect.**

As between Answer (B) and Answer (C), the trustee is entitled to a presumption that the debtor was insolvent during the ninety-day period preceding the bankruptcy filing. 11 U.S.C. § 547(f). That is only a presumption, however, and if the bank chooses to contest it, it bears the burden of overcoming the presumption. **Answer (B) is thus correct**, as it better states the effect of the presumption. Answer (C) incorrectly places the burden of proving insolvency on the trustee, and thus **Answer (C) is incorrect.**

250. **Answer (B) is the correct answer,** for the same reasons as given in the prior question (and **Answer (C) is incorrect** for the same reasons).

LargeBanc has an unperfected security interest. Security interests in consumer goods (and presumably, a painting held for personal enjoyment in one's home would so qualify) are perfected automatically (i.e., without further action), only if they are *purchase-money security interests. See* § 9-309(1). Here, the loan was not purchase money, so LargeBanc remains unsecured. **Answer (A) is thus incorrect.**

Answer (D) is irrelevant. Even if LargeBanc retains its unperfected security interest, the collateral was worth less than the debt, making the $2 million payment essentially a payment on an unsecured claim, and avoidable as a preference regardless of the trustee's other actions. **Answer (D) is thus incorrect.** The trustee would undoubtedly seek to avoid the unperfected security interest under Section 544(a) (since that section gives the trustee the status of a lien creditor under state law, and under Article 9, which is state law, a lien creditor prevails over an unperfected security interest under section 9-317). And it would likely join that claim for relief in the same action as the preference action, but that would affect whether LargeBanc could keep anything related to the painting, not whether it could keep the earlier payment.

INDEX

235

INDEX